D0895788

Devaluation under Pressure

Devaluation under Pressure: India, Indonesia, and Ghana

David B. H. Denoon

The MIT Press
Cambridge, Massachusetts
London, England

© 1986 by The Massachusetts Institute of Technology.

All rights reserved. No part of this book may be reproduced in any form by any electronic or mechanical means (including photocopying, recording, or information storage and retrieval) without permission in writing from the publisher.

This book was set in Palatino by Asco Trade Typesetting Ltd., Hong Kong, and printed and bound by Halliday Lithograph in the United States of America.

Library of Congress Cataloging-in-Publication Data

Denoon, David B. H.
  Devaluation under pressure.

  Bibliography: p.
  Includes index.
  1. Devaluation of currency—India.   2. Devaluation of currency—Indonesia.
  3. Devaluation of currency—Ghana.   I. Title.
HG1235.D37   1986   332.4'14   85-15314
ISBN 0-262-04083-2

To My Parents

Contents

Preface

This book grew out of my work experiences. After undergraduate and masters training in economics, I began working in Southeast Asia on economic development issues, first in Thailand in 1967 and then as program economist for the U.S. aid program in Indonesia in 1969. It was an exciting period for analysts and participants in Indonesian economic policy. The economic disintegration of the Sukarno period was halted by President Suharto in 1967, reversed in 1968, and by 1970 it was clear that a dramatic turnaround in economic performance had been achieved.

In the 1970s the "Indonesian economic miracle" was being widely reported in the press, and many claimants were anxious to take responsibility for the results. The record was impressive: between 1965 and 1970 inflation dropped from over 600 percent to 10 percent per year, exports recovered, economic growth resumed, and new investment surged. Some argued that the Indonesian technocrats who designed and implemented the stabilization program deserved the primary credit for the economic revival; others noted the high level of private capital inflows; considerable attention was given to the massive transfers of bilateral and multilateral aid; and still others saw the Indonesian events as evidence of the benefits of turning away from centrally directed socialism to market-oriented policies. Some even began to refer to the archipelago's performance as the Indonesian model for economic development.

Yet as a participant in the aid process, I was continually struck by how atypical the circumstances in Indonesia had been. The attempted coup in 1965 led to the decimation of the communist party and discredited the far Left. The socialist and nationalist parties were identified with the decay of the Sukarno period. This left the army and the economic technocrats as the principal source of political legitimacy. Moreover, Indonesia's rich natural resources and key strategic location made it attractive for both government aid and private capital. Also, the vast majority of the Indonesian population are relatively self-sufficient farmers who do not depend on imported goods. This overall set of characteristics meant that the Indonesian economic policymakers could vigorously attack inflation, count on large new flows of foreign resources, and be confident of minimal political opposition. Few other developing countries could make economic policy in such a setting.

On returning to the United States, I worked at the National Bureau of Economic Research where Jagdish Bhagwati and Anne Krueger were directing a twelve-volume series, "Foreign Trade Regimes and Economic Development." This outstanding project covered a broad range of less developed countries (LDCs) and analyzed how trade policy affects economic performance. I then decided that it would be useful as a complement to the economic literature on trade and development to do a study that formally linked the political setting with the economic policy choices that national leaders must make.

The first cut at this problem was in my subsequent Ph.D. thesis at the Massachusetts Institute of Technology, "Aid: High Politics Technocracv, or Farce?" This initial effort led me to the three devaluation cases presented in this book, but it focused more on aid issues and the politics of multinational consortia rather than the internal choices developed here.

In deciding on the precise agenda for this book, I set three basic goals: to explain the complexity of a currency devaluation from the perspective of an LDC government, to present devaluation as a striking political-economy problem where there are major political constraints to economic choice and economic constraints on political strategy, and to develop three devaluation cases that were historically significant and representative of the situation facing LDC governments.

Chapters 1 and 5 set the context for and draw the conclusions from the study but are written using a wide range of other cases as well and are meant to help generalize about devaluation in LDCs. Chapters 2, 3, and 4 were selected to be representative but also have a considerable body of detail that will be of interest to country and area specialists. I have thus divided those chapters into two parts: the main text, which uses the theoretical framework for analyzing the devaluations, and chronologies, which provide extra historical background and detail.

Much of the information here is new and in some cases will be quite controversial. The summary of the Woods-Mehta agreement presented in appendix 2B is the first publication of the details of a historic document. The Indian government has kept the existence of this agreement hidden from its own people for nineteen years and has expressly asked the World

Bank not to release the document. I have seen a copy of the agreement and took precise notes on it.

All three case studies include details of government decision making that cast key individuals in more or less favorable light. The only way to do this type of research was to talk extensively with the individuals directly involved and then to cross-check the material they provided with other written or verbal sources. Many individuals granted interviews on the condition that they not be quoted. I have respected their requests and thus have much material that lacks references. For readers' information, I have listed at the back of each case study the names of the people interviewed. I made it a firm rule to include material only if it had been cross-checked with at least one other participant, and in most cases the material was confirmed by several sources.

A project such as this could not proceed without advice and assistance from a large number of people I wish to thank all of those who helped me as the research, writing, and revisions proceeded. Special thanks go to Lucian Pye who chaired my Ph.D. dissertation and continuously urged me to probe for the counterintuitive aspects in the behavior of the decision makers I was analyzing; to Myron Weiner who deftly led me into the complexities of Indian politics and gave me considerable advice on conducting field research; and to Everett Hagen and Jagdish Bhagwati who made insightful comments as the project was developing. John P. Lewis and Bernard Bell were exceptionally helpful in recounting their experiences in the events and in providing perspective on the subsequent developments. The India research was aided by S. Lateef and L. Jain, the Indonesia work by N. Kairupan and A. Shakow, and the Ghana work by J. Odling-Smee and T. Killick. Travel to the countries and early research was supported by the University Consortium for World Order Studies; subsequently New York University provided a stimulating setting and encouragement as the final drafts proceeded. Mention should also go to E. Rosenthal, J. Hart, N. Abdolal, and C. Labio who helped with key research assistance and to D. Bula who conscientiously typed the manuscript.

1   The Issues

The Problems of Devaluation

During the spring and early summer of 1983 the Philippine economy faced formidable problems: economic growth had slowed, inflation had accelerated, and the deficit in traded goods and services for the first quarter of the year ($343 million) was more than twice the rate forecast by the Philippine government. On June 23, 1983, the Philippine Central Bank officially devalued the peso by 7.3 percent. In a letter to President Marcos, Jaime Laya, head of the Central Bank, said the new exchange rate "reflected the true international value of the peso" and would have "positive effects on the balance of payments," making Philippine exports relatively cheaper and imports more expensive.[1]

By the fall of 1983 the Philippine economic situation had deteriorated further. At the end of the third quarter the trade deficit had surged to $1.36 billion, the August assassination of Benigno Aquino had affected the political stability of the Marcos regime, and the Philippines faced a major problem with capital flight.[2] Although the Philippines had long been plagued by an inefficient industrial sector and its dependence on imported fuel, the crescendo of economic problems in 1983 seemed ominous.[3]

At the time of the June devaluation the Philippine government reached an agreement with the International Monetary Fund (IMF) to receive a $345 million standby credit, but this was conditioned on taking measures to slow inflation, restrict domestic credit, and contract the current account deficit. Yet as the economic news turned from bad to worse, the Philippine government was torn between possible courses of action. Should it undergo the rigors of an even larger devaluation? Impose domestic price controls? Tighten controls on capital movements? Dismiss sizable numbers of government workers? Or end subsidies to industrial firms? All of the options were unappealing. By October 5, 1983, the government decided against direct controls but tightened overall monetary and fiscal austerity measures, made a commitment to the IMF that the 1984 trade deficit would be below $1 billion, and announced a second devaluation, this one totaling 21.4 percent.

In 1976 the Peruvian government of General Morales Bermudez had faced a situation similar to the Philippine crisis of 1983. Peruvian economic growth had been rapid in the 1968–1973 period, but by the mid-1970s Peru was mired in seemingly intractable problems. Copper prices were down; expenditures for oil exploration had not been as successful as predicted; the usually abundant anchovy schools had vanished, reducing fishmeal exports; and President Morales found his government obligated to pay nearly $900 million per year in debt service and amortization on the $4 billion borrowed by his predecessor's government. The predicament was compounded by large deficits in public sector enterprises, a decline in the domestic savings rate, and an increase in inflation from 14 percent in 1973 to over 50 percent in 1976.[4] The Peruvian government began negotiations with the IMF in 1976 about receiving a standby credit but could not reach agreement on the character and extent of the stabilization program to be put into effect.

The Morales government then tried a novel tack: it did an end run on the IMF. The Peruvian Central Bank began discussions with a consortium of private commercial banks that ultimately agreed to provide a loan package of $398 million in the fall of 1976. The conditions were stringent, however. The Peruvian sol was to be devalued immediately by 31 percent and afterward by regular monthly "crawling-peg adjustments"; public sector wages were to be frozen for eighteen months; phased budget cuts were announced; and subsidies on key consumer items were to be reduced, thus necessitating nationwide price increases.[5]

Although the initial response by the Peruvian public was muted, by February 1977 the Morales government had begun violating the terms of the loan agreement in response to pressure from particular interest groups. The military received a special pay increase, the budget was expanded rather than curtailed, and subsidies were ended only on selected consumer goods. The banks thus suspended their loans in March, and the government faced a major impasse. Its trade deficit was swelling to a rate of over $1 billion per year, financing was not available for new imports, and the public was restless. On July 19, 1977, there was a twenty-four-hour general strike in Lima, and in a series of clashes between demonstrators and troops, thirteen people died. In the same month the civilian economics minister and the governor of the central bank resigned when the cabinet (which was dominated by the military) refused to accept the terms that the IMF was insisting on as a precondition for new credit.

After months of rancorous negotiations, with the Peruvian government threatening to default on its private debt obligations and the IMF stoutly refusing to offer new funds, an agreement was reached on a new standby credit in November 1977. Within a month the Morales government had violated the terms of the agreement, and the IMF suspended its credit. Not until July 1978 was a lasting arrangement worked out with the IMF. It entailed major cuts in government spending, tax increases, an end to subsidization of interest rates at government banks, and a commitment to periodic, further devaluations of the sol.[6]

Both the Philippine and Peruvian governments chose to postpone currency devaluations as long as possible. Both saw the devaluations and related stabilization programs as a major setback, and both saw the conditions imposed for receiving the IMF standby credit as a capitulation to foreign powers.

Why did these governments try to avoid devaluation for so long? Was it because of the resulting increase in prices for imported goods? The likely shifts in income to exporters and away from consumers of imports? The perceived loss of sovereignty involved in making a commitment to the IMF about internal economic policies? Or was the recalcitrance even more fundamental, with both governments resisting the IMF's urgings to trim government expenditures, reduce controls on trade, and end various subsidies? Why does devaluation still produce such wrenching changes when many economists had predicted that the introduction of the flexible exchange rate system in the post-1971 period would make parity changes a smooth and continuous process?

The blunt answer is that devaluation frequently involves a blend of all the problems raised in the questions. It is rare that a government has the good fortune to deal with these issues one at a time. In addition to economic problems, national leaders must be highly sensitive to the political implications of their economic policy choices. It is worth noting that, despite the fact that the Marcos government is a rightist authoritarian regime and the Morales government was of leftist authoritarian stripe, both feared proceeding with devaluation, and both lost popularity when the exchange rate changes were announced. We can thus be confident that regimes across a broad ideological spectrum have similar concerns about the impact of a devaluation.

Purpose of this Book

Given the dramatic increases in less developed country (LDC) borrowing in the past decade and the subsequent debt servicing problems, the growing complexity of planning and implementing a devaluation, and the likelihood that these difficulties will continue, there is a need for a systematic examination of currency devaluation as a policy problem. Although there is a vast literature on the theoretical aspects of devaluation, this book concentrates on the practical problems that policymakers face in planning and implementing a devaluation. Three central questions are posed in this study:

1. What drives a country to devalue?
2. What determines the likely success of a devaluation?
3. What are the critical stages in a devaluation process?

To respond to these questions, we will examine detailed case studies of devaluations in India, Indonesia and Ghana. Not only are these cases historically significant, but their diversity illustrates the range of problems and constraints facing a government considering devaluation. Also, in each of these cases, the governments were being pressured to devalue, and this added a special element of complexity to the decision process.

Because devaluation is a frequent, critical, and often volatile issue for LDCs, it merits particular attention.[7] Most LDC governments do not have enough foreign exchange and the financial expertise to manage a float of their currencies.[8] They choose instead to peg their currencies in a fixed ratio to one of the major reserve currencies: the U.S. dollar, French franc, British pound, or the IMF's special drawing right (SDR). In June 1984 ninety-three of the world's governments had pegged their currencies, and only four (Canada, Japan, the United Kingdom, and the United States) met the IMF's criteria for fully "independent floating."[9]

Although the current international financial arrangements are called the floating exchange rate system, virtually all of the LDC governments face a somewhat mixed situation where their parities are officially fixed (in relation to one of the reserve currencies) but do move up and down as the price of the reserve currency fluctuates.

This means that LDC governments must be ready to make two types of adjustments: (1) adapting to the daily oscillations of the currency to which they have pegged and (2) making less frequent but more fundamental shifts when they change the ratio between their currency and the reserve currency. Each time there are parity changes relative to either the major currency or the rest of the world, there are internal price changes that affect economic performance. Although the floating exchange rate system was designed to ease economic adjustment and has done so to some extent for the Western industrial democracies, in important ways it has complicated the situation for LDCs.[10]

Devaluation is a policy decision of extraordinary power. Unlike expenditure programs that require staff to implement or tax programs that the public can often avoid, a devaluation can be planned by a small group and has pervasive effects on an economy. Devaluation usually has an immediate impact on traded goods, often followed by subsequent effects on a nation's price, employment, and growth performance. Yet because a government wants to avoid a speculative attack on its currency, the preparations for a parity change are usually made by a limited number of trusted technical staff.[11] If a researcher has access to members of the staff or their records, it becomes a manageable project to reconstruct the main events and influences on the decision.

Devaluation is also of interest from a political-economy perspective because it has national prestige implications with which few other economic policies are burdened, making it an interesting case of economic efficiency versus political prestige concerns for a government.

Devaluation is a curious remedy; the costs (increased import prices, shifts in employment, and possibly inflation) come at least twelve to eighteen months before the benefits (expanded exports and employment). This makes political leaders want to get it over with, blame it on the previous administration, and find some way to blunt criticism of the decision without trying to explain the technical details to an uncomprehending public. Attempts by French President Mitterand to blame the United States for the franc devaluations in 1982 and 1983 (despite the fact that France's inflation rate was twice the U.S. rate) is a good example of this approach.

A parity change has in addition differential effects on diverse groups of people. A devaluation rewards producers in the import-substituting and export sectors and penalizes consumers or producers who use imported goods. This has significant class implications in most LDCs where middle- and upper-income groups are the main importers.[12] It also has important consequences for urban versus rural divisions because agricultural and raw material exports are often the first to benefit from a devaluation, while urban service sector consumers feel an immediate pinch. If urban consumers are unionized or politically powerful, reducing their incomes is a risky exercise.

Most important, devaluation warrants attention because LDCs have even less success than the developed countries in controlling inflation, and they repeatedly need to adjust their parities to keep exports competitive and avoid encouraging imports. So not only will the LDCs have the problem of dealing with the fluctuating exchange rate system,[13] but their difficulties in coping with internal interest groups and inflationary pressures are likely to make devaluation a continuing policy dilemma.[14] Although there has been sentiment in the United States and Europe for a return to fixed exchange rates, the advocates of this step appear to have only limited support among the major member countries in the IMF.

The Central Hypotheses and a Framework for Analysis

Among academic economists, there have been three principal approaches to analyzing devaluation. The *elasticities approach* has concentrated on evaluating the effects of parity changes on the balance of trade. Using partial equilibrium methods and assuming that all other factors are constant, advocates of this approach have shown that a devaluation will improve a country's balance of trade if the sum of the elasticities of demand for its exports and imports is greater than one.[15] Further refinements of this view have shown the conditions necessary for a country to improve its balance of trade if it starts from a position of trade deficit.[16] The advantage of this approach is that import and export supply and demand elasticities are measurable, and the analysis focuses on the odds that the trade balance will actually improve. The limitations, however, are that all other factors are rarely constant, and it does not provide a policy guide of how to handle the situation if other dilemmas (like inflation or resistance from key interest groups) are plaguing a government.

The *absorption approach* grows out of the Keynesian tradition, emphasizing that there is a fixed supply of goods and services in an economy at full employment. Under these conditions devaluation can be successful only if the domestic absorption of goods is reduced to permit either fewer imports or increased exports.[17] The absorption approach has also been used to show that instead of stimulating demand, devaluations can actually be deflationary if the resulting relative price changes favor groups in the society with low propensities to consume.[18]

The *monetary balance approach* draws on elements of both other schools but introduces two additional refinements by showing how asset balances of citizens are affected and how capital flows in and out of the devaluing country shape the balance of payments position.[19] Monetary balances are important because devaluation lowers the value of assets for holders of domestic currency. This may lead to increased savings to recoup the lost assets, a process that can be deflationary if there is a sizable decrease in consumption. Also if there is fear that devaluation may be a recurring phenomenon (clearly the case in many developing countries), the public may try to hold its assets in foreign currency or foreign bank accounts.

The monetary balance approach raises an even more troubling problem. There is evidence that it takes long periods (six to eighteen months) for producers to shift orientation and for trade balances to adjust, but with the increasing sophistication of world capital markets, financial adjustments may take place within a matter of days.[20] This means not only that capital adjustments may work in opposition to the desired trade adjustments but that there could be numerous shifts (positive or negative) in the monetary balance effects during the period when a country was trying to implement an overall program to improve its trade balance.

In sum, economists have developed a set of useful quantitative methods for identifying the constraints policymakers face when considering a devaluation. Nevertheless the effects of a devaluation depend on the circumstances under which it takes place. If the devaluing country had been at full employment and close to balance of payments equilibrium and the parity change was designed primarily to cope with a new external shock (like the oil price increases of 1973–1974 and 1978–1979), the necessary internal adjustments, though possibly large in magnitude, can be directed toward the principal goal of increasing exports and slowing imports.

As noted in the Philippine and Peruvian cases, however, many developing countries are using devaluation as part of a more complex policy package to address internal and external problems. A common situation is for the country to be facing simultaneously an internal budget deficit, inflation, a deteriorating balance of payments position, and difficulty in meeting foreign debt obligations. Under these circumstances, currency devaluation is only one of many steps that need to be taken to stabilize the economy.

Although devaluation is a frequent and often traumatic occurrence in LDCs, it has not been the subject of much commentary in the political science literature. Between 1980 and 1984 not a single article appeared in the *American Political Science Review* examining this key policy problem for LDCs.

There is relevant work in the political economy literature that analyzes the context in which LDC governments make economic policy choices. One key theme is how the character and extent of trade affect national power and bargaining.[21] There is also extensive work on how economic dependence shapes decision making.[22] There is a growing literature on how a country's national interest may be compromised or enhanced through political pressure.[23] And some recent theoretical work examines the asymmetrical relationships that typify bargaining on international economic policy questions.[24]

This book attempts to combine analysis of both the political and economic aspects of devaluation. The following five hypotheses are designed to provide a comprehensive but integrated description of the political and economic constraints that LDC policymakers face when deciding whether to proceed with devaluations:

1. The success of a devaluation requires both short- and long-run adjustments. In the short run a devaluation is successful when the respective price and income elasticities for exports and imports facilitate a marked improvement in the balance of trade, the macroeffects of the parity change supplement the government's overall policy package, there are no destabilizing capital flows, and the moves are accepted as legitimate by the public.

2. In the long run a devaluation is successful if there are fundamental shifts in resources toward export development and a slowing of the rate of growth of imports, if inflation moderates, and if the reallocation of income (toward exporters and import substituters) is not reversed through political pressure or other means.

3. A devaluation's success in economic terms is in many cases incompatible with the political constraints facing the regime in power. The devaluing government needs maneuverability to deal with the reductions in real income and reallocation of resources that occur. Maneuverability requires some tangible hope that the devaluation will lead to an improvement in the balance of payments, usually entails domestic credit constraints, and frequently necessitates external aid or credit.

4. The actual monetary and fiscal effects directly attributable to a devaluation are often thwarted by adverse foreign macroeconomic conditions or other internal economic problems that limit resource reallocation within the devaluing country.

5. Devaluations produce such complex changes that economists are frequently unable to identify and estimate the full extent of the subsidiary effects. Political decision makers are at an even greater disadvantage because they typically have little familiarity with the details of a parity change. Devaluation has the additional disadvantage that the costs to the public are immediate, while the benefits frequently take eighteen months to be felt.

Given the complexity of devaluation, the range of circumstances that precipitate it, and the differing limitations each country faces following a parity change, an elaborate quantitative effort would be required to develop a fully satisfactory model for devaluation episodes. Without initiating a vast modeling exercise, however, it is possible to identify the major groups likely to benefit or suffer from a devaluation. Additionally it is useful to distinguish the initial political and economic effects of a devaluation from the longer-run changes that occur as the rewards and disincentives of the exchange rate change work their way through the economic system. Since so many devaluations are part of an overall stabilization program, it is also worthwhile to separate the effects of stabilization measures from those of the devaluation. Table 1.1 presents the results in a simplified, schematic form.

The Questions to Be Addressed

In approaching these devaluation decisions, we will want to explain their differences, but it is also useful to organize the discussion around several key theoretical questions. Not only do we want to know why a country devalues but what systematic patterns there are in predicting the outcomes and what analytic structure to use for approaching the disparate information available about a devaluation episode.

1. *What drives a country to devalue?* Governments choose devaluation under basically three types of circumstances: under duress, when there are attractive inducements, and when the devaluation is part of an overall program that requires a parity change to be effective.

Necessity is probably the principal driving force behind most devaluations. When governments find that they are exhausting their foreign exchange and are unable to obtain additional funds from foreign creditors, they ascertain that the situation is serious. Yet there are a host of interim remedies: increased tariffs, quotas, selective credit policies, licensing requirements, and contractionary domestic macroeconomic policy.

What frequently tips the balance in favor of devaluation is the recognition that these interim steps have not worked or will not work sufficiently quickly to avoid a crisis. The Ghanaian devaluation of 1971 is a classic example of this type. The Ghanaian government was unable to meet its payments obligations and had run out of feasible alternative measures. Although few regimes wait as long before acting as the Busia government did, the threat of having to cut off new imports or default on payments is a powerful stimulant. In approaching other devaluations, some of the initial

Table 1.1
Likely effects of a devaluation in an LDC

	Groups hurt	Groups helped
Direct effects of devaluation		
Economic		
Relative price changes and resulting income effects	Consumers using imports	Exporters
	Producers requiring imported raw materials or intermediate goods	Producers of import substitutes
	Urban, middle, and upper classes relying on imported consumables, durables	Producers of nontradables (construction, local services)
Asset effects	Holders of domestic currency	Holders of foreign currency
Political		
Criticism for bad economic performance	Government in power	Opposition
Concentration of responses	Volatile, articulate urban dwellers	Rural inhabitants and those in export industries
Secondary effects of devaluation		
Inflation	Wage and salary earners unable to keep pace with inflation	Debtors
	Savers	Holders of real assets
	Holders of money and non-indexed financial assets	
Possible recession	Most wage-earning workers	Exporters due to greater price competitiveness
	Most producers for domestic consumption and investors in domestic industry	
Emphasis on exporting through relative price changes and shifts in government programs	Importers	Exporters
	Domestic sectors receiving less government support	

Table 1.1 (continued)

	Groups hurt	Groups helped
Related consequences if devaluation is part of a broader stabilization program		
Restrictive credit policies	Leveraged investors and those relying on low interest and government credit	Those trying to compete with government firms or government-subsidized firms
Price rather than quantitative restrictions on trade	Domestic industries less protected by quotas and by government's former determination of resource allocation	Efficient producers who were limited when government was allocating foreign exchange
Restrictive government budget policy	Any area of direct funding or subsidies that were cut due to general attempts to reduce domestic budget deficits	Private sector to the extent that resources are freed for nongovernmental uses

questions to ask are thus: How severe was the crisis? What would have happened had the government delayed?

Attractive inducements can also encourage national leaders to take steps that they know will be painful. In the Indian devaluation of 1966, Prime Minister Indira Gandhi certainly understood that there would be strong opposition to devaluing the rupee, yet the World Bank and bilateral aid donors were offering such an enticing package of new aid that the benefits appeared to outweigh the costs.

Inducements need not always be external resources. If a devaluation is likely to produce a substantially more efficient internal combination of production and investment, then it may well warrant the dislocations involved. Naturally different governments will evaluate the risks involved in varying fashions, but the analyst must look for patterns in how the costs and benefits were assessed.

Devaluations are increasingly being recommended as elements of overall programs for adjustment. The Indonesian devaluation of 1970 is an interesting example of this motivation for a parity change. President Suharto's economic advisers had long planned to end their dual exchange rate system, simplify export taxation, and consolidate administration into a single, market-determined exchange rate. When the IMF offered its standby agreement, the devaluation and rate consolidation became an attractive prospect.[25]

With the World Bank now offering structural adjustment loans and the IMF vigorously pursuing its enlarged access policy, LDC governments may prefer to wrap devaluations into an even broader set of policy changes. It may also be easier for a government to justify a devaluation if it is viewed as one element in an effort to adjust to higher energy prices and generate enough foreign exchange to service debt. We will thus want to identify those aspects of a devaluation that can augment or impede adjustment programs.

2. *What determines the likely success of a devaluation?* No single variable can be used to predict the success of a devaluation. Ultimately national leaders choose devaluation when they are severely constrained, and they look for flexibility in policy options. Success is a relative term. At a minimum it can mean avoiding a disastrous cutoff in imports; moderate results might entail some internal reallocation of resources and improvement in the balance of trade; and a resounding success could mean major changes in internal production and investment behavior, and the development of a dynamic export sector.

Most of the literature on devaluation has focused on the economic issues. This book attempts to set out the process in a broader context. The basic argument will be that the success of a devaluation depends on the maneuverability open to the government concerned. The freedom to maneuver is a complex blend of three factors: latitude in the economic variables, the extent of domestic political constraints, and the character and extent of international support. It may not be possible, in advance of a devaluation, to know which of these clusters of variables is most important, but they are clearly interdependent and a government must deal adequately with each area to achieve fundamental changes.

The economic factors shaping the success of a devaluation are the easiest to measure. One tangible measure is whether the devaluation improves the balance of trade. This, however, is not an adequate overall judgment on the effectiveness of a parity change. It has even been suggested that a devaluation is a success if the country's minister of finance survives in office at least twelve months after the decision.[26]

Yet there are clearly a range of economic variables that need to be assessed: how large are the foreign exchange reserves, and how long can the country wait for export earnings to improve? What are the elasticities of demand for those export products that the country can plausibly produce? How innovative and effective are the country's entrepreneurs? For agricultural goods, how predictable is the country's climate, and how easily can resources be moved into higher-productivity crops and processing? How critical are timing considerations? Are there elections, potential military conflicts, holiday seasons, or crop cycles that will make a government want to speed up or delay a decision? None of these factors alone will prevent a country from devaluing if it faces a severe crisis; nevertheless, a prudent policymaker will probe each of these issues to determine likely performance.

The most comprehensive presentation of how economic variables will affect the likely success of a devaluation is available in the series edited by Jagdish Bhagwati and Anne Krueger.[27] They and their coauthors explore the most propitious circumstances to enable an LDC to remove internal controls and reallocate resources. They show that a devaluation can be part of a building process where early success at removing the trade deficit provides resources necessary for the further removal of protection. Thus maneuverability provides promise of acceptable performance on certain key variables and creates the right sequence of steps.

The domestic political constraints are frequently given inadequate attention when devaluations are planned, yet both the Ghanaian and Indian governments ultimately failed because they encountered intense domestic resistance. Here the analyst also needs to look at a range of issues: Which businessmen are in the export trade? What are the links between business and government? How extensive is the level of protection? Which sectors are receiving subsidies? Would particular regions of the country or classes noticeably gain or lose through a parity change? Is there a religious or cultural reason why greater reliance on competition will be resented? It is not possible to quantify these variables with precision, but they are vital for determining outcomes and need to be put on a par with the economic factors in determining a national leader's room to maneuver.

National political leaders must also be concerned with how the devaluation is perceived by their citizens. If balance of payments problems are brought about by a war or by some external event the government could not control, the public may be willing to support the government despite the deprivations. Yet if the devaluation is seen as a result of economic mismanagement or as part of an overall program to shift rewards permanently in the society, the resistance can be intense.

In the Ghanaian case the devaluation of the cedi clearly helped rural, small-holder cocoa growers and hurt unionized labor, civil servants, and the military. Although Ghana was a democracy at the time and low-income cocoa farmers vastly outnumbered the urban elites, the Ghanaian political system was sufficiently fragile that it could not take the strain of such major income redistribution. There are also dynamic elements that need to be considered. If the exchange rate change is one bit of bad news for a regime generally perceived as competent, public acceptance is vastly different than in a situation of extended miasma. Since most LDC governments are not democracies, one also needs to evaluate how effective the means of coercion are if serious resistance develops.

The international environment is often viewed in exclusively economic terms: what are the export and import supply and demand elasticities, and what type and volume of credit is available? In a pre–World War II environment, this might have been a realistic way to look at devaluation. But currently a country must estimate not only what resources will be available from bilateral donors and multilateral agencies but whether these organizations will play an attentive and supportive role in encouraging further private sector participation.

Here several sensitive issues come into play: the strategic significance of the country to potential donors, the size of its internal market, the experience of the donors and multilateral agencies when they were involved in past attempts at giving policy advice, and whether the country has either critical resources or a sufficiently large debt that it could threaten other nations by its behavior. Given the high visibility of these external funding sources, few heads of government spurn them, but in each of the three case studies we will note how the outside organizations were able to shape outcomes.

In sum, an adept national leader will assess constraints and then attempt to maximize maneuverability given the economic variables, domestic political structure, and international scene.

3. *What are the critical stages in a devaluation episode?* In dealing with the range of pressures and actors involved in a devaluation, it is useful first to analyze the setting in which the decision takes place and then to focus on the actual stages of the process.

For our purposes, it is worthwhile to divide devaluations into two broad categories: those where the country is basically operating on its own, with minimal outside interference, and those where foreign advice and offers of foreign resources play a significant role in the decision process.

In the situation where the devaluing country is operating independently (either because it does not want or is unable to obtain substantial foreign advice or resources), the calculus is simplified. The aspects of the external environment that are important are predominantly economic—in particular, the relevant supply and demand elasticities and estimates of how quickly the balance of trade will change. If external resources are not available to cushion the effects of the devaluation, the adjustment may be wrenching. Thus a government in this situation needs to plan for resistance to its decision and design an overall policy package that works with limited resources and protects those most vulnerable to the parity change.

Most LDCs, however, do not operate independently. They are typically members of the IMF and World Bank, and most have some access to private credit. Therefore this group will receive most of our attention. When foreign involvement is important, the external environment is vastly more complicated. The government concerned must not only calculate the pure economic effects of a devaluation but must decide on the best negotiating strategy for obtaining the foreign resources.

There is a fundamental asymmetry between the foreign organizations and the country considering devaluation. Each side knows that the foreigners can simply withdraw funds if they so choose. Hence to sustain a relationship for months or years, there needs to be a mutually satisfactory set of guidelines for their interaction. Obviously there is considerable variety in these relationships. Typically, large numbers of individuals are involved, and they frequently have conflicting goals and operating styles. The essential element, however, is the judgment by each of the foreign organizations and the devaluing country of how significant their interaction will be. Thus we have a classic bargaining situation.[28]

The bilateral donors are commonly concerned with the location, strategic significance, volume of trade, key natural resources, level of foreign investment, commercial borrowing, and political orientation of the recipient. The international organizations, such as the World Bank and the IMF, have only an oblique interest in the military status of their clients, but the magnitude of trade and debt and political prominence strongly influence how responsive they will be.

The devaluing country must choose its patrons carefully. A government receiving outside assistance must judge whether outside resources are adequate to compensate for the costs. The costs will vary among countries, but they often entail reduced policy flexibility and create a situation in which the government can be criticized. In sum, as a country's foreign exchange reserves dwindle and balance of payments difficulties appear imminent, the donors and the potential recipient rate their respective partners. If a mutually satisfactory relationship appears feasible, the delicate art of shaping an explicit understanding commences.

Each devaluation episode is distinct. Yet certain common patterns of behavior allow us to categorize the interaction between the parties. This interaction could be measured by several indexes: volume of resource flow, publicity given to the agreements, or number of people directly or indirectly affected by the decision. Although we will look at these measures in the case studies, none is fully effective at capturing the character of relations between the foreigners and the devaluing country.

The most tangible indication of how seriously the parties take the relationship is the rank of the individuals involved. For example, in the Polish debt rescheduling and negotiations of 1981, prime ministers and presidents were directly involved. In contrast, the Turkish devaluation and debt rescheduling undertaken during 1979 and 1980 was handled predominantly by senior technocrats and private bankers. High visibility is not always a benefit, but the rank of those involved is a critical indication of what the participants expect.

Stages in a Devaluation Episode

One way to approach a devaluation is to follow the sequence of economic policy measures chosen (moves back and forth between tightness and looseness in exchange controls, quotas and tariffs, and parity adjustments).[29] Another way would be to do two cross-sections, comparing before and after for the gamut of micropolicies and macropolicies selected.[30] Each of these approaches has merit, depending on the aspects of the episode of greatest interest. Here, however, the focus will be on the decision-making process.

In the India, Indonesia, and Ghana cases, there were four essential stages common to each episode:

Stage 1: the establishment of an *arena* where the devaluing country and the foreign organizations determine the seriousness of their interaction and the character of foreign involvement in the decision

Stage 2: the *bureaucratic politics* where competing policy options are presented, and different factions maneuver to have their views incorporated into the devaluation package

Stage 3: the actual *executive decisions* where the president or prime minister determines the scope of the devaluation adjustment program

Stage 4: the *implementation* process, including the timing, the manner of presenting the decision to the public, the mobilization of support, and the myriad choices on trade, finance, and investment regulations that determine the extent of the devaluation's effect.

Stage 1: The Arena

Once it is clear that a country cannot meet its payments or faces serious difficulties, there is generally a short period of calm as both the local government and foreign organizations evaluate the circumstances. In this stage decisions are likely to be rational, reflecting the costs and benefits of involvement. Although the outside organizations have the inherent advantage of being able to exit, the ties that develop limit the flexibility of both sides.[31]

Nevertheless, fundamental changes in assessments do occur. In 1978 the Soviet Union switched from supporting Somalia to an extensive involvement in Ethiopia, and between 1966 and 1971, the United States reversed its position from strongly supporting to threatening India.[32] In each case there were dramatic shifts in resource flows. The arena thus provides for a period of mutual sizing up by potential partners, The significance of the devaluing country and the promise of the situation play a key role in determining the volume of resources to be committed.

The arena also helps shape a mutually agreeable operating style. If there is a large transfer of resources involved and decisions are being made at the chief executive level, both sides may want a high-profile relationship. IMF lending to Jamaica, U.S. aid to Israel, and Japanese support for South Korea fit this pattern. To maintain a high-profile interaction, however, there must be tangible signs of economic and security benefits. Without such benefits, the leadership in the devaluing country may be accused of making too many concessions to the foreigners. An alternative approach is to handle the interaction at a more routine, technical level. This keeps the discussion among specialists and tends to be a less volatile situation that can be nurtured for long periods because of its lesser visibility and participants' lower expectations. There is also the possibility that the devaluing country is of such minor importance that a serious relationship never develops. This is a highly asymmetric situation and can pose considerable difficulties for the devaluing country because it cannot be sure of either new resources or high-quality technical advice as the crisis develops. Yet the more usual pattern is for the initial period to circumscribe likely options and produce an agreed agenda.

Stage 2: Bureaucratic Politics

After the basic ground rules have been laid, the bureaucratic politics of the situation move to center stage.[33] The significance of this step will vary with the number, sophistication, and influence of the actors involved. Given the financial gain that could result if traders knew of a planned devaluation, the preparations are closely held. Yet the ideologies, training, and personal agendas of those who actually draft the options need to be sorted out. Dealing with a cohesive, highly skilled group like the economic technocrats in Indonesia is a different experience from negotiating with the bureaucratic disarray in Zaire.[34] In addition, in a country like India with an exceedingly wide spectrum of ideologies, the proposed policy measures reflect that political reality even if the bureaucrats themselves might prefer a different outcome. Thus it is essential to see how the competition among advisers plus the exigencies of the moment mold the final recommendation to the principals.

Stage 3: Executive Decision

Given its importance, the final approval for a devaluation is usually made by the head of government. Although only one of the three chief executives evaluated in this study was questioned directly, we have considerable information about all three from those who dealt with them frequently.[35] The purpose of focusing on the executive decision is to see how political leadership responded to economic crisis.

The first step is generally when the economic staff convinces the political leader that the situation is sufficiently serious to warrant close attention. Then as the various alternatives are brought forward, the options are narrowed. For each case in this book, I discuss the particular circumstances that led each leader to agree to the devaluation.

Once a decision has been made, a host of issues requiring political judgment arise. What should the timing be? Are there drought, holiday, or election periods to be avoided? Although preparations must be kept secret, what planning should be done to mobilize support for the decision and to thwart anticipated criticism?

It is important to know how well the technical economic analysis was presented. Was it accurate? Did the presidents and prime ministers, who are not economists, understand the pervasiveness and significance of the step they were approving? Were there patterns in the way that these political figures responded to difficult economic choices?[36] We know, for example, that Prime Minister Kofi Busia of Ghana was well aware that his finance minister favored the devaluation not so much as a means of solving the trade deficit but as a disguised tax that would yield favorable results in handling the domestic budget deficit. If Busia went that far in analyzing the effects of devaluation, we will want to know why he did not press further to estimate the likely price increases that would result and which groups in society would be most adversely affected.

Stage 4: Implementation

The Indonesian devaluation was seen as part of an overall stabilization program and received only minimal criticism, while the Indian and Ghanaian decisions were the objects of intense controversy and virulent attacks. Clearly we cannot judge the performance of the respective governments by the public reaction alone, but it is reasonable to ask how well the decision makers did with the circumstances they faced.

In 1965 India survived one of the worst droughts in its history. Because there was no record of major droughts in two consecutive years, it is not reasonable to criticize the Indian economists for failing to predict the second drought in 1966. Yet it is sensible to ask why they did not postpone the devaluation for another six to eight weeks when they could have had accurate information on crop yields, which are so important for estimating exports and food imports in India. Similarly it is curious that Prime Minister Busia chose to go ahead with the devaluation in Ghana before the holiday season was over and before he had a firm commitment on future resources from the IMF.

It is also useful to know if the government actually took the steps necessary to improve economic performance and get the benefits from the devaluation. Were export duties lowered? Were government regulations on investment simplified so that business could move into or expand in the export sector? What steps were taken to control inflation so that the new exchange rate would not quickly be overvalued? For example, in 1964 the Park regime in South Korea decided to float its currency until it could determine a reasonable parity, but it began intensive steps to encourage exports and lay the basis for its rapid growth before exchange rate policy was entirely certain.[37]

Finally, did the government make a persuasive case in explaining the need for the devaluation? In Mexico's financial crisis in the fall of 1982, President Lopez Portilla blamed Mexicans who had invested their money overseas and the private banks for his problems. Portilla then used this as an excuse for nationalizing the banks.[38] Much of the Mexican public remained skeptical of Portilla's remarks. Similarly, the Indian and Ghanaian public reactions to their devaluation was exacerbated because the sacrifices being extracted were not well explained. The analysis of implementation will therefore evaluate how appropriate the economic steps were given the known constraints.

Why Analyze Devaluations under Pressure?

It is not possible to give a precise quantitative estimate of the percentage of devaluation decisions made under pressure because many of the deliberations are secret and governments occasionally initiate a devaluation to avoid the appearances of having conceded to foreign pressure. Nonetheless, a study of recent IMF stabilization programs showed that most governments did devalue before, during, or shortly after the provision of IMF standby credit.[39]

Thus, from an analytical standpoint, the appeal of concentrating on devaluations initiated under pressure is that they are clearly an important subset of all devaluations and highlight the tension between the objectives of foreign organizations and the domestic constraints a government faces.

The initial question thus becomes, Does the threat of a foreign exchange crisis produce reasonably predictable government behavior? There is considerable evidence that economic policymakers typically view a foreign exchange shortage as a transient problem and attempt to cope by searching for internal sources of funds. When internal options are exhausted, governmental attention is then often focused on the easiest external sources, like commercial banks and some bilateral donors. Only as a last resort do decision makers acknowledge the need for harsher remedies like devaluation and borrowing from the IMF. If systematic inquiry shows that these patterns show up repeatedly, we have a useful policy guide because it is clearly suboptimal for governments to wait until crises develop before initiating a stricter regime.

An equally important issue about devaluations under pressure is whether the foreign intervention is legitimate. Part of this debate is ideological. Marxists see the foreign pressure as insidious,[40] while many social democratic critics view the process simply as an additional means of preserving an international economic system biased against the LDCs.[41] In the 1960s Western neoclassical economists tended to be confident about their ability to define precisely a country's resource needs,[42] and this led to confidence about the legitimacy of intervention.[43] By the 1970s a much broader debate about the objectives of development was occurring.[44] Some analysts stressed improving the physical quality of life in LDCs.[45] Others preferred a focus on employment and ensuring minimum living standards.[46] And a third group emphasized decontrolling LDC government regulations with renewed reliance on market principles and export promotion.[47]

In the midst of this lively debate on policy objectives, there was also considerable discussion about the effectiveness of the resources and advice provided by foreign organizations. Although certain stabilization programs had clearly been effective in the post–World War II era,[48] doubts increasingly arose about the advisability of stringent policies in a time of resource scarcity when unpopular programs appeared to be only marginally successful in solving balance of payments problems.[49]

Much of this debate has been about the IMF itself. Liberal critics have argued that the IMF is too rigid,[50] too monetarist,[51] and too market oriented.[52] Conservative critics have claimed that the fund has not pressed hard enough to get countries to select realistic exchange rates and has not put enough emphasis on supply-side considerations.[53] Mainstream critics have lamented that the IMF has been only moderately successful at meeting its own stated goals[54] and that it should shift its emphasis toward a new mix of objectives like growth, sectoral balance, and even income distribution.[55]

In the 1980s there has also been greater concern with how the entire international economic environment shaped the real—as distinct from theoretical—options of LDC policymakers. In the decade 1974–1983, there were five years of recession in the developed countries (due to the reactions to the oil price increases), and the LDCs necessarily saw this as a forbidding environment for trying to increase their exports.[56] This meant that many LDC governments had to contract their imports sharply if they were to reduce their trade deficits.[57]

Three case studies will not provide a definitive judgment on the efficacy and legitimacy of foreign-pressured devaluations, but by probing in depth we can identify particular recurring patterns that shape outcomes. Although in the past decade commercial banks have become the target source of finance for LDCs, in many cases the role of the IMF in pressing for devaluation has been strengthened because the private banks have preferred to have the IMF leading the discussion of stabilization measures.

Why Select These Cases?

The India, Indonesia, and Ghana cases illustrate both sufficient similarities and sufficient differences to allow generalizations about devaluations under pressure. Because the central objective is to explore what precipitates devaluations and what determines their success, the variety in the cases will highlight the issues involved.

There would have been some advantages to broadening the sample and making this a more statistical study. Yet work of this kind has been done, and it poses a number of problems in ensuring comparability in the circumstances being measured.[58] In addition, probing these cases in depth permits us to convey their complexity and is useful for making generalizations as long as we demonstrate that it is the differences in the key variables that produced the divergent results.[59]

There are a number of important similarities among the Indian, Indonesian, and Ghanaian devaluation episodes:

- external pressure to devalue
- anticipation that the devaluation and related policy measures would lead to an increase in external resources
- government steps to move toward a more market-oriented mix of policies
- a turning point in policy choice for the respective governments

The main differences were these:

- the structural characteristics of the countries (strategic significance, size of internal market, regime type, and past experience in dealing with foreign donors)
- the factors that drove the governments to devalue
- the breadth and quality of the analytical work that preceded the decision
- the resulting maneuverability available to the respective governments

Although there was variation in the extent of the external pressure (Indonesia getting the least and Ghana the most), each of the national leaders knew that necessary foreign resources would not have been forthcoming unless policy changes were made. Also, despite Indonesia's success at bringing down the inflation rate to 10 percent in 1969, prices had risen 85 percent in 1968, and aid was still supplying 27 percent of government revenues. Hence Suharto's economists still felt the situation was tenuous and could not afford to antagonize aid donors or international organizations.

The differences among the cases are striking. The geopolitical significance of India and Indonesia led to their being offered opportunities that never developed for Ghana. This affected not only the analytic work and style of negotiations but ultimately the maneuverability necessary for a successful devaluation.

Each case is historically significant. The Indian decision of June 6, 1966, is an extraordinary example of a foreign-pressured devaluation. The analytic work that laid the basis for the move was a fourteen-volume study commissioned directly by the president of the World Bank.[60] Chester Bowles, U.S. ambassador to India at the time, leaked a key memo by the U.S. Agency for International Development (USAID) to the *Washington Post* hoping to put extra pressure on President Lyndon Johnson to increase U.S. aid; Mrs. Ghandi's visit to Washington in March 1966 was planned with the explicit purpose of extracting more assistance from the Aid-India Consortium; in April 1966 the Indian planning minister came to Washington and worked out the details for the devaluation and decontrol package in discussions that involved direct negotiations with the president of the World Bank and several meetings with President Johnson. There are few economic policy decisions made by a developing country that involve such a profusion of high-level attention.

The Indonesian case is notable because the Suharto government brought about startling changes in economic policy without high-level foreign involvement. In fact there was a clear understanding between the Indonesian government and aid donors that discussions would be low-profile, technocratic undertakings. The U.S. government limited its aid to one-third of the total and consciously avoided public discussion of policy recommendations from the aid donors. For their part, Suharto's economists had a clear strategy left over from the Dutch: provide cheap rice to the urban areas and cheap textiles to the entire population. While meeting these minimal requirements, the Indonesians then concentrated on resource flows: attempting to maximize aid, expand private foreign investment, and encourage the repatriation of Indonesian capital.[61] This permitted a rise in living standards throughout the stabilization period and made the devaluation untraumatic.[62] The striking aspect of the Indonesian case is how atypical the circumstances were for an LDC. Few other countries may be as fortunate.

The Ghanaian devaluation of December 1971 is an example of foreign pressure producing a bitter result. The Busia government got itself into a serious balance of payments crisis but never received the attention or volume of funds that were so critical in the Indian and Indonesian cases. Because Ghana lacked strategic importance and was of minimal commercial significance, Western donors were not willing to intervene to provide any major expansion of resources or to soften the terms of the IMF. It is ironic to note how dramatically Ghana's fortunes had changed from the period in the late 1950s and early 1960s when Ghana appeared to be the darling of many donors. In that former period Ghana looked as if it had reasonable economic management and Kwame Nkrumah seemed to be extracting aid deftly from both Western and Marxist countries. By the late 1960s, however, Nkrumah had produced an economic disaster, and Ghana was no longer an appealing model for either the donors or other African countries.

This meant that Prime Minister Busia had limited maneuverability. Given Ghana's reduced importance to the donors, the poor planning for the devaluation itself, and the unavoidable reduction in consumer imports, the Busia government was seen domestically in a very unfavorable light. The circumstances created an easy excuse for antigovernment activity and dissent within the military. The Acheampong coup, which overthrew Busia, followed seventeen days later.

Ongoing Problem

Currency devaluation will remain an ongoing problem for LDCs. Virtually all countries face difficulties with a depreciating currency, but the LDCs usually have the least maneuverability. Their foreign exchange reserves are often minimal, their exports are typically concentrated in a few commodities, and structural adjustment is frequently constrained because capital mobility and changes in production technology are slow. Since these problems are relatively predictable, it is useful to examine how governments in different circumstances have taken steps that enhanced or impeded success at managing a devaluation.

One of the central objectives of this book is to provide a framework linking the political and economic constraints facing a devaluing country. Despite the vast economic literature on this subject, there has been little analysis of the political factors influencing outcomes. Foreign advice about devaluation is often purely economic, and in such a political vacuum, LDC decision makers frequently stumble by ignoring key issues. The case studies illustrate the complexity of making decisions on devaluation and how severe the consequences are for some countries.

2   India: Expectations
       Shattered

Lord Siva could drink the poison, but the Congress cannot.
Kamaraj, 1966

On the night of June 5, 1966, Sachin Chaudhuri, union finance minister, went on All-India radio with the unenviable task of announcing that the government had decided to devalue the rupee by 58 percent.[1] Chaudhuri, a courtly Bengali barrister, had taken over his post five months before as a classic patronage appointee. With little previous training in economics or finance, Chaudhuri stumbled as he read the speech prepared for him by his career, civil service staff.

In and of itself, the event should hardly be surprising. It is widely recognized that the Indian political system is a consensus one where patronage appointments are not only accepted but considered useful in muting the friction of a polyethnic state. Also the tradition of having generalists make policy decisions based on technical work by their staff is an old British habit well entrenched in New Delhi. It is not particularly startling that a lawyer who spent most of his career on tax law was not familiar with the latest arguments on effective exchange rates. What is interesting to note, however, is that the government of India, for eight years prior to Chaudhuri's speech, had employed thousands of government workers to review millions of import requests to avoid devaluation and decontrol; that the 1963–1965 Annual Reports of the Ministry of Commerce and International Trade had stoutly maintained that a devaluation was unwise and unnecessary; that most of the cabinet had not been informed until minutes before the announcement; that Prime Minister Gandhi authorized Chaudhuri's move only after intense pressure from the IMF, the International Bank for Reconstruction and Development (IBRD), and Aid-India Consortium members; and, most important, that Mrs. Gandhi took this risky decision based on her assessment of the new rapprochement in U.S.-Indian relations she felt she had engineered during her March 1966 trip to Washington.

The Nehru and Shastri Legacy

In a short discussion it is not possible to present a full evaluation of the legacy imparted by Jawaharlal Nehru, India's premier statesman.[2] The following comments highlight only those factors that had a significant impact on the economic policy options open to his daughter in 1966.

Nehru's economic strategy can be characterized as a blend of belief in Soviet-forced industrialization and fabian socialism. Given his ambiguous feelings about Western civilization, Nehru hoped that India could achieve the levels of income that he associated with the industrialized countries while retaining the strengths of traditional Indian cultures.[3] This led him to favor government ownership of industry, central direction of the economy, a bureaucracy designed to monitor even the minutest details of resource allocation, concentration on heavy industry, and an explicit strategy of import substitution to reduce dependence on trade. This set of policy preferences led him to downplay the importance of the agricultural sector. He viewed peasants as a drag on the economy and a group that needed politicization through the Community Development Program but not as a source of economic growth that could complement the industrial objectives.

Although this design for India's economic development met the test of coherence, in retrospect it appears to have been extremely inappropriate for a country of enormous size and a population of predominantly poor peasants. Despite the skills and relative sophistication of India's civil service, economic management from the center was slow, inefficient, and costly. Additionally resources were repeatedly channeled into industries where they could not be effectively used, compounding the problem of the poor, stagnant rural sector.[4] Table 2.1 shows that the mismanagement of the economy was so pervasive that there was virtually no growth in per capita net national product (NNP) during the last four years of Nehru's life. This meant that Prime Minister Lal Bahadur Shastri, and ultimately Mrs. Gandhi, inherited inefficient private and public industry, an extensive bureaucracy with a vested interest in continuing controls, a rural sector sorely in need of greater investment and incentives for production, and a family planning effort that was having little impact.

Several elements of the political system that evolved under Nehru should also be mentioned. The broad coalition of the Congress party, the splintered

Table 2.1
Indian net national product, totals, per capita, and growth rates (computations in rupees)

	Net national product at 1960–61 prices		Annual growth rates (percent)		Index numbers (1960–61 = 100)	
	Total (rupees billions)	Per capita (rupees)	Total	Per capita	Total	Per capita
1950–51	90.9	253.1			68.4	82.7
1951–52	93.1	255.1			70.1	83.4
1952–53	96.4	259.1			72.6	84.7
1953–54	102.6	270.8	3.7	1.8	77.3	88.5
1954–55	105.3	272.9			79.3	89.2
1955–56	108.9	277.1			82.0	90.2
1956–57	115.1	286.9			86.7	93.8
1957–58	113.2	276.9			85.2	90.5
1958–59	122.3	292.6	4.0	2.0	92.1	95.6
1959–60	124.5	292.2			93.7	95.5
1960–61	132.8	306.0			100.0	100.0
1961–62	137.3	309.3			103.4	101.1
1962–63	139.9	308.2			105.4	100.7
1963–64	147.7	318.3	2.6	0.4	111.2	104.0
1964–65	158.8	335.1			119.6	109.5
1965–66	150.8	310.9			113.5	101.6
1966–67	152.3	307.9	1.0	− 1.0	114.7	100.6
1967–68	166.1	328.2	9.0	6.9	125.0	107.3

Source: J. N. Bhagwati and T. N. Srinivasan, *Foreign Trade Regimes and Economic Development: India* (New York: National Bureau of Economic Research, distributed by Columbia University Press, 1975), table 1-1, p. 6.

opposition, and skillful national leadership committed to gradual, democratic change became hallmarks of Indian domestic politics. Yet despite Nehru's oft-demonstrated charisma, the Congress party was losing its vitality.[5] A generally recognized malaise had begun to develop.[6]

Part of the declining enthusiasm reflected India's reverses in foreign policy. During the 1950s Nehru had been able not only to advocate what he claimed was a moral course for India but could legitimately say he was speaking as one of the leaders of all the developing countries. Several commentators on Nehru's worldview have argued that he always considered industrialization and modernization primarily as routes to world power.[7] His concern for his international image and his known tendency for running the Foreign Ministry as his own fiefdom unfortunately kept him from focusing on much more crucial domestic problems.[8]

By the 1960s the LDCs were no longer content to let others speak for them, and India's strategic importance had declined. Also Nehru's belligerent stance toward the Chinese led to the humiliating loss in the 1962 war.[9] The government of India's tendency to criticize those that were aiding it gradually created sufficient resentment to reduce maneuverability. Although aid continued to increase during almost every year from 1954 through 1966, India's claim as a development model was on the wane, and donors were increasingly disheartened with India's perfunctory economic performance.

For a mild-mannered, self-effacing man, Shastri proved remarkably successful as a politician and leader. Nehru's strength was his vision of what the nation should be and his appeal to a broad spectrum of citizens. Shastri's strength was his pragmatism. He had learned to survive in an exceptionally competitive party hierarchy and brought these skills to policymaking. Several of his characteristics differentiated him from his predecessor and made him open to changes in economic strategy: decisiveness, a lack of foreign education or theoretical sophistication, and relatively little antagonism toward the top civil servants.[10]

Shastri was in power only for eighteen months, so he was not able to bring about any fundamental changes in the Indian economy, yet he made a number of moves that laid the basis for significant policy changes after his death. His most striking decision was to change the balance of priorities between agriculture and industry. He let his agriculture minister, C. Subramaniam, start a program for massive imports of fertilizer; committed his government to a price incentive scheme for farmers combined with decontrol of seed, pesticide, and fertilizer distribution; and authorized increased expenditures for irrigation and rural works.

Shastri took two other steps that diverged from Nehru's rigid course. He increasingly began to listen to Subramaniam and Asoka Mehta (planning minister), the two cabinet members most inclined toward decontrol and greater use of the market. Shastri also took the threat of a scandal as a convenient excuse to fire T. T. Krishnamachari (TTK). (See the Chronology for the details of the firing, which occurred in December 1965.) TTK had been a major power in his own right and as finance minister had been one of the most outspoken opponents of devaluation and decontrol.[11] Interestingly it was the top civil servants in his own ministry who became disillusioned with controls and thus the strongest inside advocates of greater reliance on the market. When Sachin Chaudhuri was picked as TTK's replacement, the civil servants themselves began to play a bigger role in policy formation. The powerful Finance Ministry thus swung around from opposition to support of decontrol.

Shastri's economic choices were not all stellar ones, however. In September 1964 he had to preside over a cabinet session where final determination was being made on budget allocations for the remainder of the Third Five Year Plan (up to 1966). At this session his weakness for seeking consensus led him to agree to a clearly inflationary budget because he was unwilling to choose among increases for the military, industrial, or social sectors. By granting increases in capital expenditures to advocates from each sector, he forced the bureaucracy to cut back on supplies of raw materials and intermediate goods to existing public and private firms. This meant that production was held below capacity, and new investment went into plants for which there were limited raw materials.

Nehru's dreams were far beyond India's economic capabilities. The focus on industry in the public sector led to a neglect of both private firms and seven-eighths of the population who still lived in rural areas. Under Shastri there were signs of moving toward decontrol and greater competition, but fiscal policy was too expansionist, and it created inflation for the first time since World War II. Clearly Mrs. Gandhi would have faced a series of fundamental economic choices even if the Pakistan war of 1965 had not aggravated the balance of payments situation.

Stage 1: The Arena

The Nehru and Shastri legacy provided the setting in which Mrs. Gandhi had to operate. Yet both of her predecessors had avoided devaluation, and both were content to continue with the controls system. What actually precipitated the devaluation, and why did Mrs. Gandhi take the risks she did? Several events stand out.

The 1962 China war had a crucial influence on Indian economic policy. The humiliating loss produced an understandable nationalistic reaction, creating popular support for increasing military spending. This in itself would not have led to subsequent balance of payments problems, except that Nehru proceeded to advocate guns and development and Shastri tried for guns, development, and the social sector. The resulting stimulative macroeconomic policy caused further scarcity of key raw materials and intermediate goods and inflation, and made exports less competitive and imports more attractive.[12] The major increases in military expenditures were for the Indian Army. Although this was not likely to have scared the Chinese (who had nuclear weapons in 1964), it probably did increase Indian confidence that they could prevail in a conflict with Pakistan.

The 1965 Pakistan war had a more immediate impact. It forced a further sharp increase in government expenditures, and the military logistics effort placed a strain on the transport system, which otherwise could have dealt with civilian requirements. The decision by the United States to cut off commitments of new aid to both India and Pakistan during the hostilities created additional uncertainty because the Indian Finance Ministry did not know how to ration the remaining aid. Interestingly, the government of India (GOI) decision to establish the defense remittance scheme and initiate even higher import duties together was a de facto devaluation.[13]

The 1965 drought was a critical event for several reasons. It required the use of additional foreign exchange to buy food and seriously hurt export earnings as jute, tea, and cotton production were down. Most important, the drought exposed the weaknesses of the Indian planning system. By concentrating on industry and providing high levels of protection, the agricultural sector had suffered, and import availabilities became a principal constraint on growth. The irony of this pattern is that reducing dependence on imported goods had been a key Indian objective, whereas the drought highlighted India's vulnerability. Because the West and the United States in particular were the only foreseeable source of adequate grain to avert famine, it was a pragmatic step to consider a more conciliatory stance toward the United States.

The success of Mrs, Gandhi's trip to Washington, D.C., March 1966 also played a key role in building momentum for the devaluation. Although it was an exploratory visit designed to let President Johnson meet the newly selected prime minister, both heads of government sensed a possibility of a rapprochement that could be beneficial to both India and the United States.

Mrs. Gandhi knew that U.S. resources were a critical element of bilateral and World Bank aid, and President Johnson saw the possibility of forging a link with an energetic leader of a key state. Soon after Mrs. Gandhi's return to New Delhi, she got a cable from her uncle B. K. Nehru, the Indian ambassador to Washington, who reported that she had made a superb impression on Lyndon Johnson and urged that efforts be made to capitalize on renewed U.S. government warmth toward India.

A growing pattern of donor disillusionment with Indian economic performance provided a background to these specific events, which made the top Indian civil servants worried about their outside sources of support. Of the $1,511 billion that India received as project, program, and food aid disbursements in fiscal year 1966–1967, only 6 percent came from countries that were not members of the Aid-India Consortium. Most of the nonconsortium aid was from socialist countries and was paid for on hard terms through barter agreements.[14] Thus, keeping the Aid-India Consortium members supportive was clearly a vital interest to Mrs. Gandhi. (Tables 2A.1 through 2A.3 summarize the actual disbursements for 1966 through 1969.) So, with foreign exchange reserves falling to very low levels, a growing concern among the donors that their aid was not being well utilized, and the effects of two wars and a major drought plaguing the economy, Mrs. Gandhi knew that there had to be changes in economic policy. Before turning to her options, it is useful to review the donor position and discuss why the government of India relied so heavily on quantitative trade restrictions and industry controls.

The Donor Position

When the Aid-India Consortium was formed in 1958, its central purpose was to mobilize support among Western nations for massive transfers of resources. The GOI was the only LDC government that had a sophisticated planning commission, it used the latest in mathematical models, and it had a twenty-five-year planning horizon as well. In fact, the 1957–1958 balance of payments crisis that highlighted the need for aid was viewed as an aberration caused by declines in export prices, not as a reflection of poor economic policy. The donors who formed the consortium thus felt that this justified increasing aid flows rather than greater scrutiny over aid utilization. The World Bank's report of 1960 (chaired by Michael Hoffman) and the comments of three independent economists brought in to assess Indian economic performance in 1961 both skipped lightly over resource allocation problems and stressed the need for increased aid to avoid the impinging balance of payments constraint (see chronology). This was poor analysis, but it was masked because NNP was growing satisfactorily at about 4 percent per year from 1956 to 1961. By 1962, however, the effects of the investment in government-owned heavy industry were being felt, and the rest of the economy was carrying the load. Yet the debate was still in ideological, private versus public sector terms, and there did not seem to be a clear alternative.

Then a change in analytic orientation evolved. It was recognized that neither U.S. nor Soviet experience was precisely applicable for investment decisions but that the Western Europeans had been coping with large public sectors for over a decade, and their choices might be relevant. The questions shifted from being, "Who owns the resources?" (Indian private firms were often just as inefficient as public ones) to the more pragmatic, "How productive are the resources?" With this change in orientation, other data from the Indian scene began to fit a common diagnosis: farmers were unproductive because incentives were insufficient and the GOI artifically skewed investment toward industry, exporters were not particularly in-novative because the overvalued exchange rate was essentially a tax, and industrial firms had little incentive to be efficient if they had a protected market. In the enthusiasm about macroeconomic growth models, price theory had been neglected. Among both socialist and liberal analysts,[15] there developed a greater interest in the micro aspects of resource distri-bution and using competition to achieve efficiency.[16]

As this new approach to Indian economic policy was gaining adherents, George Woods, president of the World Bank, decided to undertake a full-scale evaluation of the Indian economy. The IBRD chaired the Aid-India Consortium, and Woods was deeply worried that donor disillusionment with Indian progress would grow to the point where it would be difficult to maintain aid levels. Dr. Bernard Bell was picked to head the IBRD mission, and the group was given over a year to do its research and reach its findings on eight sectors and issues in Indian policy. (The Chronology provides a detailed review of the Bell mission's activities. Appendix 2B summarizes the findings.) The Bell mission did extensive data collection and had frequent contact with a range of analysts. The final report was kept secret, but it drew heavily on the growing critiques of the GOI, stressing the need for greater emphasis on agriculture, the advantages of greater competition and less governmental interference in resource allocation, the need to devalue if controls were removed because the rupee's official rate would lead to excess import demand, and the desirability of having the consortium provide a large amount of nonproject aid to ease the transition toward a decentralized, substantially decontrolled economy.[17]

Then an interesting phenomenon developed: the ideology of aid was taken seriously. Formerly the rationale for aid to India had worked to reinforce GOI preferences. Economic growth was the principal goal of aid, and during the 1950s India had a commendable record.[18] Rewarding performance was also a central tenet of aid programs, and the GOI's planning effort and ability to draft appealing justifications for aid projects had made it relatively simple to give examples of India's effort.[19] Starting with Chester Bowles in the early 1950s and extending to John P. Lewis in the 1960s, there was also a long string of advocates who argued the crucial importance of India, and this doubtless made it easier to win approval for added assistance for New Delhi.[20] India's role as a model for other LDCs was also frequently stressed by those who were impressed by its democratic form of government. Once India began to do poorly on growth and development performance criteria, many of the aid India enthusiasts failed to see they had raised expectations unreasonably. Great commotion was made over the poor performance, and the donors then justified to themselves the use of substantial leverage to redirect GOI policy. The GOI was therefore hit not only with an intellectual challenge to its policies by the economists but had to endure the criticism of some of its fondest supporters.

Persistence of Controls in India

Controls (of production, procurement, distribution, or price) are a way to deal with scarcity.[21] They are not a technique that appeals to those trained in the liberal tradition and are rarely efficient in economic terms, yet they are politically acceptable and appealing to the elite who has governed India since independence. In the Indian context, controls are both a stratagem and a protective wall; they keep economic policy within the purview of top ranks of the administrative and economic services while providing a socialist patina to wave before hostile critics from the Left. Despite the large turnover of civil servants, there is definitely an elite culture, which is passed from occupant to occupant of key jobs and provides the guiding principles of policy formation.[22]

The basic elite goal is maintenance of the integrity of the system: keeping India together as one nation. From that come three subsidiary goals: price stability, avoidance of conspicuous consumption by the wealthy, and creation of a sufficiently large, heavy industrial base to make

India an independent world power.[23] These three goals are quite different from the public ones of growth with equality, but they have come to be the balance that best fits the political demands.[24] Price stability is necessary to appease the landless laborers, urban poor, and salaried groups.[25] Avoiding lavish consumption is a legacy of earlier days, but it touches a deep populist sentiment. International status combined with the stated goal of equity appeals to intellectuals and is clearly one of the sustaining motivations of the civil service itself.[26]

In order to make choices about types of economic strategies, operational assumptions are needed. The enduring ones could be summarized as follows:

- The pricing and distribution of essential commodities must be carried out in a politically appealing manner.
- Competition among unequals leads to visibly unequal results.
- Businessmen are shortsighted and selfish, invariably extract exorbitant profits, and have no commendable history as mobilizers of resources.[27]
- Therefore, a policy of trying to raise production by increasing competition and turning over more discretion for allocational choices to businessmen will lead to increased inequality, waste, and political uproar.
- At the other extreme, a coercive socialist pattern of economic organization such as the USSR or China has used would overstrain the government's administrative capabilities and run counter to the fundamental Indian preference for individualism.
- In sum, a move toward either increased competition or increased coercion would be unpopular. Therefore, choose the middle ground of a large public sector in essential industries and pervasive controls of those resources not directly owned.

The elite had so completely accepted the essentials of this argument that Western talk of the advantages of decontrol or Soviet proddings about the need for increased discipline were of little avail.

These self-imposed boundaries to effective action had at least two important results:

1. Controls gradually lose their effectiveness, and, as the press and opposition point out problems with the system, the imperative is to impose more controls.

2. The government's attention is frequently focused on the problems of distribution (hoarders and profiteers) rather than the issue of increasing production.

This cycle of expanded controls goes directly counter to the liberal notion that if controls are not working, try something else. Consistently Westerners have argued that the Indian controls system will lose its appeal over time when, in fact, the opposite often occurred. In the summer of 1974, for example, bad harvests were causing extensive hardship among the poor.[28] Mrs. Gandhi's response was the immensely popular decision to reinstitute "raids on hoarders" and to give speeches asking the public to "keep up the vigilance against deviants."[29] Even the business-owned press reflected the view that the problem was distribution rather than demanding more fertilizer and irrigation equipment for farmers.

Because political leaders were unwilling or unable to persuade the public to move toward either greater competition or coercion, the pattern of controls persists. Yet stagnation has long been the order of the day in India. This means that no widespread demand for faster growth (which would entail either greater inequality or greater government demands on the public) has developed.

A brief look at the history of controls shows how easily they were absorbed into prevailing norms, especially the Sirkar culture of viewing the government as regulator-provider.[30] Part of the irony is that the British were the first to introduce controls in World War II, and they viewed them as only a temporary expedient to ensure public acquiescence for maintaining an adequate supply of war material.[31]

Yet controls spread in rapid succession and soon touched virtually all major sectors of the economy.[32] In September 1939 the Defense of India Act was passed, giving the colonial government authority to regulate prices if the situation warranted. In April 1942 the government licensed all food grain dealers. In December 1942 the Food Department was established to purchase and distribute steel on an all-India basis. In May 1943 the Department of Industry and Supply was established to ensure stocks of textiles and steel. In August 1943 the Hoarding and Profiteering Prevention Ordinance Act was passed to set limits for profit on all trade. In 1945 the businessman's Bombay Plan was announced endorsing Congress party demands for independence but carefully arguing for protected industry after the British departure. The British Labour government in 1945 approved the government-owned Sindhi fertilizer plant, this being the first move toward a larger public sector after the midwar takeover of the railways and the coal mines. In 1947 Mahatma Gandhi had his famous debate with Dr. J. Matthai. Gandhi argued that controls merely lead to corruption; he won out, and the independent government decontrolled textiles and food grains. In 1948 Nehru decided to reinstitute controls and issued the Industrial Policy Resolution, which divided the economy into three sectors (private, public, and joint) but reserved the "commanding heights of the economy to the public." In 1952 the Industries Act transferred the power to license industry from the states to the central government to "ensure co-ordination" and authorized the government to issue import permits according to the needs of priority sectors. Finally in 1956 in an attempt to aid the heavy industrialization effort of the Second Five Year Plan, production, procurement, distribution, and price controls were tightened for steel, cement, and fertilizer; imports were rationed even more stringently; and more extensive regulation of the sugar and food grains sectors were started.

As is clear from this list, the term *controls* is applied to three broad types of government intervention: actual ownership, distribution of resources through licenses, or monitoring of nongovernmental flows through price, profit, or distribution regulations.

Although import controls were modified by introducing tariffs and other marginal adjustments were made in assorted sectors, the system survived essentially intact until the mid-1960s.[33] The inefficiencies and growth-inhibiting characteristics of such a stragegy have been well analyzed for other LDCs, and Bhagwati and Srinivasan have estimated aspects of the static and dynamic welfare losses from two decades of controls.[34]

Besides the losses in efficiency for the society, the controls have generated the oft-discussed black economy. Because many of the government-determined prices are far below what customers are willing to pay for scarce supplies, government officials, traders, and producers often share in the premiums obtainable above the regulated prices. Because these illegal profits cannot be easily invested in productive enterprises, they often go into consumption or elaborate laundering schemes. Numerous official commissions have investigated this additional drawback of the controls system, but there is a general consensus that corruption is inevitable as long as the GOI continues to force the sale of goods below market prices.[35]

In sum, the GOI has adopted controls as a politically acceptable means of dealing with scarcity. Except for the decontrol in 1947, the brief steps in that direction in 1966, and some liberalization in the late 1970s and early 1980s, the controls system remained a characteristic Indian method of resource allocation. Not until the late fall of 1984, after Rajiv Gandhi took over the prime ministership (following his mother's assassination), did the government try a major move toward decontrol. The system avoided the volatile alternatives of competition or coercion, maintained the status and power of the bureaucracy, and, despite its warts, provided the Congress party with an economic policy package consistently accepted by the public. It is not surprising that in 1966 the donors ran into a complex maze when they pressed for decontrol as the price for increased program aid.[36]

Alternative Strategies for Mrs. Gandhi

Given the mounting severity of the balance of payments problem in the spring of 1966 and the growing consensus among the donors that aid should be conditioned on changes in GOI policy, Mrs, Gandhi had three broad types of strategies from which to choose:

1. Taking a radical Left position of forfeiting on debt payments, rallying support through attacks on the Western nations, and making an open bid for increased aid from the Soviet Union and Eastern European countries.

2. Tightening controls to deal with the balance of payments difficulties but delaying major policy changes while bargaining with the Western donors and betting they would continue resource flows without new conditions, at least until after the 1967 general elections.

3. Liberalizing controls, proceeding with the devaluation, and hoping that the increase in aid flows would produce sufficiently tangible results that criticism about concessions to the Westerners would be minimized.

A move to the Left would have had some domestic political appeal. Mrs. Gandhi used leftist slogans in the 1971 election with considerable success, and in the midst of the drought that was causing great hardship, there would certainly have been support for moves against the business community and the wealthy.[37] There would have been major costs to that tack, however. The GOI previously had been punctilious about debt payments, and its rather Victorian view on forfeiture had allowed the GOI to keep a good credit record.[38] To give up its access to Western aid and forbearance would have been a considerable risk, particularly because the likely volume and terms of Soviet and East European aid would almost certainly have been less attractive than what was available from the West.[39] Also, although greater autarky would have had emotional appeal, it was an additional risk during a drought because the West was the major supplier of surplus food grains.

Tightening controls and attempting to delay the donor-pressured policy changes would probably have been the safest course. It seems highly improbable that the consortium would have cut off aid completely if India hestitated, and there might even have been some sympathy for a plea from

Mrs. Gandhi to wait until after the 1967 election before making major policy changes. The problem with this route was that it would have meant reductions in aid (when she needed increases), and it would have failed to capitalize on her goodwill with President Johnson.

The devaluation and decontrol coupled with major increases in aid thus began to look like an enticing package. The appeal certainly warranted sending her planning minister to negotiate with the president of the World Bank about the final terms.

As the arena took shape, Mrs. Gandhi assessed her position. India's size, location, and political prominence made it attractive to the donors, and Mrs. Gandhi had an opportunity to expand significantly the country's resources. The price was the virtual certainty of criticism over the devaluation and a long series of smaller battles regarding decontrol and sectoral priorities. The donors were increasingly frustrated with India's performance and saw Mrs. Gandhi's first few months in office as the ideal time to make her an offer.

Stage 2: Bureaucratic Politics

The most important characteristic of the predevaluation bureaucratic maneuvering was its secrecy. This was necessary partly to limit the possibility of speculative demands on the rupee, but it was also used as a means of thwarting criticism by ministers and top civil servants who might ordinarily have been included but who would have delayed or altered the design of the policy package had they been involved.[40] This meant that the small number of individuals who were involved had considerable influence.

The Actors

The central figure was Mrs. Gandhi. President Johnson described her as "a combination of Barbara Ward and Lady Bird" (which we can assume were both compliments). Others found her "devious," "without scruples," "shrewd," "capable of outwitting all her male peers," and a "born politician." For this analysis, the most important aspect of the decision-making process in the spring of 1966 was that "there was a tug of war for her mind." One of her closest staffers says, "Though she always kept politics to herself, she was open to a variety of alternatives in economics."

Mrs. Gandhi had been raised on Nehru's brand of socialism, but she was a local product, not concerned with ideological purity. As home minister, she seemed quite willing to dissolve Communist state governments, and she had been promoted to prime minister because other Congress leaders felt they could control her. She thus had an ambiguous record, and each major political faction was trying to win her over. Ironically, despite the overtly political contentions, it appears that the most critical figures influencing her decision were civil service advisers. Men of similar caste, some even Kashmiris, they were a group she trusted during the extraordinarily tense beginning of her term.

With her finely honed political skills, Nehru's daughter sensed the fragility of the situation and knew there needed to be at least the appearance of action. Given the dwindling foreign exchange reserves and a recognition of the vitriol that would ensue if there was a substantial reduction in imports, Mrs. Gandhi recognized the direct causal relationship between aid resource flows and her future political maneuverability.

The opposed ministers made it clear that they preferred to stay with controls. Manubhai Shah (Commerce and International Trade) and T. N. Singh (Steel) were vociferous opponents of decontrol and devaluation. Shah, a voluble, energetic man, had long represented the interests of Gujarati and Marwari businessmen, and he personally ruled the empire of export subsidies that meant enormous profits for those who could convince the GOI that their product merited special treatment. He was convinced that the GOI should intervene to stimulate exports on a commodity by commodity basis.[41] Singh was so opposed to the Bell mission (and what he assumed its recommendations would be) that he refused to give permission for his staff to talk with the visiting World Bank personnel.

The swing ministers were Subramaniam, Mehta, and Chaudhuri. Subramaniam had made his name as an administrator and, though quite content with a large public sector, felt that controls should be minimized to avoid wasteful government intervention. Mehta, an articulate socialist theoretician of some prominence, had long been a darling of the Nehrus, and Mrs. Gandhi felt relaxed with his pragmatic approach to management. Chaudhuri was important primarily because he took the advice of his advisers who by 1966 were convinced that significant changes needed to be tried. If Mehta and Subramaniam had not been close to the prime minister and had they not been strong advocates of the donors' proposal, Chaudhuri alone is unlikely to have been successful at bringing about the changes. Nevertheless, at the moment of her decision the three together had a crucial influence.

The secretaries group was also quite important.[42] It consisted of S. Bhoo-tilingham, L. K. Jha, I. G. Patel, V. K. Ramaswamy, and S. S. Marathe.[43] Jha had the most direct access to Mrs. Gandhi and was persuasive because of his analytical ability and experience in the same job under Shastri. Bhootilingham and Patel, both strong and competent, dominated the Ministry of Finance once TTK departed. Marathe, having held Patel's job before, knew both the requirements of the Finance bureaucracy and the details of the arcane controls system in the other departments. Ramaswamy had little bureaucratic skill, but his intellect was important in the design of the eventual policy package. Each of these men was the intellectual equal of the foreign advisers and economists who descended on Delhi, and they were quite capable of probing and exploring the recommendations prof-fered to the GOI.

Foreign aid personnel and Academics were in abundant supply in India at the time of the devaluation preparations.[44] Three were the most influen-tial in identifying a new policy package and then persuading key Indians to consider it. Through his widely read paper on underutilized industrial capacity, C. E. Lindblom convinced several top civil servants that it was unwise to continue with new investments in heavy industry when there was insufficient foreign exchange to supply the extant factories. Lindblom was also one of the most articulate in showing the interrelationship of controls, protected markets, poor export performance, and inefficient gov-ernment industries.

When John Lewis returned to India (after two years as a member of the U.S. Council of Economic Advisor), he brought with him not only his extensive familiarity with the economy but his calm, persuasive manner. Lewis was known as a "friend of India," so his criticisms were not overly threatening, and he was the first high-level outsider to come up with the idea of the carrot and stick approach of proposing more aid as an incentive for GOI policy changes.[45]

Bernard Bell took these available options and (besides documenting them in detail through his mission report) began the difficult job of trying to persuade ministerial-level figures on both the donor and recipient sides to accept the policy package. Bell is a skilled economist and a reconciler superb at dealing with strident, potentially conflictual issues.[46] Thus these three foreigners complemented each other by moving the liberalization ideas from the theoretical to the operational sphere. Although there were some clear differences in orientation among them and among the broader group of foreign economists in Delhi, it is fair to say that the Westerners as a whole supported some variant of the move toward decentralization, decontrol, and increased competition.[47]

The Gathering Momentum

It was not technocrats, however, who created the environment in which devaluation seemed a reasonable risk to Mrs. Gandhi. It was the 1965 Pakistan war and the worsening drought that precipitated the balance of payments crisis and revealed the GOI's vulnerability to foreign pressure.

Once George Woods had accepted the draft of the Bell mission report, the weight of the consortium's chairman was behind an extremely critical document but one that proposed increasing the program aid component to ease the GOI's transition to decontrol. When Woods asked Bell and A. De Lattre (a top French central banker) to go to New Delhi to review the report's findings and try to persuade the Shastri government to follow the bank's strategy, the GOI's top civil servants knew the effort was serious.[48] A participant has commented, "Bell's return to Delhi was like the visit of a high-level physician to a sick patient who was refusing his medicine." With the Subramaniam-Freeman agreement on changes in agricultural policy reached shortly after, the donors were encouraged.[49]

On Shastri's death and during the first few weeks of Mrs. Gandhi's term in office, economic policy received only peripheral attention. By mid-February 1966 the patterns became quite clear, however. Vice-President Hubert Humphrey's visit had been successful at reaffirming U.S.–Indian ties; India's executive director at the IMF had committed the GOI to a "more realistic" exchange rate; and Mrs. Gandhi had accepted an invitation to Washington with the intent of sounding out President Johnson. With a successful Washington visit behind her, the previous talk of increased program aid became an imminent possibility, and Mehta was dispatched to Washington to see what the World Bank was offering in return for the devaluation and decontrol.[50]

This situation still left Mrs. Gandhi an excuse if the Woods-Mehta discussions went poorly, but it seemed to be the most attractive way out of her resource bind. While Mehta was in Washington, the civil servants she trusted were put to work on the final alternatives if a liberalization package was agreed on and it appeared politically propitious to proceed. With the momentum already evident, the bureaucratic maneuvering then narrowed to the small group of economists and administrators who debated the technical problems of attempting to restructure Indian economic policy management.

Devaluation and Liberalization: Arguments Pro and Con

In New Delhi, the arguments about devaluation and decontrol had been debated for so long that there was almost a fear of the consequences. Those advocating greater use of the market and responsiveness to international demand needed to convince not only themselves that the risks were worth taking and to develop sufficient justification for the move to overcome the deeply felt bureaucratic and public resistance. This required not only a strong commitment to pure theory but an act of faith as well because the country had been controlled for over two decades, and it was unclear how the private and public sectors would respond to greater competition.

The debate over the advisibility of the devaluation came down to three essential questions:

1. Would the devaluation solve the balance of payments problems?

2. Would the related changes in the economy necessary to get the full benefits of the devaluation and decontrol be beneficial?

3. Would the combined benefits clearly outweigh the costs of economic adjustment and political criticism?

The most commonly used argument against devaluation for India was one of elasticity pessimism. In fact, this had become the predominant view among Indian economists. This argument had two parts: (1) the claim that most of India's exports were agricultural where prices were set by world markets, not the exporter and (2) the readjustment into export-oriented production that usually accompanies devaluation would be slow or nonexistent in India. In nontechnical terms, Manubhai Shah said, "What is the sense of having a bargain sale in a department store when the shelves are bare and when the buyers only want a limited quantity of the goods anyway?"

Supporters of the devaluation admitted that a parity change for the rupee would not have any significant effect on the world price for cotton, jute, or tea. They countered, however, by noting that India had the world's tenth largest industrial capacity, which could significantly expand its export potential. They also stressed that other countries like Taiwan, Brazil, and Malaysia (which previously had exports concentrated in primary products) had been able to make the transition to manufactured exports and processing of agricultural goods by use of the market and realistic exchange rates.

On the immediate question of whether the devaluation would solve the payments difficulties in the spring of 1966, there was considerable uncertainty. Opponents of devaluation argued that targeted export subsidies were already an adequate incentive and that import tariffs and licenses were the most effective means to regulate imports. Advocates of devaluation acknowledged that it would take six to eighteen months for any substantial increase in exports, but they urged the parity change as an instantaneous means for restricting imports and a method for abolishing the inefficiency of the import licensing system.[51] To the small group who knew of the Bell mission report, there was also the clear understanding that devaluation would be accompanied by not only an increase in aid but a shift toward program assistance, exactly what India needed for covering urgent import needs.

Regarding the long-term benefits of devaluation and decontrol, the controversy was intense but even harder to resolve. The controls system was deeply entrenched, and there was little domestic pressure to change it. Yet, among the technically trained there was embarrassment and doubt about controls. The problem in estimating the long-run results was in predicting how the Indian farming and entrepreneurial community would respond.[52] If decontrol provided an adequate incentive, then there were unquestionably unused capacity and resources that could form the basis for a surge in economic growth. The fear was that decontrol would lead to a flood of imports and no substantial change in exports.

The ultimate question was whether the changes were worth the risk. Here the issue became a choice among difficult alternatives. Tightening controls and delaying the changes until after the 1967 general election would have been politically acceptable, but it would have lost or postponed the chance for the sizable increase in program aid. Since one could not do polling on the question or even do extensive private soundings without provoking rumors, judgments about the political reaction were also speculative.

Because a detailed quantitative estimate of the effects of various levels of devaluation and decontrol was beyond the computational capabilities of the civil service group looking into the policy alternatives, the final recommendations were, not surprisingly, based on personal judgment. The leader of the group, Bhootilingham, had been one of the principal designers and implementers of the controls system, and he was convinced that most controls had outlived their usefulness. Bhootilingham was willing, therefore, to propose taking the risks. Once Patel agreed with him, the course recommended to the prime minister was determined.

The Donor Package

Given that the episode is still highly classified on both the donor and recipient sides, there are at least three relevant questions about the agreement between George Woods and Asoka Mehta:[53] What were the donors offering? Would the donors have cut aid if the GOI had failed to meet the terms? What was the GOI committing itself to do in return for the aid promised by the chairman of the Aid-India Consortium?

For the donor side, Woods was pledging (for the consortium) to try to raise the nonfood aid from $1.2 billion in 1965–1966 to a level of $1.6 billion in 1966–1967. There was also the intention to change the composition of aid from predominantly project lending to about 50 percent program assistance.[54] Although there are many counterclaims based on Mehta's comments on his return to Delhi or the actual consortium pledge at the November 1966 Paris session, the record shows original numbers as agreed. (Appendix 2B contains a summary of the Woods-Mehta agreement.) Two points about the understanding that summarized the agreement are particularly interesting: Woods was pledging only to try and emphasized that the consortium was made up of sovereign governments, which would have to make their own decisions, and though it was assumed that the aid would continue at a high level, there was agreement on only the initial GOI fiscal year at hand.

It is impossible to know what the governments would have done if the GOI had refused to devalue, but we can speculate. It is highly unlikely that the donors would have cut off all aid, but with the IBRD no longer endorsing the GOI request (as might well have occurred), most donor governments would have had difficulty justifying the effort to maintain the large flows. Also, without substantial encouragement from the IBRD, the donors would never have agreed to the commitment of increased program aid and that was the GOI's highest priority at the moment. It is also not unreasonable to assume that if the agreement had been stymied, political relations between the principal donors and the GOI would have deteriorated (as in fact happened in the late 1960s after aid was reduced).

Commitments for the GOI were extremely detailed, covering specific targets for various sectors. Import controls were to be replaced by tariffs within twenty-four months, and industrial licensing was to be streamlined. Yet there was a fundamental and apparently unresolved difference in perception of what liberalization meant. Even to the most market-oriented Indians involved, talk of decontrol meant a gradual increase in the number of import permits and industrial licenses issued, possibly reaching the point of issuing licenses for every justified request. To the World Bank staff and other foreigners involved, decontrol meant the actual dismantling of control procedures. Bell thought he had an understanding that all administrative controls would be removed if program aid reached $900 million.

Although program aid disbursements never reached that level, the Indian participants in the negotiations do not even recollect that proviso.

Given the complexities of the issue, the difficulties of nomenclature, and the desire of Mrs. Gandhi to keep the details of the agreement out of the hands of her opposition and to maximize flexibility regarding the donors, the ensuing wrangling over donor and recipient commitments was not surprising.

The Final Steps

In analytic terms, the policy package proposed by the donors and accepted by Mehta can be divided into four broad areas: a GOI commitment to rationalize import distribution, reorient industrial policy, place greater emphasis on agriculture, and stimulate exports. The changes in agricultural policy were simply an extension of programs initiated after the Subramaniam-Freeman accord, but the other three choices were new decisions on the extent of decontrol and the price of foreign exchange. These choices affected virtually all sectors. Which export subsidies would be dropped? What import duties would be kept? Which industries would receive the priority for increased import licenses? Mehta's return brought information on the level of new aid anticipated, but the secretaries' group (and the junior staff they trusted to help them) still had an enormous job to do under time pressure because Mrs. Gandhi soon decided that the new policy should be announced in June.

Although consideration was given to floating the rupee, this alternative was eventually rejected as too risky.[55] It was finally decided that any system of marginal adjustments (like broader import entitlement schemes) would hinder the import rationalization and industrial policy change goals, leaving devaluation inevitable.

The final package was extremely complex, but an attempt was made to keep the regulations as clear as possible while still giving the Ministry of Finance leeway to allocate import privileges to preferred sectors:

- The rupee was formally devalued by 57.5 percent (which, after adjusting for subsidy and tariff changes, was a net 44.8 percent increase in import prices and a net 22.3 percent reduction in export prices).[56]
- Export subsidies were ended.[57]
- Import duties were cut, though assorted import bans remained.
- A list of fifty-nine priority industries was published with the under-

standing that firms in these sectors would be given quicker and larger import permits in the GOI approval process.

These were major steps. The rupee had not been devalued since directly after independence; Shah's export subsidization empire seemed to be in tatters; and power over import licensing appeared to have shifted to the Finance Ministry and away from the operational ministries. With the technical aspects of the decision reviewed, it is useful to turn and focus on the calculus at the chief executive level.

Stage 3: The Prime Minister's Decision

Mrs. Gandhi was an aloof person who rarely let her aides know her reasons for making particular decisions. Additionally, except for two years out of office, she remained in power between 1966 and 1984. Thus, few of her former advisers were willing to talk freely about her calculations. Nonetheless, she tended to be less secretive in reaching economic decisions, and, through interviews, it was possible to piece together sufficient information to make a reasonable assessment of her choices in the spring of 1966.

One of the most important aspects of the rupee devaluation was the extent and quality of the staff work that preceded it. In fact, in comparison with the preparations for the Ghanaian and Indenesian devaluation, the work was striking. The multitude of previous small sector studies and the Bell mission report combined to form an impressive empirical base for recommending policy change. In a country with a consciously intellectual civil service, these preparations helped generate some adherents. More significantly devaluation and liberalization had not been of particular interest to Indian economists, so the proposals could later (quite correctly) be branded as primarily of foreign origin. This meant that in accepting the Woods-Mehta agreement, Mrs. Gandhi was counting not only on foreign resources but relying predominantly on those Indian advisers who held alien ideas.

The decision to proceed with the Indian devaluation was a sliding one made over a number of months. The initial element was Mrs. Gandhi's overture to President Johnson and the cementing of her entente in March 1966. The political understandings that came from her Washington visit made it substantially more likely that the United States would fund its 44 percent share of the program aid Bell proposed. Therefore it is not surprising that as India's payments position worsened and Mrs. Gandhi got complimentary readings on her first foreign trip as prime minister, she was willing to take the second risk of sending Mehta to explore what the donors were offering.

Although she knew that the donors were proposing significant inducements, they also appeared to be hardening their position. Not surprisingly, the U.S. government and the World Bank saw the Woods-Mehta agreement as a binding commitment, and once the United States had informally endorsed the World Bank's position, the other donors could be more easily persuaded to comply. Naturally this gave the World Bank staff more leverage in its technical negotiations with the GOI. In addition Mrs. Gandhi knew that the IMF would be just as stringent. Since the GOI had used up all of its $200 million standby in 1965 and had nearly exhausted its $187 million gold tranche (drawn in February 1966), it was clear that further IMF resources would entail conditionality.

Mrs Gandhi not only understood this sequence of moves but actively participated in it. She approved the letter to the IMF stating that the GOI would adopt a realistic exchange rate, and she intentionally picked Asoka Mehta to deal with George Woods because he was no threat to her within the Congress party and would preserve her confidence. Once the technical aspects of the donor package were worked out, she faced one last hurdle: getting internal political acceptance for the proposed policy changes.

The initial steps went quite expeditiously, but the failure to resolve the internal political conflicts undermined the entire endeavor. This may have been inevitable given the secrecy and scope of concessions necessary to bring the donor proposal to fruition. For example, by relying on Mehta and Subramaniam for economic advice, she had to exclude Kamaraj (who still got his advice from TTK, a vociferous opponent of Subramaniam). Similarly, she could not trust Moradji Desai who was still brooding over his loss of the party leadership fight. This meant that she had to exclude her major rival and also give up some potential leverage over his supporter, Manubhai Shah.

Outside the Congress party, she could not discuss the issue with the Left, and her decision to rely on foreign resources made it impossible to generate nationalistic sentiment in favor of the devaluation. In sum, her intuition and boldness worked well in negotiating a secret understanding with the donors, but she failed to mobilize the necessary political support. The secrecy in planning a devaluation and the range of opponents to decontrol made hers an unenviable task. From her subsequent behavior, we know that she had hoped to keep her options open and not identify herself too closely with the devaluation but the last and most curious aspect of her decision process was that she seems not to have made any specific fallback plans if the venture failed.

Stage 4: Implementation: Constraints Dominate

As soon as Chaudhuri finished his June 6 devaluation announcement, the GOI began an effort to avoid discussing the planning and maneuvering that led to the decision. In his lackluster presentation to the Parliament several days later, Chaudhuri claimed that the devaluation had not been taken as a result of foreign pressure, but his distributed question and answer sheet acknowledged that the GOI had acted to "maintain the flow of foreign resources."

In the parliamentary debates that followed, the opposition pounced. The prime minister was badly buffeted. Virtually all of the Congress party leaders had been kept in the dark about the move or sounded out on it only at the last minute, so they were hardly willing to support her as the public response began to turn rancid. This left rather junior members of Parliament supporting devaluation for the Congress, while virtually all the opposition parties were critical. Even the free-enterprise Swatantra party (which felt obligated to support the trend toward liberalization) stressed that this unfortunate day had been brought on by poor past economic policy.

Mrs. Gandhi defended herself by saying, "We would have had to devalue whether or not the IBRD and IMF existed."[58] The opposition, however, saw no reason to let the ruling party escape and most of the speakers either disagreed with the substance of what was done or took the easier tack of claiming that India's sovereignty and honor had been infringed.

In the press the tone and quality of the debate was not much better. Although the main business-owned papers were generally sympathetic, no great effort was made to present a full and balanced interpretation of the events that had caused the balance of payments crisis or of the possible advantages that might come if the parity change and decontrol worked.[59] Of the business organizations, the Associated Chambers of Commerce (Assocham) took no formal position, the Federated Indian Chambers of Commerce and Industry (FICCI) supported the move with a small favorable advertising campaign, while the Indian Tea Association and Indian Jute Mills Association vigorously fought the new export tax as a disincentive for new investment in their respective sectors.

The initial reaction was extremely negative. Devaluation had become the fixation, and the GOI failed to convince any major group that the decision was laying the basis for a more promising future. The scene in

Delhi was one of glee among the opposition and despair in the Congress party. With this depressing news as a backdrop, Mrs. Gandhi flew off to Belgrade and Moscow, hoping to draw attention away from domestic troubles and emphasizing that nonalignment was still alive.

In an attempt to redress the pro-Western tilt that the June 6 announcement implied, Mrs. Gandhi signed a final communiqué in Moscow calling for an end to U.S. bombing in Vietnam and attacking "imperialist forces threatening peace."[60] This pleased the leftwing of the Congress party and the Communist party of India, but it destroyed the political understanding between Mrs. Gandhi and President Johnson. It was thus the first step in the unraveling of the entente that underlay the Woods-Mehta agreement. Lyndon Johnson was furious. He had enough problems without being scolded by the largest U.S. aid recipient and decided at that moment to shorten the leash. From that point on, President Johnson decided to approve personally all PL 480 food grain shipments to India and to limit the flows so that the GOI's stocks would dwindle to no more than six weeks of reserves.

On returning to Delhi, Mrs. Gandhi discovered how seriously she had offended President Johnson and some of its consequences. She learned also that 1966 was turning into an unprecedented second year of severe drought, with several implications: agricultural exports would not be up to predicted levels; disposable income would remain low, failing to trigger the increase in spending and production that the liberalization was designed for; speculation on food would drive up prices and thus aggravate the price increases resulting from the devaluation; and Mrs. Gandhi's domestic political fortunes would remain strongly influenced by the flow of PL 480 food. The prime minister quickly reversed her ground, claiming before the Lok Sabha that her "statement about imperialist forces threatening peace was not meant to apply to the U.S. specifically but to imperialists found everywhere: in China, the USSR, and former colonial countries."[61]

With her weakness and vacillations in full view, Mrs. Gandhi's detractors within the Congress recognized an opportunity to begin reversing the June 6 policies. Shah began telling his friends that "the devaluation had been the biggest mistake since Independence and by mid-August had succeeded in reinstating export subsidies on certain manufactured goods.[62] With Shah showing the way, the director general of technical development (DGTD) began pulling back to the Ministry of Industry some of the review functions that Finance had taken over and modified two months before.

In the early postdevaluation period, the economic situation was bleak. In the agricultural sector, food grains, cotton, jute, and oilseed production were about 20 percent below trend in both 1966 and 1967.[63] Inflation accelerated to 18 percent in 1966–1967 and 17 percent in 1967–1968.[64] Gross real investment declined in 1966–1967 and stayed roughly constant at the depressed level in 1967–1968.[65] These patterns, combined with a decline in real per capita income, were indications of a severe recession.

Although it can be shown, using econometric techniques, that most of the unwanted economic features of the 1966–1968 period were due to the two major droughts, few generalist observers have bothered to sort out the causes of the economic difficulties in the mid-1960s.[66] It is also interesting to note that the GOI was so worried about inflation from the drought that it followed a restrictive monetary and fiscal policy between 1966 and 1968.[67] So instead of operating in an era of rapid economic growth and investment shifts toward an export orientation, the devaluation and liberalization measures were engulfed by the drought and recession.

Liberalization received its coup de grace the following February as the results of the fifth general elections were analyzed. The Congress party lost control of a majority of one third of the state legislative assemblies for the first time since independence and witnessed the disgrace of having the Congress president lose in his own Tamil Nadu district. For the next four years, Mrs. Gandhi's full attention was devoted to strengthening her own position within the Congress and then making a nationwide comeback. Although some of the economists she kept around her made occasional halting efforts at decontrolling assorted sectors, the 1967 monsoon was a good one and the excitement over the advent of the green revolution took attention away from resource allocation and industrial policy questions.[68] With the liberalization package never more than partially tried, it was then given a quiet burial.

The devaluation episode affected subsequent GOI policy in several ways. The most tangible and immediate outcome was the return to the pervasive controls system. Not only did controls survive as the trusted method of dealing with scarcity, but the foreign pressure and domestic political backlash proved such a searing personal experience for some of the liberalization advocates that even the policy debate faded. This meant that it was impossible to raise decontrol and greater use of the market as serious policy alternatives for six to seven years after the Chaudhuri speech. During the 1970s and early 1980s the Ministry of Industry took steps to ease regulation on businesses, but there was nothing like the intellectual ferment of the mid-1960s. (After 1984, Prime Minister Rajiv Gandhi changed the setting, however. His emphasis on efficiency and administrative reform made "use of market" legitimate—even though the direction of change is similar to that proposed in 1966.)

An additional result of the devaluation was a shift in Mrs. Gandhi's own political strategy. It became clear to her that she was vulnerable from the Left and needed to recoup. The communiqué in Moscow had been a first attempt, but the need for PL 480 food constrained the international initiatives.[69] She naturally returned to the classic political strategy learned at her father's knee: "talk Left but hold the center." This meant getting rid of pro-U.S. ministers like Asoka Mehta and Subramaniam, which she did shortly thereafter.[70] It also meant an eventual decision on whether to compromise with the regional leaders in healing the Congress party's fissures or to strike a more independent stance. It would be placing too much importance on the devaluation to argue that it was a major cause of the Congress split, but in certain respects the later battles were being foreshadowed.

Another fundamental result of the devaluation drama was the rapid deterioration in aid relations. Performance conditioning, which had played such a large part in the academic aid doctrine of the 1960s, became a veritable anathema in Delhi. Although the U.S.-Indian aid relationship had never been convivial and this affected the entire tenor of the Aid-India Consortium's undertakings, in many areas there had been a relaxed interchange of ideas and a sense of common purpose. Yet the leftist attacks on the civil servants who had engineered the liberalization package were so severe that it became impolitic to spend much time with or have similar ideas to foreigners in the aid establishment. This trend turned the aid process in a new direction where the GOI consciously tried to divorce the capital transfers from the donors' policy prescriptions. A related GOI decision (pressed by I. G. Patel) was the determination to end indebtedness to the IMF and to build up unusually large foreign exchange reserves.[71] This, along with the other moves to limit the access and visibility of foreigners involved in aid, completed the general pattern of attempting to reduce vulnerability to donor pressure.

The mid-1960s appears as a remarkable, atypical era in donor-GOI relations. The level of expectations reached heights that were impossible to fulfill. The ensuing period has been one of restriction and disappointment.

Conclusion: Quietly Slip the Check under the Door?

At least four conclusions can be drawn from the preceding case.

First, there are two common interpretations of the 1966 devaluation episode, and neither is fully satisfactory. The argument from the Left is that this was another example of the capitalist states using international organizations to impose their will on a third world country and that the real purpose was to shift India from a socialist to a capitalist pattern of development. Although the Bell mission did recommend cutbacks in public sector investment and reductions in government intervention in the economy, none of the donors seems to have been under the illusion that the devaluation and liberalization would be creating a free market economy. What the donors did hope was that India would create the type of environment where resources could be effectively used. If the donors had any model in mind, it was probably closer to the European social democratic tradition of Sweden than the market-oriented style in Taiwan.

The second main interpretation of the devaluation is that it failed because the GOI never implemented the agreed policies. Although it is true that the GOI quickly began backing away from its commitments, it is not clear that the policies would have succeeded in the best of circumstances because the actual situation in June 1966 was adverse. Thus even true believers in the market must recognize that the drought and the deeply ensconced controls system were formidable obstacles, which should have been approached with more caution. The devaluation could have been delayed until mid-July when the major crop reports were in, and it might have been prudent to schedule a phased decontrol program to prevent the formation of a unified opposition.

Second, the episode is a striking example of the dramatic shifts in policy that can occur if heads of government take a direct personal interest in what is usually left to technocrats. The emerging understanding between President Johnson and Prime Minister Gandhi provided the momentum for implementing the technical work started two years before under the Bell mission. The dangers of such high-level attention are obvious as well: expectations were raised to unreasonable levels, the pace was rushed, and there was rank disappointment on both sides when events did not develop as anticipated.

Third, the Aid-India Consortium played its role precisely as most development economists would have recommended. It sponsored a first-rate analytical review of Indian economic performance, laid out a detailed program for change, and made a major effort not only to increase aid levels but to increase the percentage of rapidly usable program assistance. Although this represents the essence of logical policy analysis, the consortium's single-minded focus on economic performance meant that inadequate attention was devoted to political constraints.

Fourth, there are obvious limits to donor-induced policy change. In a

country with a high level of politicization, where politics consistently dominated economics, and where economic decisions are usually announced
only after extensive bargaining among regional and functional groups, the
odds are clearly against a prime minister who secretly negotiates a major
program with Western donors. There are also cultural issues: Is it possible
to change a deep suspicion of businessmen and competition? Can a leader
of a country with a long socialist tradition convince citizens that use of the
market is not malevolent?

Even if one could write the perfect political-economic blueprint for
donor-induced economic policy change, few governments or organizations
would be willing to try. This is partly because of the general donor fear of
being overinvolved but partly because of an increased LDC presumption
that aid should be quietly slipped under the door.[72] Most important,
though, grand exercises in social engineering are bad risks in any circumstances and thankless with a recalcitrant government.

**Appendix 2A   Chronology of the Key Events Related to the 1966
Indian Rupee Devaluation**

1951

India began its first Five Year Plan. Although a small, Harrod-Domar type
model of anticipated economic growth was appended to the plan, the main
focus of expenditures was on building social overhead capital: roads, ports,
power facilities, and schools. Foreign exchange was not a critical constraint
because substantial reserves had been built up during World War II and
raw material prices were high due to the Korean war. The plan explicitly
stated that India expected to become self-sufficient of foreign assistance by
the end of the fifth Five Year Plan and that the economic growth strategy
would reflect a desire to reduce dependence on foreign powers.

Chester Bowles was appointed U.S. ambassador. His relaxed, open style
was a distinct contrast to that of other members of the diplomatic corps,
and he made an attempt to convince the Indians he met that the United
States was willing to support India despite its non-aligned stance. Bowles
arranged for a wheat loan totaling $189.7 million, a precursor of future
massive food grants and loans under the PL 480 Act of 1954.

The intense U.S.-Indian hostility that developed during the early part of
the Korean war (when Nehru refused transshipment rights for UN troops)
subsided.

1953

Chester Bowles was replaced by the Eisenhower administration, but he returned to Washington and made a strong attempt to convince influential congressmen that a large commitment of U.S. resources to India would be worthwhile. In his *Ambassador's Report*, he argued that India was a bulwark against communism in Asia, the United States should support an example of such nontotalitarian forms of development, and India was in vital need of aid. He thus urged the United States to put aside its usual ideological preferences and support India's socialist government.

U.S. aid continued under the Eisenhower administration. Although it was predominantly technical assistance, it was on a very large scale. The respective fiscal year appropriations for 1953 through 1959 were (exclusive of PL 480): $44 million, $87 million, $84 million, $60 million, $90 million, $137 million, and $194 million.

1956

India announced its Second Five Year Plan. The methodology for this plan was radically different from the first. Prasanta C. Mahalonobis, one of India's most famous physicists, had designed a plan frame, which set up a modified input-output scheme for determining investment requirements in various sectors. The plan made the development of heavy industry the central objective and placed little emphasis on growth in the food or export sectors.

August
The United States signed its first PL 480 agreement with the government of India (GOI).

1957

The large investment in imported machinery for the Second Five Year Plan combined with the drop in raw material prices caused a severe foreign exchange crisis.

The India lobby (Chester Bowles, John Sherman Cooper, and John Kennedy were the key leaders) began to press for capital and budget assistance to New Delhi. The *Kennedy-Cooper* resolution urging enforced aid for India was passed.

The Millikan-Rostow proposal for assistance to developing countries was published and became part of the argument used by pro-aid advocates. The proposal's stress on getting away from short-run political and defense criteria for allocating aid, using economic performance as the new guide, and accelerating economic growth to preserve democratic forms of government all fit well with the evolving U.S. conception of aid doctrine as the Cold War eased.

1958

With substantial organizational impetus from Eugene Black, president of the World Bank and Douglas Dillon, a private banker, the Aid-India Consortium was formed. The purpose was to provide a forum for reviewing India's progress and get joint agreement on aid levels.

1959

A drought and subsequent bad harvest led the Ford Foundation to fund a drought report, which analyzed not only the impact of the bad monsoon but alternative agriculture and irrigation policies for the future. This was the beginning of donor concern over the GOI's focus on industry and neglect of the rural areas.

1960

The World Bank (IBRD) sent out a team headed by Michael Hoffman to evaluate the strategy and status of Indian economic growth. The report was optimistic and cited several major areas where policy could be improved but did not differ from the course chosen by the GOI.

1961

The Third Five Year Plan was announced. It maintained the emphasis on heavy industry and allocated relatively little to the agricultural sector. Mahalonobis's methodology was used as the basic approach, but there were critics within the Planning Commission who advocated less central direction and greater use of the price mechanism. Continued balance of payments difficulties led to import surcharges and export subsidies on selected commodities.

The appointment of J. K. Galbraith as the U.S. ambassador was seen by many Indians as a sign of possible increased U.S. aid. It was also seen as an indication that capital aid might go to GOI public sector undertakings.

Eugene Black, chairman of the Aid-India Consortium, was worried about the increasing criticism of Indian economic policy. He organized the "three wise men" (Isaiah Frank, Herman Abs, and Alan Sproul) to carry out a review mission, evaluating the intent and progress of Indian economic policies. The group evaluated the Third Five Year Plan and certified it as sound, enabling those who favored increasing aid to India to argue that the donors should be primarily concerned with increasing the resource flow.

1962

Jagdish Bhagwati, a leading economist at Delhi University, wrote "More on Devaluation," published in *Economic Weekly*. Bhagwati, with B. R. Shenoy, thus became a prominent critic of the controls system and artificially maintained exchange rates.

B. Zagorian, U.S. Treasury attaché, was so disillusioned with the inefficiencies of the controls system and Indian central planning that he advocated a substantial reduction of U.S. aid unless the GOI made more efficient use of the resources from the donors.

John P. Lewis's *Quiet Crisis in India* was published and extended the argument of Bowles by asserting that the 1960s would be particularly important for India once industrialization began accelerating rapidly. The book was critical of the Indian neglect of agriculture, the inefficient government industries, and the operation of the aid programs. It suggested a switch to nonproject lending as the most important change necessary by the aid donors.

October
The Indo-Chinese war on the Himalayan border broke out, and the Indian troops were soundly beaten. The war shocked supporters of Nehru for they had believed his continual assertions that the Chinese were friends and that the Indian Army was stronger. Krishna Menon was forced to resign as defense minister.

Both during the war and after, the GOI got military aid from the United States, breaking a U.S. precedent of refusing to give military aid to India while aiding Pakistan. The USSR sought to minimize the effect of the changed U.S. position by authorizing the sale of MIG jets to the GOI.

1963

A draft IBRD-financed study of the Indian coal industry, directed by Bernard Bell, used shadow prices for imported machinery on the assumption that the rupee was so overvalued that investment decisions should not be made using the nominal exchange rate. In reviewing the draft, the Ministry of Finance took great exception to this and accepted the report on the condition that this not be an acknowledgment of the need to devalue.

K. N. Raj, a noted and committed socialist, completed his commission report on the steel industry and was extremely critical of the operation and impact of the controls system. Although he did not advocate the end of planning, he argued for a substantial simplification of controls.

IMF consultations resulted in informal IMF suggestions that the GOI devalue the rupee. Rumors of the IMF recommendations got out to the press and opposition. GOI spokesmen vehemently denied that the government was either going to give into foreign pressure or seriously considering devaluation.

From early soundings in committees of Congress, it became clear to the Kennedy administration that an appropriation for the GOI-owned Bokaro steel plant was unlikely to get funding and that this could delay the entire foreign aid bill. To avoid a showdown, President Kennedy personally wrote to Nehru asking the GOI to withdraw the request for funding. Nehru did this but shortly after announced Soviet funding for the project. Ambassador Galbraith was put in an embarrassing position because he had initially encouraged Nehru to submit the request to the United States after the plant had been proposed by the USSR. The incident also showed that though most of the aid bureaucracy was quite willing to be involved in an Indian public sector undertaking, there was still substantial resistance to this on Capitol Hill.

October
The Planning Commission undertook a full-scale midplan review designed to assess progress since 1961 and to decide what balance of economic and military programs should be given attention and priority in the wake of the criticism of Indian preparedness during the China war.

C. Subramaniam was named agriculture minister. He invited various specialists in to see him and posed the question: "What should I do?" Representatives of the Ford and Rockefeller foundations and the U.S. embassy saw this as an opportunity to convince the dynamic agriculture minister of a need for drastic changes in policy. Although the arguments differed slightly, all of the Americans recommended an end to exhortation as a means of increasing production and advocated raising farm prices to make production financially attractive for the farmers. The common themes were that the GOI should establish a price incentive scheme by creating a national buffer stock used to keep prices up during a good harvest and dampen price movements during bad seasons; there should be greater availability of quality inputs (seed, fertilizer, and pesticide); and there should be substantially greater investments in irrigation. These basic recommendations were researched and talked about in the ensuing two years and eventually became the basis for a broad-ranging change in policy announced in December 1965. (This turns out to have been a key turning point for the U.S. mission as well. Previously Ambassador Bowles had seemed more interested in resuscitating his beloved Community Development Program than in making USAID or the embassy focus on agricultural output. Yet in preparing for the meeting with Subramaniam, Bowles was won over to the package of agricultural inputs approach and soon became its ardent advocate. He also stressed the need to spread the benefits of development in his lectures at Delhi University entitled *Makings of a Just Society.*

1964

April
At a meeting of the state chief ministers, T. T. Krishnamachari (TTK), union finance minister, had almost convinced the top state leaders that they must accept a substantially reduced allocation from the national government because military expenditures needed to go up. Nehru contradicted him and said, "The Chinese know we will shift toward increased military programs and that it will hurt our economy. We can't let this happen; we must have both defense and development." The chief ministers saw that they could get their pet projects after all, and the plan review in process was undermined.

Nehru died, and L. B. Shastri was picked as his successor. There was a feeling of gloom in the Congress party because Shastri had little charisma, and the increasing difficulties on the economic front made the politics of scarcity a central problem.

Pakistan decided to liberalize its import controls in exchange for an increase in program assistance from the United States. Although Pakistan's agricultural sector was growing only about 1 percent faster than Indian agriculture, Pakistani industry was quite dynamic, and the overall comparisons seemed to reflect poorly on Indian economic choices. Also because Pakistan's liberalization was carried out under pressure from its aid consortium, an increasing number of donor economists following India began advocating a similar approach to New Delhi.

May

George Woods, successor to E. Black as president of the World Bank, sensed the increasing disillusionment with Indian economic performance. He told close acquaintances, "If the only thing I do while I am president of the bank is to turn India around, I'll be happy." Woods also had some concern that such a large percentage of the World Bank's portfolio was going to one country. With his private sector, financial background, he was worried that concentrating loans in a poorly performing borrower would lead to a bad portfolio balance.

Woods hired Bernard Bell as a permanent staff member of the bank with the specific purpose of having Bell direct a comprehensive review of Indian economic policy. After approving the scope for the study, Woods negotiated the arrangement with the GOI, arguing that donor disenchantment with Indian aid utilization was such that a major reevaluation was necessary. For the team, Bell selected a number of internationally known economists, conspicuously trying to choose people who had no strong past ideological or personal ties with India. It was agreed that the review would cover planning, agricultural transport, exports, statistics, and administrative procedures.

June

John P. Lewis left the Council of Economic Advisers and was named the USAID mission director. His appointmented was viewed as a favorable sign by Indians who sought more aid. On the other hand, Lyndon Johnson changed the character of the Aid-Indian Consortium pledging sessions by forbidding U.S. representatives to pledge amounts of U.S. assistance. He claimed that aid levels were determined by Congress, and he was not going to make promises that could not be fulfilled. Many top GOI officials saw this as a portent of increased tension in the aid relationship.

September

In a joint meeting of the senior cabinet ministers and the Planning Commission, TTK resumed the discussion started in April over what balance of military and economic development projects to choose in the revised Third Plan. Word had gotten around that TTK had already won over Shastri to his view that new industrial projects must be sharply curtailed. At the meeting, VKRV Rao of the Planning Commission strongly attacked TTK's position, saying that the social sector should not be neglected just to build up the military. TTK charged that Rao was being irresponsible in advocating expenditures that could not be realistically financed. Shastri, who previously had supported TTK, did not like the manner of the discussion and adjourned the session until the following day. At the second session Rao again strongly argued for maintaining funds for the health, education, and related sectors. TTK, embarrassed over his previous outburst at Rao and weakened by Shastri's vacillation, was forced to accept an economic program he did not favor. The Third Plan revision thus became a strange document. Although it was purportedly designed to scale down other expenditures to enable an expanded military budget, Nehru's comments about industry and Rao's plea for the social sector meant that the only place to cut was in the supply of raw material and spare parts for existing manufacturing firms. The revision thus explicitly incorporated plans for going ahead with major new industrial undertakings while starving existing operations of their needed materials. This fateful decision (affecting the allocation of internal production and imports) significantly contributed to the low capacity utilization and growth figures, which the donors were soon analyzing in great detail.

December
John Lewis wrote a memo, "Betting on India" to David Bell, USAID administrator, arguing the case for expanded aid to India. The memo, though confidential, was leaked to the *Washington Post*, and there was increased pressure on President Johnson to aid India in the nonpolitical fashion Lewis advocated. The president was irritated and apparently resolved not to be pressured by the pro-India partisans within the aid establishment.

1965

January
Members of the Bell mission began to arrive in India. There was annoyance within the Left members of the GOI bureaucracy because the mission staff was given broad access to government information on economic policy questions. They challenged this and said that the IBRD was a U.S.-controlled organization and that if one set of foreigners got to discuss such

details, there was no reason why any other donors (socialist countries) should not have the same privilege in evaluating their aid projects.

C. E. Lindblom, Yale economics professor on leave and economic adviser to Ambassador Bowles, circulated a paper to senior economists and civil servants in the GOI. The thrust of the argument was that controls were preventing optimal use of resources in the system. The low price for imports (overvalued rupee) was encouraging firms to overbuild in capacity just to get allocations for imported raw materials and intermediate goods to sell at excessive profits. Lindblom urged that licensing be withdrawn and be replaced with competition among demanders.

March
On March 19 the IMF approved a standby agreement with the GOI for $200 million. The funds were completely used in 1965.

April
A skirmish of several days took place in the Rann of Kutch between Indian and Pakistani troops. President Johnson was annoyed because both sides were using arms supplied by the United States.

May
The Bell mission continued its work, and there was a close relationship between the IBRD and USAID staff. Although USAID was not formally involved in the bank's evaluation, Bell and Lewis had similar views on the major types of policy changes necessary, and the USAID staff had done data collecting and analysis useful or the IBRD group.

During a visit to Washington, Subramaniam conferred with George Woods over the likely outcome of the World Bank review. Woods told Subramaniam, "Let the economists play. I'll get you the resources."

In addition to the close conferring between Bell and Lewis, there was a continuous interchange between Lewis and top GOI economists. Lewis, like Lindblom, advocated greater use of the price mechanism and profit criteria (even for government-owned firms), but he went substantially further and stressed the advantages of a "Big Push" strategy to significantly accelerate growth. Lewis was convinced that if there were a much larger flow of nonproject assistance, controls could be abandoned, the excess capacity put to use, and a sharp increase in the growth rate achieved. This was appealing to GOI bureaucrats who found foreign exchange increasingly scarce and wanted more leeway in the allocation of donor assistance.

June
To broaden the donor support for the Bell mission, Woods arranged for André De Lattre to be released part time from his functions at the French Central Bank. De Lattre had extensive background in international financial negotiations and helped to diffuse criticism that the World Bank's effort was just an indirect U.S. move.

Bernard Bell and De Lattre met Prime Minister Shastri and his secretary, L. K. Jha, in London for a briefing on the progress of the Bell mission.

The four-year PL 480 agreement (signed during the height of optimism in the early months of the Kennedy administration) ran out. President Johnson decided not to make a long-term commitment of food support but adopted what he called his short-leash strategy of keeping the GOI on short supplies of U.S. food grains. He stated that this would force Prime Minister Shastri to heed U.S. advice on a variety of matters. Many influential Indians were incensed at both the name and substance of the strategy. Even many Americans in New Delhi were convinced that, far from increasing GOI malleability, this decision would force Shastri to try to be more independent to avoid domestic criticism.

Bernard Bell flew back to Washington to discuss the basic findings of the study with Woods and P. P. Schweitzer, IMF managing director. Bell covered the preliminary reaction of the GOI and noted that a devaluation seemed necessary.

July
The monsoon rains did not come, and there were forebodings of a major drought.

Bell returned to New Delhi and met with I. G. Patel, chief economic adviser, S. Bhootilingham, secretary for economic affairs of the Finance Ministry, and S. Battacharya, governor of the Central Bank. At this session, Bell raised the issue of devaluation, and Battacharya raised the question of whether it was appropriate for the IBRD to comment on IMF issues.

B. Bell flew back to Paris and met with Woods and De Lattre. All agreed that it was time to begin approaching Aid-India Consortium members to discuss the preliminary findings of the Bell mission and to start lining up support for expanded aid if India would change its policies.

Bell and De Lattre met with senior French officials and with Barbara Castle,

British minister for overseas development. Both the British and French were supportive of the Bell mission approach.

Bell returned to Washington to draft the summary portions, but the recommendations for the levels of aid were left blank until more donors could be consulted.

August
The Bell mission completed the bulk of its fieldwork. Bell consulted again informally with S. Bhootilingham and I. G. Patel. Bell pointed out that the IBRD report would be extremely critical of both the strategy and tactics of Indian planning. At the macrolevel, the report would criticize the inefficiencies of building and underutilized industrial capacity and the neglect of agriculture; at the microlevel, the analysis would stress the enormous waste coming from GOI intervention and monitoring down to the firm level. Bell accepted the thesis that India would need a large increase on the supply of intermediate goods but argued that policy change would be necessary to have it productively used.

The monsoon failed to develop, and it became clear to the GOI that it faced a severe food grains shortage. Discussions with the United States continued over further PL 480 shipments, but given U.S. policy, the atmosphere was tense.

September
A major war broke out between India and Pakistan, forcing the GOI to reallocate expenditures away from economic to military projects.

The United States cut off military aid to both belligerent nations.

USAID announced that it had suspended consideration of future economic aid for both belligerents but that aid already committed or projects underway would be allowed to continue. PL 480 food shipments were continued to both countries. In the emotional period during and following the war, press reports, many politicians, and many GOI officials stated that all aid had been cut off. This not only created animosity toward the United States but needlessly accentuated speculative hoarding of food during the drought and aggravated inflationary pressure.

Pakistan and India continued paying on their external debts throughout the suspension of new aid signings.

Bernard Bell completed a draft of the summary volume of the IBRD report and gave it to Woods. Shortly after, Woods approved the draft and concluded that the GOI needed drastic changes in economic policy and the IBRD should encourage all the consortium members to increase their aid allocations as an incentive for the GOI to make the changes.

October
Bell and De Lattre began further consultations with top GOI administrators and economists, among them I. G. Patel, S. Bhootilingham, L. K. Jha, M. Schroff, S. S. Marathe, and V. K. Ramaswamy. The discussions covered a host of issues from the details of decontrolling imports to specific changes in agricultural and industrial policy, to the size and composition of future consortium aid if the policy changes were made. Bell and De Lattre left convinced that the probability of GOI policy changes was sufficiently high to warrant a trip to the major donor capitals to generate support.

November
Subramaniam and U.S. Secretary of Agriculture Orville Freeman met in Rome while both were attending a meeting of the Food and Agriculture Organization. On the basis of extensive previous staff work, they drew up and agreed on a program for substantial changes in GOI agricultural policy (embodying many of the changes recommended to Subramaniam a year earlier by Bowles and the Ford and Rockefeller foundations). The broad thrust of the program was to develop an incentive price scheme for major food grains, increase GOI investment in both irrigation and fertilizer, and make greater use of the market for the distribution of inputs.

December
On his return to Dehli, Subramaniam announced the changes in agricultural policy. He was attacked in the Parliament after word got out that the new policy was remarkably similar to the supposedly secret Freeman agreement. Subramaniam defended himself by saying that he would take advice from anyone, even an American, if it was good advice.

USAID offered to end the suspension of new aid agreements by providing a $50 million fertilizer loan. The loan was conditioned on an extensive, secret side letter in which the GOI agreed to pursue the changes already announced by the Ministry of Agriculture, as well as to maximize output of fertilizer plants and improve distribution of pesticide and seed.

After reviewing the draft Bell report, TTK was not convinced that the GOI should follow its recommendations. He put off a final decision and avoided raising the topic with Prime Minister Shastri. Because aid distribution and the associated recommendation for a devaluation in the Bell report were the clear responsibility of the minister of finance, the decision making on the issue was stymied by TTK's inaction.

Indian newspapers published stories of malfeasance by TTK's son. TTK rebutted the stories and asked Prime Minister Shastri to clear him of charges. Shastri refused to do so without an investigation. The prime minister then offered TTK the option of having a Supreme Court justice do an inquiry. During the inquiry, TTK would step aside but with the full right to return to the minister's post if he was cleared. TTK considered this an insult and submitted his resignation, assuming that it would be rejected. Shastri not only accepted the resignation but immediately appointed Sachin Chaudhuri a Bengali barrister, as the successor. Chaudhuri was a well-known corporate lawyer who had little experience with economic policy, but his was a needed patronage appointment from West Bengal. Ironically Chaudhuri had been the investigator of the Mundra affair when TTK was charged with misuse of government funds in the 1950s. The removal of TTK greatly facilitated the discussion of decontrols because the finance minister was not opposing it and Chaudhuri's inexperience made him rely on this top staff members who were convinced that some package of import liberalization and steps toward decontrol were necessary.

1966

January

Prime Minister Shastri went to the Tashkent Peace Conference.
Quite unexpectedly, he died soon after the agreement was signed with Ayub Khan. Shastri's death initiated a bitter fight within the Congress party for the party Leadership. Moradji Desai was extremely disappointed at the Congress president's decision to back Indira Gandhi. Desai actually forced a vote (which had been avoided in the consensus selection of Shastri eighteen months before) but lost. Mrs. Gandhi became prime minister but with her power mortgaged to Kamaraj, the Congress president, and a weak base given Desai's conviction that he would eventually force her out.

Blitz, a leftist Delhi tabloid, published the full text of the side letter to the December 1965 USAID fertilizer loan. John Lewis and S. Bhootilingham, the two signatories, were sharply criticized in the press for having reached a secret agreement on changes in policy.

February

Vice-President Humphrey was sent by President Johnson to Pakistan and India to smooth over feelings ruffled by the suspension of new aid between September and December 1965. Humphrey was authorized to tell the GOI that the United States was willing to make a new commitment of $200 million in nonproject aid. Although the actual agreement was to be signed in April, the GOI was told that it could go ahead with imports of $200 million from the United States and that this could be back credited to the loan once the agreement was in effect. The GOI was, nevertheless, in a difficult foreign exchange situation due to low exports during the war and the need to purchase commercial food (to go along with the massive 10 million ton relief effort being staged by the United States). The GOI decided to draw its full gold tranche from the IMF, giving it immediately $187 million in extra reserves. Yet the IMF sent a mission to New Delhi and in the discussions over this drawing (an automatic one that the IMF could not prevent), it became clear that the IMF would not allow the GOI to draw any more funds unless major economic policy changes were made and the rupee was devalued. Although it was not a condition of the GOI drawing, Ambassador Anjaria (who doubled as economic minister in the Indian embassy and as GOI executive director in the IMF) passed a letter from Indian Reserve Bank Governor Battacharya to the IMF. It said that India would readjust its exchange rate to a more realistic rate at an appropriate time in the near future.

March

Bernard Bell returned to New Dehli for two weeks of discussions before Mrs. Gandhi's visit to Washington. During her visit, Mrs. Gandhi impressed President Johnson as a capable politician. Although there were conflicting reports over how well they got along personally, the president saw that Mrs. Gandhi needed dramatic news to strengthen her own internal position. He thus saw this as a promising moment for a change in the nature of U.S.-Indian relations.

Following Mrs. Gandhi's visit B. K. Nehru, India's ambassador in Washington, cabled New Delhi urging immediate efforts to capitalize on the recent goodwill between President Johnson and the prime Minister. He suggested that though the time might not be right for signing a long-term PL 480 agreement, it might be propitious for getting increased program assistance as Lewis and Bell had recommended.

April

Mrs. Gandhi decided to send Asoka Mehta, India's planning minister, to Washington to negotiate with the IBRD over the Bell report and future levels of consortium aid. Mehta and Subramaniam were the two ministers most convinced of the need to reduce the extent of internal controls, so Mehta's visit was not an indoctrination session but rather a series of negotiations over details of a GOI-IBRD agreement. In most of the sessions, Mehta was dealing only with Woods, Bell, and a few additional staff members. Mehta found, however, when he saw Dean Rusk, the U.S. secretary of state, that Rusk was fully briefed on the progress of the negotiations. Mehta was annoyed by this breach of confidentiality on the World Bank's part but did not make an issue of it because he wanted to return to New Delhi with a confirmed promise of increased nonproject aid. The negotiations reached a satisfactory conclusion, with K. S. Sundar-Rajan and Bell drafting a summary of the agreed points. President Johnson asked Mehta to meet other cabinet secretaries and several congressional leaders to acquaint them with the new pragmatic, market-oriented course the GOI was committed to taking.

May

Mehta returned to New Delhi, and Mrs. Gandhi approved the agreement that he negotiated. The entire cabinet was not informed, however, because Mrs. Gandhi was loath to tell those whom she knew were opposed. She also feared that telling a large group would inevitably lead to a leak, thus undermining the effectiveness of the proposed devaluation and other measures.

A small group of top civil servants was set up to plan the actual implementation of the devaluation and the import liberalization. S. Bhootilingham chaired the group, which was put under great strain because it could not divulge the nature of its work to even upper-level staff, and it had to make plans for ministries where the ministers had not been informed.

The Ministry of Finance sent a small team to the IMF to work out the technical details of the devaluation. The Indian representatives were Gobinda Nair, additional secretary, V. K. Ramaswamy, economic adviser, and M. Schroff, deputy economic adviser. There was no standby credit arrangement because the GOI did not want to acknowledge any substantial foreign involvement. Although the IBRD was kept informed of the IMF-GOI talks, Woods preferred to have no direct World Bank involvement.

After the Woods-Mehta agreement and the agreement on the devaluation were completed, Bell and De Lattre made an additional trip to London, Paris, and Bonn to give detailed briefings on the proposed changes in Indian economic policy and to line up support for increasing donor aid.

June

During early June, Mrs. Gandhi called in a few top Congress leaders and asked their opinions on a devaluation. Although the agreements had been signed and the preparations complete, she acted as though the issue was still up for debate. Leaders were opposed to the devaluation because they feared the inflationary impact of increased import costs and the appearance of weakness.

Mrs. Gandhi went ahead with her plan, however, and the devaluation was announced June 6. This followed some earlier indicative policy changes where decontrol had been permitted in eleven domestic heavy industries.

The devaluation was met by intense political debate in India, both within the Congress and by the opposition parties. In Parliament, only relatively junior Congress members supported the move.

Given the principle of ministerial responsibility, Finance Minister Chaudhuri was required to explain and defend the devaluation. Not only was he unfamiliar with the economic principles involved, but he was not present when the agreement was negotiated with the IBRD in Washington. Thus Chaudhuri was in the difficult position of defending something that he did not understand analytically. He made three appearances: a radio address on All-India radio, at a press conference, and at a defense in the Lok Sabha during the weekly question and answer period. Before the last, he distributed an information sheet covering the basic issues. None of these presentations appeared convincing to the skeptical audiences.

The Federation of Indian Chambers of Commerce and Industry (FICCI) supported the move. Its president, L. N. Birla, gave a radio speech favoring the devaluation but argued that the export duties imposed (to tax windfall profits) were thwarting the directions of the move. FICCI took out a series of ads in newspapers supporting Mrs. Gandhi's decision but took no other action except to press for reductions in the export duties. The Associated Chambers of Commerce (Assocham) took no public stand, but given its high percentage of foreign firms, its members were not enthusiastic as foreign employees had their salaries cut substantially.

Of the well-know economists, only Shenoy, Raj, and Bhagwati supported the devaluation before the event, while Ganguli, Vakil, and Minhas supported it afterward.

In the press, the *Times of India*, *Statesman*, and *Hindustan Times* were mildly supportive, but the Left papers and the economic ones (*Economic Times*, *Financial Express*, and *Eastern Economist*) were sharply critical.

Bell and De Lattre went to Japan to elicit support for the increased aid to India. They found considerable resistance because Japanese government officials were not confident that the aid would be well utilized.

July
The monsoon rains did not come for the second year in a row. The GOI could not judge the effect on the harvest at this point, yet there was fear of a second drought, which exacerbated the difficult nutritional and inflationary situation.

The GOI announced the partial decontrol of forty-eight additional industries.

Mrs. Gandhi visited Moscow and agreed to a joint communiqué with Leonid Brezhnev condemning "imperialist bombing and aggression in Asia." President Johnson was furious; he felt he was having enough domestic troubles without having India add to the chorus of critics. He decided to take an even firmer stance over the release of PL 480 shipments to India. For all other countries, the Department of Agriculture was authorized to release the grain once purchases were made. But for India, the president would personally approve each future release so that Mrs. Gandhi knew exactly how involved he was in the decision process.

July
The Aid-India Consortium had an interim meeting to review recent Indian economic performance. Bernard Bell opened the discussion by saying that import controls had been kept and that the policy moves were a significant beginning but were not yet extensive and needed close scrutiny. Peter Cargill, the India country director for the World Bank, argued that it was impossible for the GOI to go further in decontrol unless a significantly increased amount of program aid was provided. W. Macomber of the U.S. State Department said he was struck by the change in climate surrounding Indian-donor relations and that he was pleased with the increasingly pragmatic approach that the GOI appeared to be taking.

September
The extent of the drought was known, and estimates of the food shortfall were made. It appeared that India would need as much or more imported food than in 1965. With President Johnson taking his tenacious stand about releasing PL 480, Mrs. Gandhi became increasingly worried about the effects of the food shortages on the upcoming election.

Finance Minister Chaudhuri, I. G. Patel, and Reserve Bank Governor Battacharya went to the IMF-IBRD annual meeting. Before the meeting started, they asked Bell and De Lattre to come to New York to meet with them and discuss the implications of the devaluation and policy changes. The GOI officials made it clear that Mrs. Gandhi has suffered politically from the decision and that she needed as forthcoming a donor position in the upcoming pledging session as possible.

November
Mehta made a trip to Moscow to arrange for Soviet aid and returned with pledges for projects worth 100 million rubles. The Western donors immediately pointed out that the Soviet aid was paid for through barter agreements that were on very hard terms. Nevertheless, Mehta felt he had recouped some of his independent status by being able to negotiate large aid packages from both the capitalist and socialist countries.

The Aid-India Consortium met in Paris and pledged $900 million in non-project assistance, plus $300 million in project aid. The total aid level had thus not changed, but the composition of the aid being provided had shifted substantially toward program aid, which could be more easily used to fill the gap in the supply of capital equipment and intermediate goods.

Mrs. Gandhi was intensely annoyed at Manuhbai Shah's performance as minister of commerce and international trade. As the top decision maker under the former scheme of export subsidies, Shah had tremendous power, which was immediately reduced by the shift from export subsidies to export taxes. Shah therefore had fought the move on both a personal and bureaucratic basis. Mrs. Gandhi wanted to remove him from contention by shifting him to the Ministry of Science and Industry and leaked to the papers the rumor of his transfer. Shah blatantly said he was not going to move, and no major Congress leaders came to Mrs. Gandhi's support. Because the Congress party needed the campaign contributions of the big businessmen who supported Shah for the 1967 elections, Mrs. Gandhi eventually backed down and left Shah in his post. This revealed the extent

of her weakness within the party; no previous minister could have succeeded in challenging either Nehru or Shastri on such an issue.

December
The effects of the drought were pervasive, and, though the civil service was
managing the second year of food crisis well, there was great hardship for
the bulk of the lower-income populace.

1967

February
In the fourth general election, the Congress party lost six of the seven-
teenth state legislatures, and in the Lok Sabha its majority declined to forty
seats. The Congress president, Kamaraj, lost his seat in Madras, and increased tension in the Congress surfaced. Party leaders forced Mrs. Gandhi
to take Moradji Desai as her deputy prime minister and finance minister.

April
The droughts of 1965 and 1966 brought on a major recession. Because of
the underutilization of much industrial capacity, demand was insufficient to
encourage businessmen to import goods at the rate anticipated during the
planning for the devaluation.

June
In a conversation with J. D. Rockefeller III (who had a strong interest in
India), Woods said, "The devaluation was a flop; India didn't make the
policy changes we expected."

July
The U.S. Congress delayed a vote to replenish the World Bank's soft loan
affiliate, the International Development Association (IDA). Because India
had been receiving much of its bank lending from IDA, this put a major
stumbling block in the path of bank staff members who wanted to maintain
the pledged level of aid to the GOI. There was nevertheless severe dissatisfaction among some bank analysts at the halting steps at decontrol made
by the GOI. Some felt that this was a sign of bad faith on the part of the
GOI; more sympathetic interpretations were that the food crisis made it
politically infeasible to go ahead with the full range of planned decontrol.

September
Mrs. Gandhi remained openly critical of U.S. policy in Vietnam despite
low-key requests from Americans to play down her statements. Her position made it harder for the administration to get funds from Congress.

October
At the Paris pledging session of the consortium, the GOI reported that it had not used up all the committed program aid from the previous year but that it still wanted the donors to commit the same level as in 1966. Most of the donors found this unacceptable. By March 31, 1968, India had $768.1 million in committed but unutilized program aid.

1968

October
Although donor enthusiasm slackened in 1967 due to the slow utilization rate and the GOI failure to make the promised policy changes, the GOI was anxious to get as large a pledge as possible for the coming year. The donors, on the other hand, were deeply disappointed over the retrenchment in economic policy that had taken place during the intervening two years since the devaluation. Import licensing was still in force; decontrol of industry had been maintained only in a few sectors; and the expected changes in fertilizer policy had been only haltingly implemented. The pledging thus fell below the 1966 and 1967 commitment level. For the consortium countries, in 1966–1967 total disbursements (including food) were $1.4 billion. In 1967–1968 total disbursements rose to $1.5 billion, while by 1968–1969 they had dropped to $1.1 billion. After the meeting, I. G. Patel returned to New Delhi and vented his frustration on Ambassador Bowles and AID director Lewis. Patel argued that India would never again let its foreign exchange reserves get so low that the GOI would be forced to accept the pressure of foreign donors as in 1966.

Appendix 2B   The Bell Mission Report

The Bernard Bell mission report, *Report to the President of the IBRD on India's Economic Development Effort* (Washington, D.C., October 1, 1965), is still a classified World Bank document.

The authors of the respective volumes were as follows:

Bell:	Summary
King:	Planning
Crawford:	Agricultural policy
Hopper	
Ladejinsky	
Goreux	
Garnier	

Bohr: Manufacturing
Please: Financial policy
Segal, Taeuber: Family planning
Owen: Transport
Holland: Exports
Crompton: Statistics
Baneth: Administration

Although the summary volume is not a synopsis of the respective sector studies, it does condense the major arguments and present a unified alternative policy to deal with the problems addressed. For purposes of this review, it is thus satisfactory to cover the main arguments in the summary volume.

The discussion begins with a list of the major macrocharacteristics of the Indian economy during the period 1961–1965:

- Growth of GNP was disappointing, as it failed to exceed the rate of the Second Five Year Plan.
- Per capita income showed minimal increases; overall growth was about $4\frac{1}{2}$ percent annually and population growth approached 3 percent.
- The growth of GNP was low despite a 6 percent annual growth of imports, with the import-export gap rising from $700 million in 1961 to $1.3 billion in 1965.
- The rate of internal savings was not the prime constraint on growth. The bulk of expanded resource availabilities went into new investment consumption (because of expanded population) and the military budget (after the 1962 war with China).
- The basic investment problems were due to a shortage of foreign exchange and administrative weaknesses. The constraints on imported intermediate goods prevented production from reaching capacity, and overly bureaucratic decision-making procedures delayed virtually every essential function.
- Agriculture had become another key constraint in the economy as food production lagged (necessitating imports) and traditional export crops showed little growth.

The summary report then reviewed several major interrelated policy areas where changes could be made to improve the performance of the Indian economy:

1. Foreign exchange management: Government controls should be removed and import privileges sold on a competitive basis. The controls system was inefficient, slow, prone to corruption, and discriminating

against new small firms trying to break into new markets. Above all, selling foreign exchange at too low a price was an incentive to import.

2. Defense expenditures had gone up substantially after the China war. Although the World Bank group was not trying to assess the extent of the threat posed, it was clear that the bulk of the new outlays had gone for purposes that could add only marginally to economic development. There also appeared to be signs of a further arms race between India and Pakistan. Given these patterns, the mission recommended a return to concentration on economic objectives as soon as politically feasible.

3. Transportation expenditures by the GOI appeared to have been overly concentrated in railways, producing an underinvestment in roads and the truck fleet. This reflected a government desire to maintain control over transportation (through the state railways) but had reached the point of causing excessively high transport costs for short-haul traffic. If alternative transport facilities were provided and competition maintained, production and distribution costs would certainly decline.

4. Family planning appeared to be understaffed and poorly organized, with no significant effect on the total population growth rate. Given the extraordinary difficulties the government was already facing in providing services and a structure for employment of the rapidly growing population, greater attention and efficiency needed to be centered in this area.

5. Foreign investment was so severely restricted and encumbered in bureaucratic requirements that opportunities for outside investment had been lost even in sectors where the GOI was anxious to have foreign capital. New regulations should be designed to speed the review process and broaden the areas of permissible foreign investment.

6. Public sector industries were poorly planned, operating without economic efficiency criteria as the governing ones, and suffering from physical controls rather than competitive means of supply and distribution. Controls over distribution of state-managed steel, cement, and coal industries were leading to particularly serious misallocations.

7. Agriculture was the most neglected area of the Indian economic effort yet probably the most important. Underinvestment in agriculture produced a situation where fertilizer, irrigation, seed, pesticides, and credit were not available at sufficiently attractive prices to induce greater production. The GOI should divert resources away from government-owned industry toward agriculture, and price incentive schemes should be established, letting profit serve as the inducement to farmers. In addition, underutilized rural labor should be mobilized for more extensive local construction of roads, dikes, and dams.

8. Finally, although tax officials had shown considerable resourcefulness at designing and implenting levies, additional effort should be put into streamlining the rules and eventually increasing agricultural taxation.

After reviewing this long series of major policy problems (and referring readers to the individual sector studies for documentation of the generalizations), the summary volume presented an argument to explain why this interrelated set of difficulties had developed. The assertion was that pervasive government controls had led to serious distortions in the economy. Not only had government industries been inefficiently run, but resources had been kept from lighter industry and agriculture, which could have more effectively accelerated economic growth. To maintain its desired investment strategy, the GOI had been forced to set up an elaborate series of control measures that slowed growth, fomented corruption, and allowed artificially high profits for those fortunate enough to secure government permits. The solution was to maintain government supervision of macroeconomic policies but to decontrol as much as possible to allow resources to flow to areas where they would yield their maximum returns.

The Bell report concluded by reviewing the outlook for India. The report was optimistic as it stated that government policy was capable of accelerating economic growth, yet substantial changes in direction were needed to avoid the current stagnation. It was very pessimistic, though, about growth prospects if policies remained the same. To speed growth significantly, Bell estimated that an additional $300 million to $500 million would be needed in maintenance imports. Additionally the donors should recognize that as debt repayments came due at increased levels, new aid commitments had to grow even faster if real resource transfers were to increase. It was estimated that $300 million of new imports would lead to an increase in output of $1.2 billion (due to underutilized capacity) and that this might accelerate overall growth rates to about 5 percent per year. Bell stated that the increased aid would be justified (given India's salutory political system) if the donors could be sure that the GOI would accept the recommendations of the mission and move toward a more open, competitive, and decontrolled economy. Without these assurances, there was not sufficient evidence to conclude that the aid resources would be well utilized.

Appendix 2C   The Woods-Mehta Agreement

The April 1966 agreement between George Woods, president of the World Bank, and Asoka Mehta, Indian planning minister, remains a highly classified document in the IBRD files. The government of India has refused to give permission for its own staff seconded to the bank to see the document without the approval of the relevant IBRD vice-president. The following is a summary of the key aspects of the agreement.

Woods and Mehta did not sign a legal agreement. They did not even sign a minute of understanding. Initially Woods and Mehta simply had discussions on the broad outlines of the Aid-India Consortium's role and the types of anticipated policy changes by the GOI. Mehta then met for technical talks with various World Bank staff members. At the end of the specific sessions, Mehta and Woods met again to summarize their understanding. It was then agreed that K. S. Sundar Rajan and Bernard Bell would exchange notes on the essence of the expected obligations by both the bank and the GOI. This interchange of notes is the written record of the Woods-Mehta agreement.

The agreement cited specific policy directions and targets for eleven areas: agriculture, population control, mobilization of internal resources, export promotion, import policy, industrial licensing, private foreign investment, fertilizer production and distribution, the public sector, transportation, and tourism.

The GOI commitment to replace import controls with tariffs, to simplify procedures and reduce backlogs in industrial licensing, and to make no new investments in the public sector unless the expected rate of return was equal to that of the private sector were startling changes in economic policy management. It is noteworthy that there was no specific mention of devaluation. It was assumed a devaluation would be necessary if import liberalization proceeded. Mehta made it clear that he felt discussing a parity change was the purview of the IMF. Woods agreed.

On the consortium's behalf, Woods pledged to attempt to raise the total aid level to $1.6 billion from its previous level of approximately $1.2 billion. For the 1966–1967 Indian fiscal year (April 1–March 31), the expected totals were as follows (in millions):

Project:	$339.15	Non-U.S.
	348.00	IDA (World Bank soft loans)
	108.24	United States
Program and fertilizer	804.61	
	$1600.00	

In the concluding remarks, however, it was noted that the consortium would try for an even higher level of program aid if the negotiations between the GOI and IMF were successful. So although there were targets for GOI performance, on the essential issues of devaluation and the extent of decontrol, the agreement left substantial room for ambiguity.

Appendix 2D Aid Statistics and List of Interviews Conducted on the 1966 Rupee Devaluation

Table 2D.1
Gross and net aid flows, 1966/67 (million U.S. dollars)

	Project aid disbursements	Nonproject aid disbursements[a]	Food aid and nonfood PL 480	Total[b]	Debt service payments	Net aid transfers[c]
Consortium members						
Austria		4.97		4.97	1.30	3.67
Belgium					0.40	−0.40
Canada	15.80	16.14	75.00	106.94	5.60	101.34
Denmark	0.75	2.97		3.72	0.10	3.62
France	9.16			9.16	7.70	1.46
Germany	61.15	25.88		87.03	50.10	36.93
Italy	0.22			0.22	3.40	−3.18
Japan	40.21	2.51		42.72	27.90	14.82
Netherlands		8.79		8.79	1.00	7.79
Norway	0.87			0.87		0.87
Sweden	4.88			4.88		4.88
United Kingdom	32.36	88.45		120.81	57.50	63.31
United States	151.64	168.81	488.00[d]	808.45	58.60[e]	749.85[f]
IBRD	34.43			34.43	85.30	−50.87
IDA	70.12	109.56		179.68	3.40	176.28
Subtotal	421.59	428.08	563.00[g]	1,412.67[h]	302.30	1,110.37

Table 2D.1 (continued)

	Project aid disbursements	Nonproject aid disbursements[a]	Food aid and nonfood PL 480	Total[b]	Debt service payments	Net aid transfers[c]
Nonconsortium						
Bulgaria						
Czechoslovakia	17.47			17.47	0.70	16.77
Hungary						
Poland	1.30			1.30	1.00	0.30
USSR	49.43			49.43	48.80	0.63
Yugoslavia	7.43			7.43	0.70	6.73
Switzerland	10.16			10.16	2.30	7.86
Others		2.97	10.00[i]	12.97	9.80[j]	3.17
Subtotal	85.79	2.97	10.00	98.76	63.30	35.46
Totals	507.38	431.05	573.00	1,511.43	365.60	1,145.83

Source: IBRD, *Economic Situation and Prospects of India* (SA-32a, May 10, 1972), vol. 2.

a. Including debt relief.

b. Excluding such other forms of aid as technical assistance and U.S. PL 480 Title II.

c. Net resource transfer in a number of cases would be higher if technical assistance or PL 480 Title II were included.

d. PL 480 Title I, food and nonfood.

e. Excludes debt service payable in rupees, of which that portion allocated to U.S. use would represent a real resource transfer to the United States.

f. Real resource transfer would be higher by amount of U.S. technical assistance and PL 480 Title II and lower by amount of U.S. use counterpart rupees actually utilized.

g. May be incomplete.

h. Largest single omission is probably PL 480 Title II, but technical assistance grants may also be significant.

i. Australian food aid.

j. Includes repayments to Kuwait, Qatar, Bahrain, and other countries for which no figures on new credits are available.

Table 2D.2
Gross and net aid flows, 1967/68 (million U.S. dollars)

	Project aid disbursements	Nonproject aid disbursements[a]	Food aid and nonfood PL 480	Total[b]	Debt service payments	Net aid transfers[c]
Consortium members						
Austria		4.27		4.27	1.50	2.77
Belgium		2.50		2.50	1.70	0.80
Canada	18.75	18.30	49.00	86.05	6.00	80.05
Denmark	0.01	3.82		3.83	0.10	3.73
France	35.20	9.89		45.09	7.10	37.99
Germany	35.38	55.57		90.95	52.30	38.65
Italy		1.95		1.95	6.80	−4.85
Japan	23.39	36.45		59.84	35.30	24.54
Netherlands	3.87	7.30		11.17	2.80	8.37
Norway	0.68			0.68		0.68
Sweden	1.91			1.91	0.10	1.81
United Kingdom	25.92	82.13		108.05	50.10	57.95
United States	77.80	284.80	464.00[d]	826.60	79.00[e]	747.60[f]
IBRD	30.33	15.00		45.33	85.50	−40.17
IDA	47.35	167.47		214.82	5.00	209.82
Subtotal	300.59	689.45	513.00[g]	1,503.04[h]	333.30	1,169.74

Table 2D.2 (continued)

	Project aid disbursements	Nonproject aid disbursements[a]	Food aid and nonfood PL 480	Total[b]	Debt service payments	Net aid transfers[c]
Nonconsortium						
Bulgaria						
Czechoslovakia	9.85			9.89	3.80	6.09
Hungary						
Poland	2.40			2.40	3.30	−0.90
USSR	63.33			63.33	85.80	−22.47
Yugoslavia	4.59			4.59	4.60	−0.01
Switzerland	4.13			4.13	2.30	1.83
Others		0.44	10.00[i]	10.44	10.40[j]	0.04
Sub-total	84.34	0.44	10.00	94.78	110.20	−15.42
Totals	384.93	689.89	523.00	1,597.82	443.50	1,154.32

Source: Ibid.

a. Including debt relief.

b. Excluding such other forms of aid as technical assistance and U.S. PL 480 Title II.

c. Net resource transfer in a number of cases would be higher if technical assistance or PL 480 Title II were included.

d. PL 480 Title I, food and nonfood.

e. Excludes debt service payable in rupees, of which that portion allocated to U.S. use would represent a real resource transfer to the United States.

f. Real resource transfer would be higher by amount of U.S. technical assistance and PL 480 Title II and lower by amount of U.S. use counterpart rupees actually utilized.

g. May be incomplete.

h. Largest single omission is probably PL 480 Title II, but technical assistance grants may also be significant.

i. Australian food aid.

j. Includes repayments to Kuwait, Qatar, Bahrain, and others for which no figures on new credits are available.

Table 2D.3
Gross and net aid flows, 1968/69 (million U.S. dollars)

	Project aid disbursements	Nonproject aid disbursements[a]	Food aid and nonfood PL 480	Total[b]	Payments	Transfers[c]
Consortium members						
Austria		4.44		4.44	2.10	2.34
Belgium		2.18		2.18	2.70	−0.52
Canada	13.43	37.32	44.17	94.92	6.10	88.82
Denmark	0.06	1.98		2.04	0.10	1.94
France	11.49	6.82		18.31	15.80	2.51
Germany	23.37	59.86		83.23	70.00	13.23
Italy	119.31			119.31	7.40	111.91
Japan	23.88	66.76		90.64	63.20	27.44
Netherlands		6.90		6.90	4.30	2.60
Norway	0.71			0.71	0.30	0.41
Sweden	3.71			3.71	1.40	2.31
United Kingdom	15.71	57.71	7.44	80.86	53.20	27.66
United States	40.45	238.56	242.84[d]	521.85	91.60[e]	430.25[f]
IBRD	25.72	15.00		40.72	81.50	−40.78
IDA	24.90	51.76		76.66	6.20	70.46
Subtotal	302.74	549.29	294.45[g]	1,146.48[h]	405.90	740.58

Table 2D.3 (continued)

	Project aid disbursements	Nonproject aid disbursements[a]	Food aid and nonfood PL 480	Total[b]	Payments	Transfers[c]
Nonconsortium						
Bulgaria						
Czechoslovakia	21.50			21.50	12.20	9.30
Hungary						
Poland	1.80			1.80	4.60	−2.80
USSR	76.32			76.32	58.20	18.12
Yugoslavia	4.80			4.80	5.50	−0.70
Switzerland	2.87			2.87	2.90	−0.03
Others		0.45	4.38[i]	4.83	10.40[j]	−5.57
Subtotal	107.29	0.45	4.38	112.12	93.80	18.32
Total	410.03	549.74	298.83	1,258.60	499.70	758.90

Source: Ibid.

a. Including debt relief.

b. Excluding such other forms of aid as technical assistance and US PL 480 Title II.

c. Net resource transfer in a number of cases would be higher if technical assistance or PL 480 Title II were included.

d. PL 480 Title I, food and nonfood.

e. Excludes debt service payable in rupees of which that portion allocated to U.S. use would represent a real resource transfer to the United States.

f. Real resource transfer would be higher by amount of U.S. use counterpart rupees actually utilized.

g. May be incomplete.

h. Largest single omission is probably PL 480 Title II, but technical assistance grants may also be significant.

i. Australian food aid.

j. Includes repayments to Kuwait, Qatar, Bahraim, and others for which no figures on new credits are available.

Interviews Conducted on the 1966 Rupee Devaluation

Interviewee	Organization*	Place
R. G. Agarwal	FICCI	New Delhi
M. Balakrishna	Assocham	New Delhi
B. Bell	IBRD	Washington, D.C.
N. N. Bhardwaj	Indian Institute of Public Opinion	New Delhi
G. S. Bhargava	*Hindustan Times*	New Delhi
V. V. Bhatt	IBRD	Washington, D.C.
S. Bhootilingham	Retired secretary, Ministry of Finance	New Delhi
P. Burleigh	U.S. Consulate	Calcutta
C. Chakravarty	Indian Tea Association	Calcutta
B. P. Chandra	Indian Jute Millers Association	Calcutta
J. Cool	Ford Foundation	New Delhi
M. Desai	Former minister of finance and deputy prime minister	New Delhi
M. Ghosh	Bengal NCC Gen. Sec.	Calcutta
R. Gilmartin	IBRD	New Delhi
K. B. Gokhale	Burmah Shell	New Delhi
S. Guhan	Ministry of industry	New Delhi
C. Gulick	USAID	Washington, D.C.
D. Hopper	C. D. Howe Institute	Correspondence
H. Houston	USAID	New Delhi
M. Irani	*Statesman*	Calcutta
G. Jain	*Times of India*	New Delhi
L. Jain	Industrial Development Service	New Delhi
L. K. Jha	Governor Jammu and Kashmir	Srinagar
K. Kamaraj	Former president, Congress party	New Delhi
M. N. Kaul	Former parliamentary secretary	New Delhi

*Organizational affiliation at the time of the interview.

S. Kashyap	Parliamentary reference Service	New Delhi
A. M. Khusro	Institute of Economic Growth	New Delhi
M. Kutty	Commission on Taxes	Calcutta
P. Lande	U.S. embassy	New Delhi
S. Lateef	*Statesman*	New Delhi
J. P. Lewis	Princeton University	Princeton and New Delhi
C. E. Lindblom	Yale University	New Haven
W. Lundy	U.S. embassy	New Delhi
D. Maitheson	Office of Management and Budget	Washington, D.C.
M. M. Malhotra	Assocham	New Delhi
S. S. Marathe	Indian Bureau of Costs and Prices	New Delhi
A. Mazoomdar	Ministry of Finance	New Delhi
A. Mehta	Congress (Opposition)	New Delhi
B. S. Minhas	Indian Planning Commission	New Delhi
S. N. Mishra	Congress (Opposition)	New Delhi
A. Mitra	Formerly member, Agricultural Prices Commission	Calcutta
A. D. Moddie	Hindustan Lever	New Delhi
D. P. Moynihan	U.S. ambassador	New Delhi
P. N. Narvekar	IMF	Washington, D.C.
K. Nayar	*Statesman*	New Delhi
I. G. Patel	UN Development Program	New York
S. Please	IBRD	Washington, D.C.
R. A. Raghavan	*Blitz*	New Delhi
V. K. R. V. Rao	Former Agriculture Minister and Member of the Indian Planning Commission	New Delhi
H. Rees	USAID	Washington, D.C.
M. Schroff	Ministry of Finance	New Delhi
D. Schneider	U.S. embassy	New Delhi
A. Sen	Former Minister of Law	New Delhi

S. C. Sen	Barrister	Calcutta
J. Sengupta	*Economic Times*	Calcutta
M. Shah	Former Minister of Commerce and International Trade	New Delhi
J. Shepherd	*Time*	New Delhi
M. Singh	Economic Adviser's Office, GOI	New Delhi
B. K. Sinha	India Museum	Calcutta
D. Souza	India Tea Association	Calcutta
G. Verghese	*Hindustan Times*	New Delhi
L. Viet	U.S. embassy, Delhi	New York
A. White	USAID	Washington, D.C.

Indonesia: Stabilization Reinforced

Storming the last bulwarks of imperialism.... A new Asia and a new Africa have arisen. Let us build the world anew. Let us create a new world, free from exploitation of nation by nation, free from exploitation of man by man! Let us build a new world free from imperialism, free from colonialism, free from neo-colonialism! Onward, no retreat! Ever onward, never retreat!
Sukarno, April 18, 1965[1]

It has been two decades since the world has heard emotional or revolutionary language coming from the presidential palace in Jakarta, Indonesia. For eighteen months after the abortive coup attempt on September 30, 1965, Sukarno vainly held on, maneuvering for some type of comeback. Yet with the excesses of his last years in full view and a strong coalition behind General Suharto, President Sukarno's dreams faded, and the new regime proceeded to act.

In quick succession, Suharto reinforced his own power base, set up a new cabinet, ended confrontation with Malaysia, had Indonesia rejoin the United Nations and the IMF, arranged for a postponement and then a settlement of the country's $2.1 billion pre-1966 foreign debt, negotiated to receive new flows of aid, and began a stabilization program in earnest.

By 1970 new aid commitments were running at over $600 million per year, the USSR and East European countries were pressed into settling their earlier debts on equal terms with the Western country agreements, inflation had declined from 635 percent in 1966 to 9 percent annually, and average per capita rice consumption had increased from 84 to 97 kilograms per year. To any development economist focusing on the macrostatistics, the results were impressive. Per capita income (which grew at about 1 percent per year from 1952 to 1959 and actually declined during the period 1960–1965) grew at approximately 4 percent between 1966 and 1971; a new foreign exchange system was established giving incentives to exporters but also resulting in increased government tax revenues; the government set up a program to ensure moderate prices for the nine basic commodities most needed by the public; Indonesian capital was being repatriated; new foreign capital was being committed at a record rate; and rehabilitation of the country's power, transport, and communications networks had begun.[2] By most conventional standards, the stabilization program had been a success, and the team of economists who planned it were lauded as a national resource.

By the mid-1970s, however, the excitement that permeated many of the initial analyses on the Suharto years had begun to fade. The drought and subsequent rice shortage in 1972 were poorly handled, much of the proceeds from the 1973–1974 and 1979–1980 oil price rises were being misused, and it was becoming more widely understood that the skills needed for planning a stabilization program are far different from those needed to manage a plethora of new capital projects. Analysts' attention began to turn from macrostatistics to examination of the results for different microgroups within the population. This new revisionism was far less complimentary toward the economic planners.[3]

It appeared that although income and consumption of rice and cloth had increased substantially from 1966 to 1970 among even the poorest groups, afterward the benefits of the stabilization and development programs were primarily accruing to urban dwellers and upper-income groups.[4] Even by the end of the 1970s, there seemed to be little evidence that the great bulk of the rural or urban poor were achieving any sustained growth in living standard.

This chapter will focus on the main factors that shaped economic policy-making in the 1966–1970 period and then comment on how the patterns of decision making changed as the political climate and economic performance evolved. The April 1970 decision to consolidate the exchange rate and devalue is taken as an example of policy choice when the donors still had substantial influence and before the economists faced any substantial competition internally.

How can we make a balanced assessment of the whirlwind of activity in the early post-Sukarno years? To concentrate just on economic indicators or the redoing of political factions is to miss the fundamental restructuring of the Indonesian political economy that occurred. To understand the transformation, we need to explain the process by which the military government was able to force a bond between itself, the domestic economists, and those foreign donor and private organizations that wished to be involved. This merging of talents and resources produced an era of technocratic dominance that continues in modified form today.

The discussion will examine four main questions:

1. What specific set of factors produced this amalgam of the military, economists, and foreigners?

2. What reinforced this coalition once it was established?

3. What role did the donor consortium play in bringing about this set of changes?

4. What was the significance of the 1970 devaluation?

The Argument

The basic contention is that the 1966–1970 period in Indonesia represents the quintessence of a public strategy to maximize economic growth. The measures used were balanced budgets, tight monetary and credit policy, reductions in unproductive state enterprises, and greater use of the market and profit incentives as criteria for resource allocation. The results were dramatic.

Some analysts have concluded that the Indonesian results were just the logical outcome of following appropriate policies[5] and that this experience does not reveal unusual characteristics of developing economies trying to achieve effective stabilization programs.[6] Far from these rather conventional conclusions, this chapter will stress that the Indonesia case is distinctly different from many other stabilization efforts, and it was those differences that made it possible to control inflation and reinitiate economic growth. Although similar policies have been tried in other developing countries, they have often achieved mixed results.[7] What were the special circumstances that explain why Indonesia got such a large flow of aid promptly? Why were large amounts of capital repatriated and foreign investment attracted? Why was there so little resistance to the new, restrictive economic policies?

The second main contention of this chapter is that political, not economic, factors were the primary ones in creating the ideal environment in which the Indonesian stabilization program was implemented. It will be argued that prudent economic policies are a necessary but not sufficient condition for successful price stabilization measures. The analyst needs to examine both the internal political constraints and external scene before being able to explain the level of resource flows and the feasibility of carrying out an anti-inflation program.[8] The significance of political constraints (or lack thereof) for economic policy-making is well demonstrated in the Indonesia case by the different pattern of economic decisions that emerged after 1971 once the internal political picture began to change and economists no longer had the room for maneuver that they enjoyed during the 1966–1970 period.

Indonesia's Special Circumstances

To illustrate how unusual the circumstances were during the early Suharto years, we need only look at the specific interest groups that regimes typically contend with while trying to control inflation.

First, the political reversal in the fall of 1965 had virtually decimated any opposition. The Communist party (PKI) was forced underground, the Nationalist party (PNI) was in disarray, and the splinter parties had lost the ability to make viable demands on the state. Additionally any government at the time could have counted on a yearning for order among the great bulk of the Indonesian people. The last Sukarno years had been exhausting, turbulent, and frightening for many. Suharto and his technical advisers could thus count on a broad climate of opinion favoring calm and the possibility of improved living conditions.

Second, Indonesia has a mild climate and remarkably fertile soil, and generally the monsoons supply enough water for two seasons of farming. Thatch is sufficient for housing, and fruit is easily obtained. The basic necessities of life are thus available for most of the population as long as rice and cloth are plentiful and inexpensive. Thus a cardinal rule of all Indonesian governments (from the Dutch Ethical Period onward) has been to ensure cheap rice and cheap textiles. Given that the masses were un-mobilized and apolitical at the time, the Suharto regime could assume a quiescent public if these basic commodities were available. The aid donors were conscious of the situation. Between 1966 and 1969, USAID supplied $210.5 million worth of food grains and $101.2 worth of cotton and yarn. In addition, both the Japanese and member countries of the European Economic Community supplied food, and the former allowed its aid credits to be used for textiles. The minimal nature of the public's demands and an adequate supply of critical items buttressed the government's position.

Third, Suharto did not have to worry about powerful and entrenched labor unions or business groups opposing his will. The Federation of Indonesian Workers (SOBSI) was banned because of its PKI dominations, and the PNI unions gradually dissipated. The business community was also in a weak position because the leading figures were almost entirely Chinese, and they suffered not only from the usual antagonism against outsiders but from reputed Chinese government complicity in the September 30, 1965, coup attempt. With the rural areas subdued and business and labor muted, the government had only the urban poor and middle classes to be immediately concerned with. The poor were unorganized and no threat. The middle classes were receiving most of the subsidized imports and were glad to see Sukarno eased out. So though it would be an overstatement to say that there were no internal political constraints, they were clearly less onerous than in recent Chilean and Italian situations.

Fourth, General Suharto was fortunate to have a shadow cabinet of competent, highly trained economists ready to assume positions of importance and in whom he had personal confidence. All of the top economists were on the faculty at the University of Indonesia and had been teaching courses at the Army Staff College in Bandung where they had met Suharto. The economists functioned as a cohesive group.[9] Widjojo Nitisastro became the unquestioned leader.[10] Widjojo gradually developed a symbiotic relationship with Suharto, and equally important, he became a symbol of competence and market-oriented economics for the donors and foreign investors. This corps of economists was thus another asset that Suharto did not need to create, which he could draw on at limited cost and reinforced his appeal to Western suppliers of aid and capital.

Fifth, the capital transfers were not only timely but massive. Official grants and loans were $359 million in 1969–1970, $494 million in 1970–1971, and $545 million in 1971–1972. These are annual per capita aid transfers of $2.66, $3.60, and $3.92, respectively. In addition, during 1970–1971 and 1971–1972 private capital inflows were, respectively, $116 million and $126 million.[11] Although these per capita transfers do not equal receipts by Israel, Taiwan, or South Korea, their magnitude is impressive nonetheless, and these funds clearly gave the Indonesian government flexibility that other countries might have wished for during their stabilization programs.

Aid and Indonesian Politics

It is impossible to characterize a relationship as complex and convoluted as Indonesia's aid affairs in a few paragraphs. Nevertheless, since the 1940s there have been a few consistent patterns, which are useful for understanding post-1966 developments.

Despite U.S. memories of Sukarno's "To hell with your aid" speech, the most striking aspect of aid in Indonesia has been its acceptance and perceived legitimacy by both the elites and masses. It should be remembered that while Sukarno was telling Americans to depart, he was encouraging a competition between Soviet and Chinese aid. It has always been assumed that aid has strings and that the government will have to make concessions; the issues debated are usually not the basic acceptance of the process but the incremental costs and benefits of various programs.

Despite the acceptance or inevitability of aid in Jakarta, there has long been a recognition that foreign assistance can be both an asset and a liability. The early success at putting pressure on the Dutch to end their 'police action' (by lobbying in Washington, which eventually led to U.S. threats to cut Marshall Plan aid to Holland) may have led some Indonesians to conclude that aid was going to be a benign foreign policy tool.[12] Yet, by 1952, when the Wilopo cabinet fell over the clumsy handling of the Mutual Security Agreement Treaty with the United States, it had become painfully obvious that concessions for aid had to be linked to tangible domestic benefits that were integrated with a broader internal political strategy[13] One thus sees throughout the 1950s and 1960s an increasingly sophisti-cated Indonesian competence at playing off competing donors. This pat-tern is illustrated in the late 1960s when the Suharto government knew that it could not realistically expect to play off Socialist and Western countries but that there were advantages to be gained by fostering a U.S.-Japanese competition.

The Indonesian institutionalization of competition among outside powers is a key element in the 1970 devaluation episode where differences be-tween the IMF and the World Bank over policy led to a delay in the deci-sion. In 1974 the Suharto government continued this tactic by reopening contacts with the Communist countries after the Western donors became increasingly critical of internal development plans.

An additional element that pervades Indonesian aid relations is the sense of déjà vu. In any interaction that has had as many oscillations and con-tinued over twenty-five years, this is understandable, but the important point is that most of the elements of the successful Suharto policies had been tried before. Yet the components had never been brought together in a cohesive package, and the political environment had never been as fa-vorable. For example, stabilization programs had been tried in 1953 and 1963, allowing exporters to keep part of their earnings in free foreign exchange had been tried in 1962, and the IMF's advice had been a consis-tent (but often unheeded) voice since the 1950s.

The history of Indonesian aid relations thus has a cyclical pattern. What needs to be explained is not the tension within the country or the reasons behind the choice of specific policy recommendations but the factors that produced the 1966–1970 interval when the technocrats dominated resource distribution. The chaos of the early 1960s and the increasing divisiveness in the 1970s show the uniqueness of this interval in both Indonesian affairs and among comparable developing nations.

Transition: Suharto's Search for Order

Except for magazine articles, one highly controversial academic paper, and one reasonably authoritative book, remarkably little has been written on the early months of Suharto's rise to power.[14] This is understandable. The Indonesian government has refused to let the issue be researched, and there has been no change of government since then to facilitate revisionist interpretations of the events. These comments on his first year of power thus rely primarily on information from interviews and try to isolate the patterns in Suharto's behavior rather than recounting a series of individual maneuvers that are extremely difficult to document.

Suharto's initial problem was to consolidate his military power. He was projected into the limelight only because six of the more senior generals had been murdered, and one remaining prominent general was both Sumatran and too controversial. Given this highly unstable situation, Suharto had President Sukarno put under house arrest. Suharto then turned to a group of close military confidants to design a strategy for preventing a full-scale Communist uprising and maintaining a modicum of public order. The working relationships formed in the first weeks of October 1965 lasted in most cases until 1971.

Ali Murtopo had been Suharto's assistant when the latter was regional commander in East Java. Murtopo had distinguished himself primarily as an organizer and through his personal loyalty to Suharto. Sujono Hamardani was a friend of comparable nature from the command Suharto had in Kalimantan. Generals Sumitro and Maraden Panggabean were acquaintances from the Staff College. Achmad Tirtosudiro, Alamsjah Ratuperwiranegara, and Ibnu Sutowo were useful because of their functional specialities. Achmad had been an organizer of the conservative Muslim students in Bandung and had logistics experience in the military; he was thus the choice to head the national logistics agency aimed at supplying civil servants, the military, and urban areas with essential consumer items. Suharto had not previously known Alamsjah, but Franz Seda (subsequently minister of communications) vouched for him, and Seda provided a key link to the Catholics. Sutowo had run the State Oil Company, Pertamina, under Sukarno, but he was quite skillful in using revenues under his control to purchase rice and supplies for the army and thus played an early part in shoring up interest group loyalty for the emerging regime.

By late November 1965, it had become clear that the Communist organization was shattered. Suharto was still worried that Sukarno would try to foment an uprising in East Java, but with rampant inflation proceeding apace and the formal structure of government in disarray, long-term plans needed to be made.[15]

With his military group firmly behind him, Suharto began a search for advice on economic and nonmilitary domestic policy. Two working groups subsequently were set up to meet these needs. The one designed to plan domestic social and political strategy consisted of a psychologist, an education professor, and an artist. Although the group met frequently into 1966, it was unable to come up with any broad conception of or short-term tactics for achieving a new political system that Suharto favored. It would be overstating the significance of this group's failure to argue that it was responsible for the following six years of direct military rule. Nevertheless, Suharto did not see any viable alternatives to military control of the civil apparatus, and two patterns developed: internal political matters were increasingly given to Murtopo and thus viewed from a military security perspective, and Suharto's main advisers coalesced into two groups: the economists and the military.[16]

The economists thus became the crucial nonmilitary link to the palace, and this was essential for establishing the military-technocratic symbiosis. From the early contacts that Suharto made to the economists, it might have been hard to predict this outcome. Although Widjojo and his colleagues were well known from their presence at the Staff College, Suharto dealt with them in a typically Javanese way. The Sultan of Jogjakarta was asked to put together an economic team, but, since it was obvious that he was primarily a symbol, he needed specialists to do the analytic work.

The Sultan thus had his fellow Jogjakartan, Selo Soemardjan, contact Widjojo. This circuitous route preserved some distance for Suharto while allowing the economists to see (after several interchanges) if their advice was going to be followed. From this tenuous beginning came a tighter bond (soon short-circuiting the sultan), which hardened into a permanent link.

Although the economic development literature usually ignores the role of individual economists, to do so in the Indonesian case would be a serious mistake. The series of economic decisions that Suharto made during his first year reflected not only Widjojo's thinking but his increasing ability to persuade the general to take bolder steps toward using market forces and competition as means of distributing resources. The December 1965 devaluation and the February 1966 establishment of the bonus export system started the process. Then in quick succession, the sultan's April speech on foreign investment, the invitation for the IMF to return, the preliminary creditors' meeting in May, the formal creditors' meeting in September, and the major announcement of the comprehensive stabilization program on October 3 were all incremental moves part of a broader strategy. (See the Chronology for a discussion of the timing and diplomatic consequences of these moves.) It is clear, however, that their measures would never have been made without the general's faith in his chief economist, Widjojo. Although there was a slowing of the inflation rate in 1967 and a sharp drop in 1968, the surge in prices was actually increasing during 1966, so it was in no sense certain that the new policies were going to yield the desired results in time to buttress Suharto's other attempts at creating order. Yet, the steps were taken.

The pattern in Suharto's moves is consistent: consolidate military power, separate areas of responsibility among loyal lieutenants, take elaborate steps to ensure loyalty among potential new advisers, divide responsibilities among the new advisers, and view governance as the establishment of authority and the issuing of decrees to the public. Suharto's conceptual model was similar to that of a Javanese king dividing his courtiers into military and economic fiefdoms. From these roots sprang the stabilization program.

Stage 1: The Aid Arena Is Set

Once order had been restored and Suharto had picked his key subordinates, his central problem became obtaining resources for managing the state. Internal tax collections were meager given the abysmal condition of the Ministry of Finance and the low national savings rate.[17] Similarly there were limits to taxes on exports because the infrastructure needed to facilitate trade had deteriorated and high export taxes encouraged smuggling. Like his many predecessors, Suharto turned to foreign nations and international organizations for revenue.

In early 1966 Suharto sent representatives to contact the U.S. government, hoping that there might be a quick sign of U.S. support with subsequent aid flows. At this point, the government of Indonesia (GOI) seemed to be quite willing to have the U.S. as the major donor.[18] But the United States was preoccupied with Vietnam, and most of the top State Department staff were anxious to avoid deeper commitments in Southeast

Asia. Indonesia was also not sufficiently stable to make easy predictions of the future: Sukarno was weakened but still nominally president, and the military was not showing any astounding expertise at governing. The U.S. government thus initially held back on aid offers.

By mid-April 1966, though, the sultan had announced a major change in GOI policy toward private foreign investment. Sukarno and his supporters were beyond hope of a comeback, and the climate for Western aid and involvement seemed highly favorable. This led immediately to token contributions of U.S. and Japanese aid. It also set in progress steps linking the settlement of the forfeited Sukarno Debt to the provision of large amounts of new assistance.

Two preliminary meetings in Tokyo of Indonesia's creditors produced an agreement to meet in December 1966 in Paris.[19] At this formal conference in Paris, a minute was signed where the GOI received a temporary moratorium on its debts in return for promises that it pay all its obligations once an independent assessment of the debt profile had been made and that it follow strict anti-inflationary domestic policies.[20] It was also agreed that the Paris Club of creditors would ask the IMF to monitor the GOI's economic performance.

The Paris Club and the understanding on outside monitoring of economic policies were followed two months later by the formation of the donor consortium, the Inter-Governmental Group to Indonesia (IGGI). Before forming the IGGI, the donors had wanted assurances that the projects requested for funding were essential for Indonesia's economic growth and that overall economic policies would be prudent. With the IMF performing this function for the creditors, it was easy to set up a similar understanding for the new donors. Although the IGGI countries have never published a precise list of the consortium's objectives, the group was performing a number of functions:

- integrating planning of debt rescheduling with allocations of new aid
- providing an internationally recognized system for establishing aid requirements
- centralizing the aid pledging process

  establishing international monitoring of the aid resource utilization

At the first official IGGI session, the GOI could make only crude estimates on its aid needs.[21] Yet the initial session set some interesting precedents that distinguished the IGGI from aid consortia set up earlier in the 1960s: the GOI was allowed to participate as a member in all sessions, the

United States government let it be known that it would try to limit its nonfood commitments to one-third of the total requested by the GOI, and the Dutch (particularly generous donors) were selected as permanent chairmen of the group.

Each of these decisions proved to be significant. Having the Dutch in the chair meant that a country guilty over its former involvement in Indonesia would set the tenor for the meetings; the U.S. limitation of its contribution meant the group was not under U.S. domination; and the presence of the GOI tended to keep the discussion in a collegial rather than an examining vein. The formal pledging process was somewhat similar to that used in the Aid-India Consortium. The IBRD and IMF reports were presented in the fall to the donors for review along with formal GOI requests for a specific level of aid funding. To illustrate the project aid request, the GOI presented a detailed list of the capital and technical assistance projects ready for funding.[22] When the donors met again in the spring, each mission knew how much its government was willing to commit, so the pledging was formally completed.

The IGGI thus served as a convenient clearinghouse for the donors, with the IBRD (and the IMF to a lesser extent) acting as executors in the field.[23] Yet most substantive negotiations over specific projects or aid levels were handled directly between the countries concerned and the GOI. For this reason, it is more appropriate to call the IGGI multinational than multilateral.[24]

The IGGI's only regulatory power was in the ability of its members to cast doubt on the substantiation for the GOI's aid request or in a challenge to internal economic policies being pursued. Even this potential sanction was limited, though, because the IGGI had no permanent analytical staff, and questioning the GOI too strongly would mean challenging the IMF and IBRD recommendations. Also, even if several individual country members were dissatisfied with some aspects of GOI policy, it is likely that they would have great difficulty in convincing the other members to curtail aid over a single issue. Given the GOI's close adherence during the 1966–1970 period to the types of policies advocated by the IMF and IBRD, the IGGI review thus became a convenient formality. To examine the real operation of and reasons for the aid relationship, one needs to go beyond the consortium itself and see the individual donors' organizations interacting with each other and with the GOI.

A final and crucial aspect of the aid structure between 1968 and 1969 was the special role of the IBRD field mission.[25] Not only was the mission large and well staffed, enabling it to help generate and monitor virtually all the capital projects underway, but Dr. Bell, its director, was preeminent among the aid and adviser chiefs of mission. His superb negotiating skills were used to deal with both intradonor issues, as well as the usual donor-recipient conflicts.[26] His role as honest broker thus became a key element in the complex negotiations that developed in a consortium with twelve members and five observers.[27]

In sum, the formal IGGI arrangements were a construct that suited the purposes of both the donors and the GOI. Although the IGGI had little power, it was an aid-channeling device that lent an aura of objectivity to the resource transfer process. The significance of the consortium obviously depended on how seriously the recipient needed the foreign assistance and the stakes for the donors. The most critical period for the GOI was in 1966 and 1967, but the rapid growth of 1968 and 1969 would never have been possible without continued and expanding levels of aid.

The Technocratic Pattern Emerges

In the chapters on Ghana and India, the analysis moves directly from stage 1 where the arena is set to stage 2 where the bureaucratic politics surrounding the devaluation takes place. The Indonesian case is quite different because the 1970 devaluation was preceded by four years of a stabilization program and three years of currency float.[28] This section thus focuses on the main decisions during this interim period and illustrates how critical groups benefited, cushioning the eventual political and economic impact of the 1970 devaluation and exchange rate reforms.[29] Also, it elaborates one of the main themes of the chapter in showing how a technocratic approach to stabilization succeeded in the Indonesian context.

In approaching the hundreds of economic policy decisions made during the 1966–1970 period, it is useful to divide the sequence into three phases:

1. December 1965–October 1966 when the broad conception of the stabilization program was developed and the initial policy moves made.

2. November 1966–June 1968 when incremental modifications in policies were made but the planners wanted to assure themselves that the system was functioning as anticipated.

3. July 1968–April 1970 when there was a muted competition among the economists over the future priorities of the system.

Future historians might look back on the first months of Suharto's power and conclude that the economists had an intricate plan for every detail of the program that unfolded during the following four years. Although

Widjojo and his colleagues had goals and a set of policy preferences, they were under such pressure for day-to-day decisions that they never had time to devise a detailed written stabilization plan. Their main worry was inflation. Initially it was also unclear how serious Suharto would be in following recommendations. The economists thus scrambled to devise a system that would work during a period of rampant inflation but also be roughly the desired structure once stabilization was underway.

The basic recommendations were for a balanced budget, tight credit, and a realistic exchange rate, goals that had to be tempered to conceivable resource availabilities. Once the request for advice had been received through the sultan, the economists went to a nearby mountain vacation area for several days of intensive planning.[30] The proposals they decided on were almost entirely drawn from the experience of previous Indonesian stabilization planning, principally the 1963 attempt by Djuanda.

The strategy that the economists preferred was to maintain tight control over a few policy variables and let market competition determine the distribution of resources in areas beyond the government's capability to administer. The long-term goal was cautious macropolicy with close government supervision of large sectors. They did not advocate massive state employment programs on expanding public sector industry and the state trading companies, though they kept extensive regulations as a means for intervening in any sector that appeared to be causing difficulties. Firing large numbers of civil servants, closing the inefficient state enterprises, and immediately reducing the bloated military were considered too politically risky. Suharto accepted the recommendations for a gradual transition. The public sector was in essence cordoned off and the private sector used whenever possible. This meant a freeze on government hiring, no new resources to the state industries, and private competition for the state trading monopolies.[31]

With this broad, overall construct the economists then worried about specific sectors. In February 1966, the bonus export (BE) system was set up to establish a legal private market for foreign exchange, create incentives for exporters, and start a procedure where the Central Bank (rather than the dubious Customs Service) would be responsible for collecting export taxes.[32] (Appendix 3A provides detailed information on the design and changes in the bonus export system before the 1970 reforms.) The spring and summer was devoted to obtaining rice and textile imports and laying the groundwork for debt rescheduling and new aid. With the formal announcement of the stabilization program on October 3, 1966, the initial phase of uncertainty was over, and Suharto was fully committed to the effort.

The second phase began when the restraining policies really took hold, but the major directions as outlined in 1966 were followed. The macrostatistics are dramatic. The budget deficit was 124 percent for 1966 and only 3 percent for 1967.[33] Donor aid rose from token amounts in 1966 to commitments of quickly usable program aid worth $200 million in 1967. Table 3.1 illustrates the significance of aid for the program and the speed of the antiinflationary results. This phase was primarily one of working the kinks out of the system. The BE system was periodically modified to give exporters greater incentives and reduce the percentage of government imports; lending rates were lowered from 6 to 9 percent per month to 3 to 6 percent per month as a result of complaints from businessmen, and the GOI found how tenuous stability could be when its buffer stocks proved inadequate for the 1967 Christmas and Muslim New Year celebrations.

Table 3.1
Inflation and aid flows

	1966	1967	1968	1969
Annual inflation	635%	112%	85%	10%
Aid counterpart as percentage of GOI revenues		28	19	27
Aid as percentage of nonoil imports		34	35	39

Source: J. Newmann, "Inflation in Indonesia" (Ph.D. diss., Tufts University, 1974); IMF, "Background Material for Article XIV Consultation" (Washington, D.C.: IMF, October 27, 1969), table 13.

In the third phase, beginning in July 1968, more venturesome policies were tried. It is difficult to ascertain how many of these policy departures should be attributed to the presence of Sumitro in the cabinet because his nominal area was the Ministry of Trade, but he made serious attempts at influencing other sectors.[34] Between July 1968 and the April 1970 devaluation, four major policy changes were made. (1) In July 1968 the GOI briefly quit selling regular BE, forcing importers either to use aid BE or purchase free foreign exchange (DP). (2) In October 1968 a savings plan was started in the state banks paying very high interest rates to attract deposits from domestic sources and to encourage repatriation of overseas capital. (3) In October 1968 and May 1969, respectively, the BE and DP rates were unofficially set at specific rates with active intervention by the Central Bank to maintain the rate stability.[35] (4) In late 1969, the Trade Ministry began organizing the export trade so that syndicates of government and non-Chinese traders were allocated exclusive collective and exporting rights in certain geographic regions.

All four changes were attempts to bring government pressure to bear on problem areas that were not adequately responding on their own, yet all the steps adhered to the principle of using price incentives rather than fiat for resource distribution. The withholding of the BE sale was to build up foreign exchange reserves for market intervention and drive up the DP rate as an incentive for capital import; the high interest rate program was to encourage savings and give state banks the ability to channel funds to desired sectors; the fixing of the BE and DP rates was done as a symbol to business of the GOI's determination to avoid destabilizing speculation; and the syndicates were conscious anti-Chinese steps to broaden the ethnic base of those involved in trade. Along with these macromoves, the GOI was continuing to subsidize the distribution of the nine basic commodities (staples like rice and cooking oil) and was trying various schemes at increasing domestic rice production. In the economic decisions leading up to the April 1970 devaluation, we thus see remarkably consistent patterns: cautious macropolicy with market intervention to fit particular sectoral problems.

If we now shift to the politics of the 1966–1970 period, we can see how the economists' policies were integrated with a domestic political strategy. The first objective was to control inflation. The groups benefiting from this effort were the wage earners, civil servants, businessmen who made long-term productive investments, and foreigners who needed market and labor stability to operate effectively. The people hurt were debtors who had anticipated repaying in inflated currency, speculators, and traders who often had access to subsidized credit.

Although the economists initially viewed the civil servants as an unproductive and potentially hostile group, as the stabilization effort continued, the civil servants realized that Suharto was at least arresting the decline in their living standard.[36] Similarly many of the non-Chinese indigenous businessmen were Sumatrans who had been neglected by Sukarno and obviously favored moderate economic policies that gave incentives to exporters.[37] Thus, by early 1967, the policies chosen primarily for their macroeconomic effectiveness were already appealing to key interest groups.

Another aspect of econmic policy was to establish programs for ensuring the urban population adequate supplies of rice and for the entire population supplies of cheap textiles. The rice supply problem was initially approached by increasing imports (commercial and PL 480) and then by a series of programs providing high-yielding seed, fertilizer, and pesticides in various combinations. Although the rice production schemes were hardly resounding successes and had to be reorganized in 1970, they provided favorable publicity in the rural areas that never expected much from the central government anyway.

The rice import program, on the other hand, was essential for the urban dwellers (poor and middle class), and they were the first to notice the sharp increase in rice availabilities once the stabilization program was under way. In addition, the cheap textiles policy appealed to all consumers; the low duties on textile imports hurt some home weavers, but that was a relatively small loss in comparison with the appeal to every family that bought cloth.

After the process of halting inflation and providing essential commodities to key interest groups, the GOI's efforts were designed to provide a wider range of better-quality public services through health programs, transport improvement, power rehabilitation, and expanded educational opportunity. By 1970 the central government had also begun a direct grants program providing each village with a small amount per capita but allowing the village leaders to spend the funds as the villagers desired.[38]

Although the broad thrust of economic policy was toward increasing use of the market and decreasing direct management by government, aid was available in sufficient quantity for the GOI to systematically provide benefits to interest groups it needed for support.[39] The technocratic approach was thus implemented in a political environment where opposition was foolhardy and where resources were provided in sufficient volume to achieve increases in living standards and stabilization simultaneously.

Stage 2: Bureaucratic Politics: Elegant Shadowboxing

In evaluating the moves that led up to the Indonesian devaluation of 1970, we notice several fundamental differences from the situations prevailing in the Ghana and India cases. First, the Indonesian political environment was supportive or at least not openly hostile. The extent of currency overvaluation was less as the rupiah had floated between 1966 and 1969, making the devaluation primarily a means to correct for the inflation during 1969. Additionally the decision in Jakarta was not part of a decontrol package because these steps had proceeded incrementally during the preceding four years. Also the GOI was not being pressured by a combined front of all the major donors. There was some early difference of opinion between the World Bank and IMF over the desirability of the move, and most of the bilateral donors were not even consulted until the real decisions had been taken.[40]

Nevertheless there are some important similarities: foreign organizations did the main analytical work during the preparations, foreign organizations hurried the timing of the decision, there was still a devaluation with subsequent increases in import commodity prices, there were risks in giving up the dual exchange rate because the DP rate was, at least theoretically,[41] an escape valve for the GOI if speculative pressure developed, and the policy change was unquestionably linked to the provision of more foreign resources.

The basic contention here is undramatic. It is that, unlike the India or Ghana cases where the governments were pressured into changes, the government of Indonesia was very concerned to keep its exchange rate from getting overvalued. Thus the IMF pressure simply speeded the timetable for the decisions, and the GOI saw advantages in acting as if it was making significant concessions. In fact, the GOI might have done the devaluation on its own.[42] Concessions were made, mostly in the decision to consolidate the exchange rate.

Economics of the April 17 Decision

Table 3.2 is the IMF's description of the exchange rate system before the rate consolidation and devaluation; table 3.3 is a portrayal of the system's functioning afterward. What were the principal changes? And what was the expected economic effect of the combined moves? Four steps are worth noting.

First, the devaluation was achieved by raising the BE rate from 326 to 378 rupiahs per U.S. dollar. This meant a 15 percent increase in the cost of importing goods that moved through the regular BE market, or about 50 percent of all merchandise imported at the time. On the export side, the parity change was even more important because the 5 percent exchange tax was repealed.

Second, ending overprice meant that exporters could no longer lobby to receive a given percentage of their export proceeds at a special rate. This was a disincentive to exporters but was necessary to simplify the complexity of the system.

Third, paying the export duty to the central government strengthened

Table 3.2
Exchange rate structure, at April 16, 1970 (rupiahs per U.S. dollar)

Buying	Selling
277 (BE rate[a] less 5 percent exchange tax and 10 percent ADO[b]) Eight major export commodities[c,d]	
293 (BE rate less 10 percent ADO[b,d]) Other export commodities (excluding petroleum products)	
326 (BE rate) Purchase of that part of export proceeds that must be surrendered to a foreign exchange bank. Rate applied to transactions of oil companies. Capital transfers associated with approved foreign investment.	326 (BE rate) All government imports and aid imports. Imports on BE list when financed with BE exchange. Invisibles paid for with exchange granted by Bank Indonesia. Rate applied to transactions of oil companies.
378 (DP rate[e]) All receipts from invisibles, including diplomatic expenditures and repatriated capital. Purchase of that part of export proceeds that need not be surrendered ("overprice")	378 (DP rate[e]) Imports on DP list. (This rate may also be used for imports on the BE list); other invisibles, including private capital transfers.

Source: IMF, "Indonesia—Changes in the Exchange System," memo to the IMF executive board (Washington, D.C.; IMF, April 13, 1970).
a. Transferable foreign exchange designated as bonus export.
b. Exchange tax on nonoil exports allocated to regions according to port of shipment of exports. ADO is *Allokasi Devisa Otomat*.
c. Coffee, copra, palm oil, palm kernels, pepper, rubber, tin, and tobacco leaves.
d. Effective export rate when there is no overprice (actual sales price in excess of f.o.b. net price) or when any proceeds received over and above as commissions, rebates, and refunds.
e. *Devisa Pelengkap*, or complementary foreign exchange.

Table 3.3
Exchange rate structure, April 17, 1970 (rupiahs per U.S. dollar)

Buying		Selling	
		326	All commodity imports and related services financed by foreign government aid
340[a]	Foreign exchange receipts from all export commodities other than petroleum products, batik, and other handicrafts		
378	All other foreign exchange receipts	378	All other foreign exchange payments

Source: Ibid.
a. 378 less 10 percent ADO tax.

Jakarta's tax-collecting abilities and also made the regional governments more dependent on the center. It had the additional advantage of reducing the incentive for regional governments to build small, inefficient ports just to get the benefit of taxing an export that originated in its jurisdiction.

Fourth, allowing goods imported via aid programs to be sold at a cheaper exchange rate (known as Aid-BE and set at 326 rupiahs per U.S. dollar) was a measure that went against the general principles of the exchange rate consolidation. It was viewed as a practical necessity, however, because there was approximately $75 million of unutilized program aid. If aid had been made more expensive, by raising its price, there would have been even less incentive to use resources available from donor organizations as the GOI wanted. An elaborate modeling effort would be needed to measure the precise effect of these assorted changes, but they made half of the country's imported goods 15 percent more expensive and gave an even greater percentage incentive to exporters.

Three main factors pushed the GOI in the direction of the devaluation and exchange rate consolidation:

1. Some real concern that the BE rate was getting overvalued and that the loss of foreign exchange between October 1969 and February 1970 represented a "fundamental disequilibrium."[43]

2. A desire to strengthen central government control over foreign exchange earnings.

3. Basic agreement with the IMF that rate consolidation was a good

objective and a lack of interest in friction with the IMF over a step that would eventually be taken away.

The balance of payments issue is the easiest to deal with because some unambiguous quantitative information is available. During the last four months of 1969 and the first two months of 1970, Bank Indonesia used $114 million of its foreign exchange reserves to defend the chosen BE and DP rate levels.[44] Although the utilization varied a bit from month to month and seemed to be declining somewhat early in 1970, this was clearly an intolerable loss rate for a country with negative reserves. Given that the reserve loss was not indefinitely sustainable, the options were (1) waiting to see if things got better in the spring, (2) go back to a float and let market forces determine the rate, (3) devalue both the BE and DP rates but keep the spread concept, or (4) devalue by rate consolidation (devaluing only the BE rate and assuming that the DP rate was the appropriate level). Were the decision entirely up to the GOI economic team, quite possibly options 2 or 3 would have been selected.

The institutional questions about the functioning of the system are complex and valid. Once the GOI was satisfied that the Customs Service was sufficiently improved to do an acceptable job of collecting (close to the stated levels) import duties, there was no longer a reason for the essential/less essential goods split on the import side. And if it was useful to increase government control over export proceeds and the exchange rate was sufficiently attractive that requiring full surrender of proceeds would not just increase export smuggling, then there was no compelling reason to keep the DP market. This was expecially true if the GOI was going to give up the attractive option of having the DP function as an escape valve (as had been done for eleven months preceding the 1970 decision). Additionally if one wanted to discourage the seeming perverse effects of the functioning of the Allokasi Devisa Otomat (ADO) and establish greater central government control, then setting up a regional subsidy scheme based on a formula was an acceptable way to proceed.

Thus most cautious observers would have counseled a devaluation if presented with similar evidence. Whether one would have favored the institutional changes depends on one's assessment of the importance of increasing central government control over export proceeds and modifying the ADO. The dual exchange rate is something that the IMF strongly opposes. Since the GOI had come down in favor of stable rates (thus favoring stability over the policy option of free floating), the eventual move to a consolidated rate was a predictable compromise.

Political Maneuvering

The bureaucratic infighting that preceded the adoption of the April 17 exchange rate changes is interesting because though there was substantial opposition from various groups, none of the opponents had sufficiently similar positions to form an effective counterweight to the IMF pressure.[45] The maneuvering took place in four areas.

IMF Versus World Bank:
The confrontation between the two international organizations was not so much ideological as a dispute over the case being made by the IMF for the devaluation and associated changes. Several members of the World Bank's Jakarta staff felt the IMF paper advocating the changes was poorly argued and based on insufficient evidence. The bank was beginning to replace the fund as the leading monitoring organization for the IGGI consortium. Also, because Bernard Bell, the IBRD resident representative, was slowly taking on his role of broker among competing factions, it is understandable that the two bureaucracies clashed. The bank staff felt that the fund was being overly doctrinaire, and the fund staff saw the bank encroaching on its usual purview (exchange rate and monetary affairs). Senior fund staff still claim that the bank backed down (it quit opposing the devaluation) only after the McNamara-Schweitzer meeting where McNamara agreed to keep the bank on the periphery of the topic. Bank staff members involved saw the serious reserve losses of December and January as the key factor that convinced them a devaluation was necessary. Once the balance of payments turned decidedly pessimistic, the bank no longer had an analytic or a bureaucratic reason for opposing the fund proposals.

IMF Versus Bilateral Donors:
Most of the donors were not brought in on the discussions concerning the devaluation. Secrecy was part of the reason, but additionally the IMF and GOI knew that few donor missions had economists who could have contributed substantially to the debate. The United States (and Britain to a lesser extent) were anxious not to see the price of their aid go too high because their currencies were already overvalued and that would create the embarrassment of further pledged but unused program aid. Yet once the IMF had agreed to the GOI's proviso to keep the program aid at the old BE rate, the bilateral donors had no major reasons for opposing the proposed changes.

Sumitro Djojohadikusomo versus Widjojo

Here the stakes were sufficient to warrant a skirmish if either protagonist had thought it to his advantage. After being named to the cabinet, Sumitro had taken virtual control over trade-related economic policy and even tried to exert his influence over credit decisions by the state banks. Sumitro's usual pattern of operation was to announce with great public fanfare a new program and then later go to the Stabilization Council for approval.[46] This type of behavior hardly endeared him to the tightly knit group of economists around Widjojo.

Sumitro quickly saw that the IMF proposal for doing away with the overprice would deprive him of the great power and financial pressure he wielded through administrative authority over check price levels. Similarly he recognized that the termination of overprice flexibility would limit options for providing greater returns to areas that concentrated on one main export crop. Although it is not known exactly what his political ambitions were in 1970, his leadership role in the 1958 rebellion against President Suharto and constant defense of the interests of the non-Javanese made him a distinct force to be reckoned with.[47] It appears that Sumitro would have preferred to have Widjojo press for the IMF proposals so that he could have opposed them, later saying he was looking after the outer islands. Yet Widjojo was too adept at this sort of bureaucratic situation to have himself caught. He gave Sumitro substantial authority for the presentation to the Stabilization Council on the issue. When he was being questioned about his own preferences given the intense IMF pressure, Sumitro was thus forced into a corner and admitted that "if the IMF really pushes and we need their standby, what alternatives do we have?" This allowed Widjojo to summarize and conclude that the consensus of the group was to accept the IMF recommendations.

GOI versus IMF

Both protagonists knew that they had come to the last act. The IMF's power was clearly on the wane because the World Bank and bilateral donors had more resources to offer, but the GOI still needed the convenient supply of reserves in the standby. Since no major group (among the donors or inside the GOI) was willing to oppose the fund, GOI negotiating tactics became simple: make the IMF staff think that they were getting something for their money by appearing to be tough but concede if the overall agreement seemed in danger. The GOI team thus wanted it to appear as if they were making major concessions but did this primarily to ensure that they could use this loss with the IMF in the future if there was any need to resist subsequent attempts at pressuring.

Both the economic and bureaucratic politics side of the preparations for the devaluation thus ended in shadowboxing, a time-tested Indonesian art. Once the IGGI was established and the stabilization program was going well, the stakes were too high to allow a falling out over the IMF proposals. Then once the devaluation was inevitable, the World Bank was not inclined to argue over changes in the BE system. Similarly the bilateral donors and Sumitro recognized that their long-term interests were best served by going along.

Stage 3: The Presidential Decision

Unlike the situation in the Indian or Ghanaian cases where the chief executive was involved at each critical turning point, President Suharto played no active role in the Indonesian devaluation decision and chose merely to approve the recommendations forwarded to him by the Stabilization Council. We are thus left to speculate on his rationale for accepting the advice of his economic team.

The most immediate and compelling concern for Suharto must have been the balance of payments. Although he could hardly have been expected to follow the intricacies of the payments gap forecasting, he assiduously followed the progress of the "Nine Basic Commodities Index" and clearly understood the connection between the maintenance of import flows and the ability of the GOI to continue price stabilization. He would thus have been loath to risk antagonizing the donors when their leverage was obvious.

Second, he was not an intense nationalist like his predecessor and was not inclined to view conditioned aid as an affront to sovereignty. His early encounters with the U.S. military had been reasonably favorable, and he brought an unantagonistic set of expectations to his reviews of relations with the donors and international organizations. This attitude was important because it was neither so trusting as Busia's nor as suspicious as Mrs. Gandhi's. This reinforced the economists' ability to keep such issues at the technical level, avoiding their emotive aspects.

Moreover, as we might predict for a military man, Suharto preferred to use the layers of bureaucracy as a buffer. To stop the devaluation or even to make any significant changes in the implementation, he would have needed critical substantive reasons to make such a move and technical economic advice that differed from what he was receiving. In 1970 there was not yet any major competition for the economists, and the issue was not one where the president could see any great benefits from being involved.

Finally, Widjojo's personal relationship with Suharto made it extremely unlikely that the president would turn down a critical proposal that had gone as far as the Stabilization Council. Widjojo's personal style with Suharto was always to be extremely courteous and deferential and to use go-betweens at preliminary stages if the issue warranted extreme caution. Also, at this point, Widjojo had become a symbol for Indonesian performance, and the president needed him as long as foreign donor resources remained critical.

In sum, until outside assistance declined in importance, the technocratic pattern maintained its own momentum. Both Suharto and the economic team needed each other; it was to their mutual advantage to handle this delicate matter in a routinized, bureaucratic fashion.

Stage 4: Implementation: Economic Policymaking with Limited Constraints:

The public reaction to the 1970 devaluation was almost imperceptible. A review of the major Jakarta newspapers for the weeks following the decision turns up only an occasional story and a few confused editorials but nothing close to either outrage or jubilation. The economic team put on television show explaining the decision, but this could hardly have influenced many because the presentations were far too technical for the typical audience.[48] Although a few of the exporters of specialty agricultural goods and handicrafts complained to the Trade Ministry that their increase in gross revenues was insufficient to compensate them for the rise in taxes they faced; and there were some murmurs from regional governors about their loss of direct control over the ADO, even the behind-the-scenes reaction was rather tame.[49]

We are thus faced with the question of why the reaction to the devaluation in Jakarta was so different from the responses in Delhi and Accra? In India, the opposition parties immediately branded the move a "sell-out to the imperialists," and in Ghana the rancor surrounding the devaluation created a convenient excuse for the subsequent coup. The most satisfactory answer is that strong factors mitigated against protest: the size of the devaluation was relatively small, a generally favorable political climate made protest an extreme response when it was well known that living standards were rising rapidly, and no interest groups were so adversely affected that they were willing to form a focused opposition.[50]

The political environment in which the stabilization program was initiated was remarkably congenial to the economists' strategy. Then as the program demonstrably succeeded, the improvement in living standards, particularly for the articulate urban populations, became pronounced. These results helped create a reservoir of support for the regime. Given this context, the stakes had to be high to warrant a protest or make trying to organize a challenge to the regime a worthwhile exercise.

This did not mean that protest was impossible or ineffective if well articulated. Ironically three examples show how relatively easy it was to reverse policies of the military regime. The first protest to the stabilization measures came in 1967 from Chinese businessmen who were eminently successful at getting the GOI to reduce state bank lending rates. A second protest, only four months before the 1970 devaluation, led to massive street demonstrations after it was announced that the state oil company was sharply raising prices for gas and kerosene. A third protest, which almost developed into a noncompliance movement, came after the Jakarta city buses announced increases in fares. All three reactions led the central government to back down. So although the environment was not conducive to challenge, it could occur if the adverse policy impact affected a large or volatile group.

If we now turn from the environment to the microlevel and look at the specific details of the April 1970 policies, we see that on balance, the impact was insufficiently adverse to trigger a strong reaction. First, the decision was sufficiently technical that it took considerable time for those involved to estimate the costs and benefits of the tax and earnings provisions. Second, exporters generally benefit and, given the export-oriented nature of the Indonesian economy, this had favorable multiplier effects. More important, though, the GOI maintained its subsidies on rice, textiles, and the nine basic commodities, so the poor were not inconvenienced by the increase in import prices. This meant that middle- and upper-income groups bore the brunt of the import price rises.[51] Since middle- and upper-income people had benefited most from the general thrust of the stabilization effort, a 15 percent increase in prices for half their imports was not terribly threatening.

Three patterns were evident in the handling of the April 1970 devaluation and may be typical of countries where economic policymaking is conducted with limited political constraints: (1) the origin of the proposals and the direction of the implementation was entirely from above, (2) consultation with those likely to be affected was minimal or nonexistant, and (3) the low level of politicization and infrequent cross-issue brokerage of interest groups reduced the impact of potentially complementary groups.

Several other examples of economic policymaking under the Suharto technocrats show that these patterns reappear. An especially interesting comparison is between the April 1970 and the August 1971 devaluation. Here though the foreign organizations played almost no role in the deliberations leading up to the decision, the economic team chose an even larger devaluation than in 1970 and was apparently not worried about adverse political ramifications. In fact, the prime concern seems to have been to keep the rupiah fully competitive, and increasing import prices 17 percent did not cause major apprehension.[52]

The various changes in the official rice production improvement programs were handled similarly. The switch from the *Bimas Gotong Royong* strategy, which relied on foreign contractors to supply a package of seed, fertilizer, and pesticide inputs, to the *Rumus Tani* (farmer's price incentive formula), was made entirely from the top and only because the farmers did not pay enough rice in return to justify the cost outlays.[53] The farmers' complaints throughout the stabilization period—that rice price subsidization in the cities was keeping farm-gate prices too low—had little impact until the real fiscal cost of increasing production became apparent.

The decision to end the subsidies on cotton, which occured gradually between late 1970 and early 1973, is an example of an area that was initially considered too politically sensitive to touch. Yet the technocrats eventually felt they could stand the strain of local price increases and thus forced competition with textile imports. Here the Ministry of Industry represented its clients, the spinning and weaving mill owners, while the Ministry of Finance pressed for increased revenue from the sale of the PL 480 and commercially imported cotton. The compromise led to a four-step reduction in the subsidy, with complete elimination by 1973. In this instance, there is no question that the spinners and weavers brought great pressure on the GOI to maintain the subsidy, yet the economists arguing the need for efficient industry won out.[54]

Suharto's economists thus seem to have operated in a situation where they could implement their technocratic preferences without the normal entanglements facing a country with opposition parties, a higher level of politicization, or a challenging hostile populace. This environment can bring reasonably quick results for technocratic policies and tends to reinforce the proclivities of specialists to keep decision making a closed affair. This style of operation blended well with the political scene in the late 1960s but came under much greater pressure in the early 1970s.

The economists were sufficiently adaptable to adjust to changing circumstances. In 1973–1974 they had to accept General Ibnu Sutowo's flamboyant management of Pertamina, the Indonesian State Oil Company, because President Suharto was not willing to intervene. Once scandal had begun to envelop Sutowo, though, the economists brought Pertamina under closer supervision of the Ministry of Finance.

Similarly, the economists have been comfortable with extensive government intervention through investment regulations, credit allocation, and price controls, despite their overall identification with using the market mechanism.[55] This toleration for ambiguity represents either compromise with political pressure or a true ambivalence about government micromanagement of the economy.[56] It is also striking to see that, two decades after they first started advising Suharto, the economists still have coherence as a group. Although the president dismissed Widjojo from the cabinet in April 1983, Ali Wardhana, the second most prominent economist, was retained and has kept the allegiance of most of the economists.

Summary and Conclusions

The Indonesian stabilization program during the years 1966–1970 was remarkable in its achievements: a virulent inflation was stopped, many inefficient government enterprises were closed, a freeze on government hiring was imposed, the previous controls system was disassembled, and per capita income began to rise consistently for the first time in a decade.

Some analysts have been tempted to attribute this fundamental restructuring of economic policy to a single cause—the skill of the local economists, the innate superiority of the neoclassical policy followed, or the large flows of outside resources received. Although parsimony is to be valued, the Indonesian economic recovery requires a more complex interpretation. The early post-Sukarno period was extraordinary not only in comparison with other countries trying similar stabilization programs but even in contrast to previous and subsequent phases of Indonesian economic policy.

The peculiar circumstances Suharto faced in 1966 provided an ideal environment for a technocratic approach to Indonesia's economic problems. The absence of political constraints allowed the economic solutions to work effectively.

There were both external and internal reasons for the persistence of a supportive aid relationship. From outside, the Vietnam war made it unlikely that the United States or any other Western donor would want the visible, potentially entangling commitments necessitated by high politics. On the other hand, Indonesia's location, natural resources, and future market made it too important to be ignored. The evolving technocratic milieu was thus a mutually satisfactory middle ground.

Suharto also found that stressing economic performance was optimal for internal political reasons. During his first eighteen months, the general was preoccupied with security problems and much to his satisfaction found that the economists were content to follow orders and avoid intrigues. This created a personal bond that was strengthened when it became obvious that Widjojo and his team were going to be expert at extracting resources from the aid consortium. Suharto was hardly an intellectual and had no particular ideological preferences in economic policy. With domestic spheres of influence clearly carved out, the initial relationship between the economists and the military was symbiotic, producing strong support for the economists' choices.

After the military-economist bond was established, performance reinforced it. In a country that had long known deteriorating living standards, order and growth were compelling endorsements for a regime. Suharto saw this and reaped the political rewards. A few other countries have done the same—Western Europe under the Marshall Plan, Japan, South Korea, Israel, and Taiwan—but these are the exceptions. Most other countries have found it extremely difficult to conduct an effective stabilization program and raise living standards simultaneously.

In the Indonesian case, the combination of private foreign investment, public assistance, and a favorable debt settlement helped to provide a resource flow level that greatly aided stabilization efforts. Nevertheless, it is not impossible to find examples of other countries with this volume of per capita foreign transfers. The two most distinguishing characteristics of the Indonesian scene were the efficiency of resource allocation and political quiescence.

With the Communist party and the militant unions destroyed, the Nationalist party drifting without its leader, and the military in control of all major resources, the economists were able to act with limited restraints. Not surprisingly, this is precisely the sort of situation where technocrats are most effective.

Appendix 3A   Chronology of Indonesia's Aid Relationships and Key Events Leading to the April 1971 Rupiah Devaluation

This summary of the major events in Indonesia's aid and economic policy history is particularly detailed for three reasons. It shows the extraordinary role that aid has played in Indonesia's development. It highlights the oscillations in the influence of foreign powers and their doctrines in Indonesian policy debates. And it shows that virtually all of the parts of the Suharto stabilization program had been tried before but had never been put together in a coherent package with a favorable political climate.

Indonesia's aid relations can be divided into five main periods:

1. 1948–1955 When most members of the Indonesian elite preferred to remain nonaligned but (except for Ali Sastromidjojo's followers and the PKI) were willing to accept a substantial Western involvement and hoped for a large U.S. aid program.

After the bitterness over the Mutual Security Administration (MSA) agreement and the fall of the Sukiman cabinet, though, there was increasing recognition that aid was not likely to be available in large quantities and that it could be both a political liability and an asset.

2. 1956–1960 When Sukarno consciously began to play off the United States and Soviet Union in an attempt to maximize resource extraction from the two superpowers. Sukarno succeeded at raising commitments for over $1 billion worth of aid during the period, but his flamboyance and lack of interest in efficient resource allocation meant that much of the aid was wasted. During this period, both the United States and Soviet Union saw aid primarily in political terms, and aid pledges were made in a competitive, publicity-seeking environment.

3. 1961–1963 When the USSR, East European countries, and China seemed to be getting the upper hand in influencing Indonesia. Internal politics became increasingly fractious with most groups forced to join with three main factors: the army, PNI, or PKI. Simultaneously Sukarno orchestrated the drama of West Irian and Malaysian disputes, hoping to perpetuate his dominance and diverting attention away from the domestic economic decline. The United States, watching its influence fade, adopted a more realistic attitude by recognizing that aid was not a particularly good lever to get changes in Sukarno's foreign policy. Ironically, in the midst of the economic disarray, United States-funded research efforts laid the base for the abortive 1963 stabilization program, which was revived and effectively used after 1966.

4. 1964–1965 When the role of the non-Communist donors was trivial and the main donor competition was between the Soviet Union and China. The United States gradually withdrew its aid and finally negotiated to end all aid except a few technical assistance projects in Indonesian universities.

Although relations with the West were strained, there were no diplomatic breaks, and observers waited for the resolution of the bitter internal struggle for power.

5. 1966–1972 When the success of the army countercoup moves and General Suharto's ascension to power dramatically reversed the roles of the donors. The GOI broke relations with China, refused to atone for the decimation of the PKI as the Soviet Union demanded, and sought Western aid. The United States was cautious about becoming overcommitted and agreed to reinstitute aid on the condition that a multinational group of creditors and donors jointly establish uniform policies about GOI debt and new aid. The Suharto government proved so congenial to Western political and business interests that the Western donors committed $3 billion of new aid by 1971 and agreed to reschedule the old debt on very soft terms. Although the Communist countries eventually agreed to the same terms for debt rescheduling, their new aid was minuscule and their involvement minimal during the period.

1948

May
M. Rammed Hatta refused to conclude the consular agreement negotiated with the Soviet Union, reputedly because he assumed that relations with the Soviet Union would endanger possible support and aid from the United States.

December 29
Sumitro Djojohadikusomo, chief Indonesian representative in the United States, tried to get the State Department to reduce aid to Holland because of the Dutch police action, which violated Indonesian-Dutch accords. The State Department rebuffed Sumitro.

1949

January
U.S. Ambassador Phillis Jessup gave a speech to the United Nations sharply critical of Dutch military repression in Indonesia, thus taking a stand considerably more pro-Indonesian than the State Department previously had taken.

February 27
Senator Brewster introduced an amendment to the Marshall Plan funding appropriation with the intent of cutting U.S. aid to Holland unless the

police action was terminated and the Dutch returned to the terms of the Renville agreement.

April 22
Sukarno and other members of the Indonesian government captured by the Dutch were released from prison because the Dutch were worried about the eventual passage of the Brewster amendment.

October 1
The victory of Mao Tse-tung in China jolted the U.S. public and put pressure on President Harry Truman to define a new explicit foreign policy toward Southeast and Northeast Asia.

December 27
The Dutch transferred full sovereignty to the Republic of the United States of Indonesia. During the round table conference where the independence agreement was negotiated, the United States put considerable pressure on the Indonesian delegates to accede to the Dutch demand for payment of $300 million in fees. Merle Cochran, then of the UN but later the first U.S. ambassador to Indonesia, evidently gave verbal assurances that the United States would substantially aid Indonesia and that $100 million would be available from the Export-Import Bank (Eximbank) if the Indonesians went ahead with the agreement.

1950

January
The government of the Republic of United States of Indonesia (GOI) adopted a nonaligned stance.

March
As part of the process of developing an aid strategy for Asia, President Truman appointed the Griffin mission as his emissaries to visit each major Southeast Asian nation. Members of the mission felt they were under great pressure to produce a program that would avoid the fall of further nations to communism. Guerrilla fighting was intense in Vietnam, Burma, and Malaya, and the plans of the 1948 Comintern meeting in Calcutta (for revolutionary movements throughout the region) seemed to be coming to fruition.

The Griffin mission considered four sources of funds for aid programs: Eximbank credits, Mutual Defense Act military aid, Point Four technical assistance grants, and the unutilized appropriation from the China aid program. The mission concluded that the political and military interests in the region were the dominant ones for the United States. The political objectives were to avoid a second China, to fill the power vacuum left by the weakened colonial powers and yet achieve the strengthening of the region without alienating the developing nationalism. Military goals were to avoid the potential domino effect of success by insurgency in one country. U.S. economic interests were seen as far less compelling in Southeast Asia; the supply of a few raw materials was advantageous, but the main economic significance of the region came from the U.S. desire to see Britain, France, and Holland sufficiently prosperous (not caught in costly wars) to repay Marshall Plan loans and maintain defense obligations.

April
The U.S. Economic Cooperation Administration office was established in Jakarta. Many of the staff members had been formerly posted with the Marshall Plan in Europe or in parts of the aid programs to Chiang Kai-shek's China.

June 21
The GOI did not immediately condemn the North Korean invasion of South Korea.

August 15
Hatta signed a U.S. military agreement for $5 million of "constabulary equipment."

October 3
Colonel Melby of the U.S. Army made a week-long visit to Indonesia. The GOI turned down offers of military assistance as having too many conditions placed on receipt of the aid.

1951

November
The J. F. White firm, contracted by the GOI with Economic Co-operation Administration funds to do a series of engineering feasibility studies, was unable to fulfill its scope of work which was to identify useful projects that the Export-Import Bank loan could be used for and the United States could consider for future aid. The firm claimed that there was insufficient information to make even prefeasibility studies. The GOI claimed that the J. F. White staff was incompetent and unhelpful. Within seven months of the aid

program's operation, there was thus a soon-to-be-familiar debate over the quality of assistance being given.

February
The GOI blamed the United States for trying to reduce the tin price by releasing stockpiled tin.

June
Although the original discussions between the United States and the GOI on possible technical assistance projects had used $24 million as a target figure, the J. F. White firm doing the prefeasibility studies was unable to come up with projects warranting more than $8 million. This figure requested by the Jakarta office of ECA was cut to $6 million by the Washington headquarters.

October
The United States passed the Battle Act requiring termination of trade between states receiving U.S. aid and states at war or in belligerent status with the United States. The GOI reluctantly agreed to embargo rubber trade with China.

October 10
The U.S. Congress passed the Mutual Security Act requiring a consolidation of technical assistance, budgetary support, and military aid under the same organizational structure.

December
The U.S. embassy in Jakarta began discussion with the Indonesian Foreign Ministry over an exchange of notes to comply with provisions in the new Mutual Security Act. The act gave recipient nations two alternatives: option A: to receive military as well as economic aid but agree to six requirements including using the assistance to enhance the military security of the United States, or option B: to forgo military aid and simply agree to efficient use of only economic assistance. U.S. Ambassador Merle Cochran evidently did not fully explain that Indonesian negotiators under pressure to obtain aid agreed to conditions necessary for obtaining both military and economic aid.

1952

January 4
An exchange of notes between the United States and GOI took place

in Jakarta, finalizing the terms of the Mutual Security Administration agreement.

January 29
The ECA director in Jakarta, Everett Hawkins, stated in an interview that the GOI need not have signed the option A provisions just to get economic assistance.

February 21
After intense debate in the Indonesian Parliament and in the press, Foreign Minister Achmad Subardjo resigned over his handling of the MSA agreement.

February 23
Prime Minister Sukiman Winjosandjojo and his cabinet resigned over the MSA affair. The incident was considered an unacceptable infringement of Indonesia's nonaligned position. Subsequently a reasonable consensus developed among centrist politicians that Indonesia should have an active but independent foreign policy.

July 1
Working in tandem with the Economic Cooperation Administration, the United States also had the Technical Cooperation Administration (TCA), which provided only technical assistance. TCA Administrator, Andrews, arrived in Jakarta and offered to sign an aid agreement with the GOI that provided economic assistance only under option B of the Mutual Security Act. The negotiations took place against the wishes of Ambassador Cochran but led to an understanding.

December
The GOI finally signed the agreement negotiated by Andrews but in the meantime, the TCA had cut the budget from $6 million to $3.1 million, leading to further disillusionment with the U.S. aid promises.

1953

The Sastromidjojo cabinet brought a considerable shift to the left in ideology of pronouncements and actions taken. The cabinet decided to recognize the Soviet Union and China and vociferously criticized the United States for releasing rubber from its stockpiles and thus hurting the world price.

Sumitro was made minister of finance and tried to initiate a stabilization program of tight money and a balanced budget. He failed.

1955

April
The Bandung Conference of Afro-Asian States brought Sukarno the world attention he craved and ushered in a period when China took a less militant tack. This gave Sukarno the opening to develop a more flexible foreign policy and to begin courting both Eastern and Western aid sources.

September
The first national elections in Indonesia showed the intricate splintering of the electorate that had developed, the lack of broad popularity of the Socialist Party of Indonesia and Masjumi, and the growing strength of the Communist party. The deep bitterness that characterized the election period became reflected in the increasing intransigence of political leaders.

1956

March
The United States offered and concluded a $90 million PL 480 agreement with soft currency repayment provisions.

April
Sukarno took an extended trip to Western Europe and North America. He stopped in Britain and Canada and arranged increased aid from British Commonwealth countries before going to Washington.

May
In his Washington discussions, Sukarno was able to get verbal commitments of increasing aid from an average of $6 million per year in the early 1950s to an average of $30 million henceforth.

August
Sukarno had an extremely well-publicized trip to Soviet Union, which led to offers of substantial aid.

September
The GOI and Soviet Union signed an agreement for $100 million of technical assistance and project aid.

1957

January
The Masjumi party withdrew from the Sastromidjojo cabinet, leading to

Sukarno's announcement that Indonesia needed to establish a new political structure that he would direct and labeled "guided democracy."

March
Martial law was declared due as signs of rebellion in Sumatro and Suluwesi and the open warfare of the Darul Islam in West Java grew.

April
The Ford Foundation began its training and faculty support program at the Economics Faculty of the University of Indonesia. Professors Sumitro, Sadli, Subroto, and Sarbini were the only seasoned economists on the faculty, but Widjojo, Salim, and Wardhana (later to become the core of the Suharto economic team) were identified as being promising.

July
The GOI requested $60 million of military equipment from the United States but was refused. Eventually a $15 million arms sale was arranged.

December
The GOI nationalized all Dutch assets and expelled Dutch citizens, asserting that the Dutch were refusing to negotiate over West Irian and were using the economic interests in Indonesia to weaken the country.

1958

February
The PRRI rebel government was announced in Padang, and the Permesta rebellion broke out in North Suluwesi. Although Sumatran resistance folded quickly, the fighting in North Sulwesi continued for over three years.

May 10
Allen Pope, a pilot paid by the CIA, was shot down and captured in North Suluwesi by GOI troops. Anti-U.S. feelings within the central government reached a new high.

1959

August
The GOI devalued the currency by 90 percent and nationalized all bank accounts worth more than 25,000 rupiah. These steps combined with regulations forbidding Chinese to own land or to live in villages became part of Sukarno's socialist and Javenese attack on the wealthy, primarily

from Chinese or other minority groups. The GOI also established a mono-
poly of all foreign trade through its own state trading companies. At a time
of deep outer island resentment of the central government,this attempt to
get greater control over exporting led to the growth of a sophisticated
smuggling trade.

1960

February
Premier Nikita Khrushchev had successful visit to Indonesia where he
dedicated a $100 million sports complex being constructed with Soviet aid,
lauded Soviet advances in science, and promised a fully equipped 200-bed
hospital for Jakarta.

1961

April
President Kennedy invited Sukarno to Washington, and, in line with a new
flexibility in aid policy, they issued a joint communiqué that made no
mention of Indonesia's increasingly autocratic guilded democracy, the
West Irian dispute, or the nationalization of Dutch property.

May
Sukarno announced that the GOI would not renew foreign oil concessions
and would allow renewal only if the firms agreed to production-sharing
contracts. Sukarno also began a virulent campaign against the Dutch for
their continued pressence in West Irian. Simultaneously the USSR agreed
to an increased supply of Soviet arms with landing craft and other weapons
necessary for invasion from the sea.

1962

January
The competition between Western and Communist donors had led to
rough equality in pledges of aid credits from either side. Western pledges
had totaled $689.2 million since 1950; Communist country commitments
(all barter agreements or loans) totaled $691 million. In addition to the
Western loans, there was a total of $187 million in grant technical as-
sistance and commodities.

February
Robert Kennedy visited Indonesia to assess the seriousness of the West

Irian Dispute. Kennedy offered-a new PL 480 agreement worth $72.7 million for the following three years and got Sukarno to agree to have Ellsworth Bunker as the negotiator between the Dutch and the GOI.

May
The USSR speeded up its arms deliveries, and there was discussion in Jakarta of the possibility of obtaining Soviet missiles.

June
The survey report of D. D. Humphrey was available in draft in Jakarta. It supposedly helped form the basis for the Eight Year Plan to begin in 1963. The report argued the strategic importance of Indonesia, the country's favorable prospects for economic recovery if properly managed, and its possible long-term role in the Pacific. The report also concluded that Communist country aid had been poorly executed and that further U.S. aid should not focus on a publicity-seeking competition with the USSR but be directed to maximizing economic growth. The conclusion recommended a major series of changes in economic policy and an aid package of $325 million to $390 million during the subsequent five years. The report came at a time when there was considerable tension between the GOI and the USSR over how much and with what speed the arms would arrive. It briefly appeared as if Sukarno might take a turn back toward the West, especially given the impression that the United States might significantly increase its annual commodity aid.

July
Britain and Malaya agreed to the formation of Malaysia. Sukarno immediately condemned the move as an example of neocolonialism.

August
The Dutch and Indonesian governments agreed to settle the West. Irian issue by a plebiscite in 1969 but that the GOI would occupy and govern the territory in the intervening seven years.

A new system announced for handling foreign exchange allowed exporters to keep 15 percent of their export earnings and set them on a free market. Given the rapid inflation, the official exchange rates were quickly overvalued, so this became a means of retaining some realism in export earnings. This principle was later incorporated into the BE system as established in February 1966.

October
Chaerul Saleh, Indonesian Minister of industry, met with E. Black, president

of the World Bank. Without waiting to hear what Saleh wanted to discuss, Black immediately made it clear that the IBRD would not lend anything to Indonesia as long as the GOI refused compensation for the Dutch assets nationalized in 1957. Saleh departed in a huff, claimed he had come only to pay a courtesy call, and demanded an apology. The next day Black apologized but Saleh said this was not enough and the World Bank should quit being a tool of the imperialists. This affair reduced the possibility that the GOI would receive IBRD lending. Interestingly, from the late 1950s into the most hectic days of Sukarno's denouement, the IMF seemed able to maintain cordial relations with the GOI, and the GOI withdrew from the fund only when it was abandoning the other "Western-controlled" international organizations.

1963

February
Sukarno formally announced the initiation of confrontation: his move to "crush Malaysia" diplomatically and militarily. Troops were mobilized and guerrilla raids executed against various parts of Malaysia.

March
The United States offered a $17 million capital loan and planned to support the Indonesian Eight Year Plan, making clear that the aid was not tied to concessions in Indonesian foreign policy.

Sukarno gave his *"Declarasi Economi—DEKON"* speech, stressing the Indonesia had to develop its own variant of democratic socialism. He claimed that there would be increasing use of the private sector and the price mechanism.

May
Prime Minister Djuanda announced a new stabilization plan with fourteen major regulations. The overall construct of the plan was market oriented and included such anticipated steps as dismantling price controls, increasing imports of raw materials and spare parts, and balancing the federal budget. Sukarno promised his full support. This new approach to economic policy within the GOI was the result of increasing recognition that inflation was seriously undermining the regime's popularity. The stabilization plan also drew heavily on the advice of three Western groups of advisers: Humphrey's mission, the IMF, and a U.S. consulting firm, DMJM. The Humphrey report stressed the need for long-term plans and economic efficiency; the IMF provided its frequent urgings of fiscal and monetary

caution; and DMJM did estimates of the raw materials and spare parts needed to revive industry even to its pre-1957 levels.

August
The IMF agreed to a $50 million standby agreement for GOI use over the subsequent twelve months in conjunction with the new May stabilization measures.

September
Sukarno escalated confrontation, producing a budget deficit of 103 percent for 1963. An even more rapid rate of inflation ensued. They May 26 regulations were increasingly ignored.

1964

March
In a talk before foreigners with newsmen present, Sukarno said: "If strings aren't removed from aid, Indonesia will say 'To Hell with your aid'!" The remark was later clarified, explicitly at U.S. Ambassador Jones's urging, to mean that the strings on the aid were the key problem.

April
The May 26 stabilization regulations of 1963 were repealed.

August
The USSR tried to avoid becoming involved in the Confrontation. Unlike the West Irian dispute, where the Soviet strategic and ideological interests were identical with Sukarno's, the Soviet leaders saw some advantages to the reduction of British power in Southeast Asia. The USSR was thus opposed to the Indonesian threats to Malaysia because they made it unlikely that the British would depart quickly.

Given the diplomatic aspects of confrontation, the United States was anxious to avoid triggering promises of increased Soviet aid. Although the United States was willing to put some diplomatic pressure on the GOI, British support of Vietnam was not sufficiently vocal to make President Johnson interested in taking a strong pro-Malaysia stand.

1965

January
U.S.-GOI relations deteriorated rapidly. Increasingly critical statements by Sukarno over the U.S. role in Vietnam and further splintering of the In-

donesian armed forces led many Westerners to conclude that the GOI was on the verge of a Communist takeover.

February
Mobs attacked the U.S. Information Agency offices and the U.S. library in protest over U.S. bombings in Vietnam. Indonesian police made no attempt to protect U.S. facilities, and the demonstrations were clearly carried out with GOI consent.

Secretary of State Dean Rusk clarified a change in U.S. policy, stating there would be no new technical assistance for U.S. fiscal year 1966, although ongoing projects would be allowed to proceed.

Sukarno's cabinet, swollen to 100 members, had become an unmanageable agglomeration and deadlocked given the three-way split among the PKI, army, and PNI. Sukarno spoke increasingly of the Jakarta-Hanoi-Peking axis. The inflation rate rose to over 100 percent per year.

April 11
Sukarno's *Berdikari* ("standing on your own feet") speech stressed that Indonesia had to produce its own food and clothing and should not import goods that could be produced locally. He claimed that the people also needed character-building projects like national monuments and conference halls for the new emerging forces.

May
Ellsworth Bunker visited Jakarta as President Johnson's representative. After negotiations, the United States and GOI issued a communiqué saying that the U.S. aid program should be continuously revised to conform to the wishes of the respective governments. In practice this meant that capital assistance was ended, the Peace Corps withdrawn, and on technical assistance projects at universities continued.

July
The Foreign Investment Law was repealed, and, like the previous regulations for the oil sector, new investment was allowed only a production-sharing basis.

September 30
The attempted coup by Colonel Untung and other Indonesian Air Force and Navy officers resulted in the death of six of the top eight army generals.

October
Sukarno fled to Halim Air Force base and initially appeared to side with the coup planners; then as the coup failed, he claimed he was uninvolved.

The subsequent three months were a period of turmoil bordering on civil war when General Suharto solidified his military power, and Sukarno's grasp slipped.

December
The rupiah was devalued and set at a rate of 10 rupiah per U.S. dollar.

General Suharto sought advice in three main areas: military security, economic, and political. The military group members were General Murtopo, Alamsjah, Hamardani, and Sutowo, each with special links to resources or key interest groups. The political group consisted of Faud Hassan (subsequently dean of psychology at the University of Indonesia), Dilar Noer (subsequently rector, IKIP Jakarta), and Asrul Sani (later a member of the Indonesian Parliament). The political group was unable to develop a coherent strategy for Suharto, and after several sessions filled with broad generalities it was quietly ignored. The economic advisers were initially Widjojo Nitisastro, E. Salim, M. Sadli, and Subroto. The economists, all from the University of Indonesia, were initially quite hesitant about being involved because they were not sure that Suharto would survive and had no way to judge if their advice would be taken seriously. Yet the economists were on call to Suharto and in one instance left a dinner party to go first to the sultan and then to the general's home. Both the military and the economic groups provided concrete advice that Suharto followed, though each was kept relatively separate and responsible for sharply deliniated areas.

1966

January 3
The GOI announced increases in gas and kerosene prices and was met within twenty-four hours by massive street demonstrations.

January 21
Although not wanting to act as if it could be coerced by demonstrations, the GOI dropped the prices of gas and kerosene.

February 11
The BE system was established. See Appendix 3B for the details of the evolution of the system from February 1966 until April 1970.

March 12
Generals Jusuf Ramli, Sarbini, Prasuki Saleh, and Suharto visited Sukarno and forced a transfer of power. Suharto became acting president, the sultan of Jokjakarta was named minister for economic affairs, and Adam Malik was chosen as foreign minister. Suharto retained the Ministry of Defense and Security for himself.

Prof. Sarbini of the University of Indonesia became frustrated with Widjojo's dominance of the economic team. Sarbini, a committed socialist, resented not only the younger man's ability to control the group but also the market-oriented, nonsocialist route being planned for GOI economic policy. Soon after assuming the acting presidency, Suharto asked the economists for a presentation on specific economic decisions to be taken. When Sarbini lost out in the discussions among the economists, he drew up his own plan for economic policies and took it directly to Suharto without telling the other economists. When Widjojo found out about this, it led to a permanent split between Sarbini and the rest of the economists. Sarbini then became the most vocal critic of the economists. He had little audience until 1972 when the rice shortage and subsequent inflation raised increasing numbers of questions about the efficiency and equity of the programs devised by the economists.

April 12
The sultan announced a change in GOI attitude toward private foreign investment and the GOI's intent to pay off on all previous long-term debts and to compensate those whose property was nationalized.

April 18
China withdrew its previous offers of aid because the GOI showed no signs of apologizing for the sacking of the Chinese embassy. The same day the United States offered $8.2 million in PL 480 rice for immediate delivery.

May 24
The Ministry of Trade announced the first of several steps to increase the percentage of export proceeds that exporters may keep for sale in the BE market. See Appendix 3B for comments on the subsequent changes and the rationale behind them.

May 28
The GOI and the government of Japan issued a joint communiqué stating that Indonesia's debt and aid problems were of sufficient scale and complexity that they needed to be handled by a multinational group.

June
The GOI convinced the IMF that it was serious about rejoining the fund and establishing a new, effective stabilization program. The IMF sent a team to evaluate alternative future economic policies.

July 5
Indonesian parliamentary decision 23, presented to the Parliament by Acting President Suharto, created the parliamentary basis for the economic stabilization program. It stated the broad goals of the new administration and delegated to the government the authority to carry out appropriate policies.

September
Indonesia's non-Communist creditors met in Tokyo to form a working group to reschedule GOI debt. They agreed that the creditor position on debt and discussions of new aid would be linked to GOI economic performance. The IMF team, which played a substantial part in preparing their papers on the GOI debt position, was given an informal role as executor in Jakarta for the creditors.

October 3
GOI economic policy goals were enunciated. The main ones included establishing and maintaining price stability on essential commodities consumed by the bulk of the population, expanding food production, rehabilitating existing transport, communication, and irrigation systems, and promoting exports and production of cost-competitive import substitutes.

December
The creditors met formally in Paris, agreeing to a one-year moratorium on debt payments on two conditions: the GOI would pay all debts once an independent assessment of obligations was made and future rollovers on debt payments would be conditioned on economic performance.

1967

February
The donors willing to give new aid to Indonesia met and formed an aid consortium, the Inter-Governmental Group (IGGI) for Indonesia. The members were Britain, France, West Germany, Japan, Italy, Holland, Belgium, Australia, Canada, Denmark, and the United States; New Zealand, Australia, Switzerland, India, and Norway sent observers. At this first IGGI meeting, the GOI requested $200 million, primarily of commodity as-

sistance for 1967. The pledge was met with the understanding among the donors that the United States would provide roughly one-third, Japan roughly one-third, and the remaining donors one-third of the nonfood aid. This ratio was agreed after considerable pressure by the United States to make Japan a major contributor in the IGGI.

April
The IMF established a full-time resident mission in Jakarta with Kemal Siber as the representative.

Chinese businessmen complained to the GOI that they were being bankrupted by the extremely tight credit policies; their complaints led to some reductions in state bank interest rates for lending.

May
Sumitro returned to Indonesia for the first time since he had been forced to flee after the collapse of the PRRI rebellion in 1958. His safety was guaranteed by Ali Murtopo, which implied that although Suharto may have been satisfied with the advice he was receiving from the economists, the president was still anxious to have an internationally recognized economist associated with the government.

Bank Indonesia opened the Bourse where the BE certificates and free foreign exchange could be traded. From February 11, 1966, up to this point, the trading of both BE and DP was in a more informal, less centralized fashion among the various dealers in foreign exchange.

July
The BE system was again modified to give exporters increased incentives.

December
A poor rice harvest, low procurement of buffer stocks by the Logistics Agency, and the coincidence of having the Muslim New Year, Christmas, and the Chinese New Year all within a brief period (which led to a concentrated surge in consumer spending) triggered a sizable year-end inflation. The overall rate of inflation was 112 percent for 1967, down considerably from the 635 percent of 1966, but the rapid destabilization at the end of the year jolted both the GOI economists and the foreign donors. This led to an increased receptivity on the donors' part for supplying large buffer stocks of food and using aid to meet the demand for nonproject durable imports. Richard Gilbert, leader of the Harvard Development Advisory Service (DAS) team in Pakistan at the time, visited Indonesia shortly after and proceeded to blame the IMF for not insisting on adequate buffer stocks

of rice and basic consumer goods. Gilbert then went to Washington, where he made a strong plea for increased PL 480 flows. This sequence of events led to his selection as the subsequent Harvard DAS director in Jakarta but also ushered in an era of competition among the foreign economic advisers to the GOI.

1968

January
Monetary policy was tightened again despite complaints from businessmen that credit restrictions were forcing a major recession.

Bank Indonesia tried an unannounced policy of market intervention to help stabilize the DP rate. It was found that the market was thin and that a relatively small amount of purchasing rupiah was sufficient to slow down the depreciation. The policy was eventually decided to be counterproductive because the overall rate of inflation was still high, and holding down the DP rate would make the exchange rate artifically low and thus reduce incentives to exporters.

February 29
The Ministry of Trade announced that check prices for all goods would be at least 5 percent below world f.o.b. prices to ensure that exporters had an adequate margin to cover commissions, claims, and payments to foreign agents.

June
The development cabinet was named, with Sumitro Djojohadikusomo as the trade minister. The economic team's status was enhanced, but (except for Wardhana at Finance) the members still held primarily subministerial posts.

July 10
Because Bank Indonesia reserves of foreign exchange had declined sharply, Sumitro convinced the Stabilization Council to suspend trading in regular BE funds, thus forcing importers either to use aid BE or DP. This increased demand reduced the unused aid BE and widened the premium between BE and DP from 16 percent to 30 percent, beginning a trend where the DP reached a peak of 50 percent more than BE in October 1968.

October
Price increases slowed substantially.

The state banks started a new high interest rate savings plan offering depositors 6 percent month. The intent was to encourage people to save and to channel their funds into the banking system and thus allow the system to meet investment needs. The high DP rate at the time made repatriation very attractive, and, given that the authorities asked no questions about the origin of the funds, there was substantial appeal to the program.

The Stabilization Council decided to hold the BE rate at 326 rupiah per U.S. dollar. Members of the Stabilization Council were worried that a sharp increase in the BE rate would not only fuel speculation but lead to cost-push inflation given the large amount of imports. A decision was also made to repeat interventions in the DP market, as was done in January 1968. The argument for stabilizing the DP rate was slightly different from those advanced for a stable BE. Although officials wanted a relatively high DP rate to encourage capital repatriation, a rapidly fluctuating DP rate would be an incentive for traders and investors abroad to hold their foreign exchange off the market in hopes of obtaining a higher rate in the future. This pattern of behavior might have led to destabilizing speculation and was the situation the GOI's top economists hoped to avoid by small market interventions.

November
At the IGGI meeting, the GOI, with IBRD and IMF endorsement, requested $500 million in aid (food, project, and commodities) for 1969.

December
With $4.7 million of purchasing since October, Bank Indonesia lowered the DP rate from 480 to 413 rupiah per U.S. dollar.

1969

January
With price increases having slowed to less than 1 percent per month and substantial amounts of capital being repatriated, Bank Indonesia found that it had to sell rupiah ($10.9 million in January) to maintain its October 1968 policy of keeping the DP rate stable.

Sumitro started establishing syndicates of export traders handling rubber, copra, pepper, and coffee similar to the ones involved in handling the import of the nine basic commodities. These export syndicates were designed to cut down profits of middlemen and were thus clearly to aid indigenous export crop producers while simultaneously creating business for non-Chinese traders.

March
From January through March, Bank Indonesia sold $52 million worth of rupiah, an example of the demand for the currency and allowing the first post-1966 non-aid or IMF reserve buildup.

April
At the IGGI pledging session, the donors overfulfilled the GOI request and offered $507 million for 1969.

May
Sumitro took a strong hand in the decision to keep the DP rate fixed through continued market interventions (rather than simply dampening fluctuations). The Stabilization Council approved.

August
P. P. Schweitzer, IMF managing director, visited Indonesia. Along with other comments, he urged the GOI to begin plans to eliminate the multiple exchange rate system.

September
Increasing import demand led Bank Indonesia to sell $15.3 million in foreign exchange reserves to defend the DP and BE rates.

October
An IMF review team arrived from Washington and joined with local IMF staff in inviting R. Saleh (deputy governor of Bank Indonesia) and E. Salim (BAPPENAS) to go to Bali with them for an extensive review of alternative future economic policies. The IMF team tried to persuade the Indonesians that a devaluation was ultimately necessary and that a consolidation of the BE and DP rates should be the way to solve the overvaluation and administrative problems simultaneously.

Declines in rubber prices, increasing general import demand, and a failure of rice procurement (necessitating an unanticipated import of 200,000 metric tons of rice at commercial rates totaling $20 million) led to an increased demand for exchange reserves.

November
The GOI requested and received IMF and IBRD endorsement for $600 million in aid for its fiscal year 1970–1971.

December

Bank Indonesia was forced to use $55.7 million of its foreign exchange reserves in November and December to defend the BE and DP rates.

Kemal Siber, IMF resident representative, wrote a discussion paper for the GOI arguing that devaluation was necessary and that it should be combined with a consolidation of the BE and DP rates. In verbal comments, the IMF staff intimated that the next fund standby (to be negotiated in March 1970 to take effect in April 1970) would be hard to obtain unless the GOI agreed to end the multiple exchange system.

The Indonesians resented the IMF pressure and refused to agree to the proposed steps. Emil Salim took the IMF balance of payments estimates to Widjojo on his return. Widjojo subsequently gave the IMF numbers to Bernard Bell, the World Bank representative. Bell asked his chief economist, Anthony Churchill, to review the IMF work and make suggestions. Churchill critiqued the paper, arguing that the balance of payments figures available (through November 1969) were not sufficient evidence for the IMF recommendation of devaluation and definitely not an argument for ending the multiple exchange rate system. The IMF's resident staff in Jakarta saw the Churchill memo and was irritated at IBRD involvement in a "monetary issue."

1970

January

The IMF staff eventually convinced P. P. Schweitzer to meet with R. McNamara, president of the World Bank, to press the issue of the IMF's jurisdiction over monetary and foreign exchange rate policy. McNamara apparently agreed not to have the bank staff interfere in the fund's area.

February

In Jakarta, the December balance of payments figures were in, and the seriousness of the reserves loss was obvious. In a follow-up memo, Churchill argued that a small devaluation might be necessary. Since he and B. Bell had no strong feelings on the rate consolidation, they were no longer opposed to the IMF recommendations. W. Hollinger of the Harvard DAS, on the other hand, argued that the exchange rate consolidation would remove a substantial safety valve in the system and thus needlessly give up a flexible policy tool. Hollinger wrote two memos for Sumitro giving the reasons for continuing with roughly the present system.

March
After extensive debate in the Stabilization Council, the IMF proposals were accepted by the GOI. Sumitro, after initially opposing the move, became the swing figure; he concluded that the negative consequences were likely to be less onerous than the loss of an IMF standby.

April 2
The IMF Jakarta staff submitted a recommendation to Washington to go ahead with the standby and the changes in the exchange system.

April 10
Ali Wardhana submitted a letter to P. P. Schweitzer outlining the proposed changes in the exchange system and requesting IMF assistance. He stated that the new system would go into effect April 17.

April 14
The IMF board approved the standby, the GOI special drawing rights availability, and the changes in the structure of the exchange system.

April 17
The new system was put into effect. See Appendix 3A for details of the new arrangements. At the subsequent IGGI pledging session, the GOI received commitments of $622 million in aid, overfulfilling the request by $22 million.

December
Bank Indonesia, after Stabilization Council approval ended the preferential rate of 326 rupiah per U.S. dollar being applied to aid BE since the April 17 devaluation. It was decided to charge the 378 rupiah rate for the aid BE, as well as for all other exchange, but to rely on special concessionary credit provisions to overcome the cost disadvantages of tied aid.

December 31
The annual rate of inflation for 1970 was only 9 percent. Most economic observers feel that the stabilization policies had succeeded. The attention of most of the top GOI and foreign economists began to turn to longer-run planning and investment problems.

1971

April
The mild creep in the inflation rate after May 1969 when the DP rate was fixed worried the economic team about what could be done to keep

exports fully competitive. The Harvard DAS was thus asked to look into means whereby the GOI could still keep receiving its export taxes but not price Indonesian goods out of international markets. A devaluation seemed a bit difficult to justify but, if there were a suitable excuse for one, would have been looked at seriously.

August 15
President Nixon announced the 7 percent devaluation of the U.S. dollar, plus a temporary 10 percent import surcharge.

August 16
The economic team met to begin consultations on the Indonesian response to the U.S. devaluation.

August 17
Major currency traders expected the rupiah to appreciate against the dollar and were quoting the new rate at about 330 to 340 rupiah per U.S. dollar.

August 18
Sumitro gave both formal and off-the-record talks saying that the GOI would support the dollar.

August 23
The GOI announced that it would devalue even more than the dollar was devalued, making the new rate 415 rupiah per U.S. dollar, or 6 percent lower than the previous rupiah-to-dollar parity. This was a full 16 percent devaluation against currencies that did not follow the dollar down.

This decision to devalue was made almost entirely by the GOI economic team, which had only a brief conference with B. Bell of the IBRD and no special consultation with the IMF resident team. In contrast to the 1970 moves where the IMF had dominated the discussions and suggested the major options, the 1971 decisions conspicuously excluded the IMF. The fund merely received the announcement of the GOI's intention the prescribed number of hours before the public statement.

Appendix 3B   Evolution of the BE System 1966–1970

In December 1965, the government of Indonesia (GOI) devalued the rupiah and set the new rate at 10 rupiah per U.S. dollar. Yet by February 1966 inflation was running at approximately 50 percent per month, and the exchange rate set two months before was clearly inappropriate.

As an incentive for the exporters to continue to use legal channels, the GOI thus decided to let exporters retain a given percentage of the value of goods sold for foreign exchange. There were thus two problems: determining how much of the sale price the exporter should be allowed to keep and checking to see what the goods had actually been sold for.

The government decided to keep the practice set by the Dutch and Sukarno regimes of publishing monthly check prices that were at or close to world market prices for the goods and then simply ensuring that the exporters had received at least that much foreign exchange.

General Suharto's new economic advisers were also committed to a greater use of the market for distributing resources, so they set up the bonus export (BE) system, modeling it closely on the operations of the Pakistani foreign exchange system. Once a product was sold, the exporter was required to submit most of the foreign exchange to the government at the official exchange rate, but he was issued BE certificates at the market rate. BE purchasers were private individuals or firms who wanted to import goods allowed from a list of essential commodities. Yet there remained one other source of foreign exchange. If an exporter was able to get more than the check price for his commodities, he had free foreign exchange, or *Devisa Pelangkap* (DP). Because the government knew that it could not collect this amount and wanted to encourage exporters to keep their foreign exchange in Indonesia or convert it to rupiah, the sale of DP was legalized for the import of less essential goods. As the legal market with the highest rate of exchange of rupiah per foreign currency, the DP market also became the means for repatriation of capital from overseas.

As the export payment system was set up on February 11, 1966, it worked as follows:

Percentage of check price	Result	Exchange rate	User
90	Surrended to GOI	10 rupiah per U.S. dollar	GOI
10	Converted to BE certificates	43 rupiah per U.S. dollar	BE importer
"Overprice" was any proceeds above the check price that the exporter was able to obtain.	Kept as foreign exchange or sold in DP market	47 rupiah per U.S. dollar	Importer of less essential DP goods

As the system was first established, there was one additional important characteristic. The GOI decided to have different percentages of the check price surrendered for different goods. In fact, three distinct categories were set up. Category I, which encompassed 75 percent of Indonesia's nonoil exports, included rubber, copra, coffee, tobacco, palm oil, palm kernels, pepper, and tin. Category II, with roughly 22 percent of nonoil exports, included tea, spices, and other specialty nonmanufactured exports. Category III was for batiks and handicrafts. Category I goods were at world market prices, while categories II and III were exports where checking on actual prices would be time-consuming and difficult. The GOI thus decided to give exporters of these two categories incentives to use the legal system by giving them the option of greater percentages of BE out of the check price.

The returns to the exporters depended on four factors: (1) the amount of overprice (the difference between the real sale price and the government check price), (2) the percentage of the check price that had to be surrendered at the official rate and the percentage that could be sold as BE, (3) the official rate, and (4) the varying exchange rates for officials, BE, and DP exchange.

The system was thus designed to allow competitive forces to determine the rates for BE and DP but still retain for the government the ability to collect most of the foreign exchange for its own use and to have control over the earnings of the exporters by varying check prices the percentage to be surrendered at the undervalued official rate. The system thus introduced the market but in a *dirigiste*, incremental fashion.

Suharto's economic advisers clearly intended to reduce the amount of government handling of traded goods, but they wanted a system that still let them control the returns to different types of exporters and even geographical areas (certain goods were grown predominantly in certain provinces).

Increasing Use of the Market and Creation of Export Incentives

The evolution of the BE system from its inception in February 1966 until its major restructuring in April 1970 was primarily a series of steps designed to get the government out of importing on its own account, attempts at improving the efficiency of the foreign exchange market mechanisms, and moves to keep up tax collections without reducing incentives to exporters. The initial rules required that category I exporters receive only 10 percent of check price in BE, category II goods were allowed 15 percent, and category III exports were allowed 50 percent. The greater use of the market thus meant a progressive increase over time in the percentage of check price allowed to move in the BE market.

The actual changes were as follows:

	Percentage of check price allowed to BE categories		
	I	II	III
February 11, 1966	10	15	50
May 24, 1966	20	60	90
October 3, 1966	50	75	90
	Group A	Group B	
May 28, 1967[1]	75	90	90
August 20, 1968	85	90	90
April 17, 1970	90	90	90 (BE became equal to DP)

1. On this date, categories II and III were consolidated and called group B; category I became group A. There was some movement between categories. As timber exports became more important, for example, they were moved from group B to group A.

As increasing amounts of BE were made available for private purchases, there had to be a system for allocating the import chits. The GOI used tariffs and very tight credit policy to dampen demand but allowed competition among importers to determine the price and therefore which people were willing to import. Because inflation was not yet under control, this float in the exchange rate allowed the rupiah to stay in alignment between its domestic and foreign purchasing power.

Overprice versus Tax Collection

Throughout the operation of the BE system, there was continual debate within the GOI and among foreign advisers about the choices to be made between the goals of increasing incentives and garnering more tax revenues from exports. Overprice existed from the beginning of the system since it was impossible to keep the check price right at the world price for each commodity. Yet, there were strong differences of opinion about what percentage of overprice there should be. Exporting groups favored a large overprice because that got them more of their proceeds at the maximum rate, while tax experts tended to argue that it was better to keep the foreign exchange in centralized markets even if average tax rates had to be reduced.

There thus tended to be something of a seesaw pattern of increased

taxes following along with increased incentives. Many government departments were hesitant to see the official (subsidized) exchange rate changed,
which meant increasing the rupiah costs of their imports.

The timing of the overprice and taxing decisions was as follows:

May 24, 1966: Along with the decision to roughly double the percentage
of export proceeds going to BE, the GOI instituted the automatically
allocated export tax (ADO) of 10 percent on all goods. The ADO was to
go directly to the treasuries of the provinces from where the goods
originated, thus encouraging the regions to increase their export sectors
and to reduce smuggling.

May 28, 1967: By consolidating category II & III exports and removing
the Group B exports and raising the percent of check prices allowable for
BE, the GOI was simplifying administrative procedures and creating further
export incentives.

July 28, 1967: Two months after the third increase in export percentage
going to BE, it was decided to add a 15 percent tax on category A exports
and drop the 15 percent of check price surrendered to GOI at the official
rate.

February 29, 1968: The Ministry of Trade agreed to set all check prices at
least 5 percent below estimated world market price levels to help exporters
compensate for commissions, claims, and administrative costs.

August 20, 1968: The Stabilization Council agreed to use overprice as a
conscious method of encouraging exports in specific sectors. It was decided
that trade associations representing firms exporting category B goods
should have the right to set their own check prices. Category B check
prices would then drop to about 60 percent of world market prices for the
respective goods. On category A goods, increased BE percentage was
obtained by dropping the special export tax from 15 to 5 percent.

April 17, 1970: In the eventual changes of the BE system pressured by the
IMF, one of the arguments used in favor of the devaluation was that this
would give an adequate incentive to exporters to compensate them for the
fact that overprice had been abolished.

Oil and Aid

Oil and aid posed slightly different problems for the BE system. By the end
of 1969, the oil sector was 10 percent and aid BE was 28 percent of the toal
import bill.

In February 1966, the exchange rate for oil was set at 10 rupiah per U.S. dollar, the same as the official rate. In March 1967 this was raised to 85 rupiah per U.S. dollar but still trailed behind the BE and DP rates. The oil rate continued to lag until 1970 when, with the major exchange rate changes, it was raised to the free market rate. This lag of the oil rate was a tax on the oil companies because they were converting dollars to rupiah in their capital investment programs. This was also a subsidy to the state oil company, Pertamina, which was getting more dollars per rupiah than other state enterprises that had to import at the BE rate (after July 28, 1967, when the subsidized official rate was abolished).

Aid posed a delicate problem for the system because the requirements necessary to use it were often time-consuming and expensive, and some of the major donors (especially the United States) had overvalued exchange rates, which made the aid worth considerably less than its nominal value. The GOI tried to compensate in several ways. Beginning in December 1966, credit BE was sold at a 5 to 20 percent discount from regular BE generated from export proceeds. On May 28, 1968, credit BE was integrated into the regular BE market, but more lenient credit terms were offered for those willing to take the aid. In 1969 there was an increase in unutilized program aid of $75 million, while official reserves dropped by $20 million, indicating the degree of unattractiveness of some aid when compared with similarly priced regular BE. In April 1970 the GOI concluded that the aid would not be utilized unless it was, once again, sold at a discount. Aid was thus the only form of foreign exchange sold at less than the rate of 378 rupiah per dollar. Once the aid had been drawn down upon, the aid rate was raised to 378 in December 1970, though special credit provisions were needed to make it attractive to importers.

Appendix 3C   Interviews on the 1970, Indonesian Devaluation

Interviewee	Organization*	Place
R. Baker	U.S. embassy	Jakarta
W. Barmon	U.S. embassy	Taipei
B. Bell	IBRD	Washington, D.C.
R. Cashin	Director, USAID/Jakarta	Jakarta
Chudori	*Antara*	Jakarta

*Organization affiliation at the time of the interview.

D. Cole	Harvard Development Advisory Service	Cambridge, Mass.
A. R. S. Djoemena	Ministry of Industry, GOI	Jakarta
M. Gillis	HDAS	Jakarta
B. Glassburner	University of California Davis	Jakarta
D. Gordon	IBRD	Jakarta
M. Grossman	Economic adviser, GOI	Jakarta
S. Hasibuan	BAPPENAS	Jakarta
E. Heginbotham	U.S. embassy	Jakarta
B. Joedono	University of Indonesia	Jakarta
D. Joesuf	Center for Strategic and International Studies	Jakarta
R. Jufri	*Tempo*	Jakarta
S. Kawasaki	Manager, Loan Department, OECF	Tokyo
K. Kojima	Hitosubashi University	Tokyo
S. Kuriyama	Ministry of Finance, Japan	Tokyo
M. Lubis	*Indonesia Raya*	Jakarta
I. Miyamoto	Ministry of Finance, Japan	Tokyo
T. Okabe	MITI, Japan	Tokyo
S. Okita	OECF	Tokyo
S. Sakai	Ministry of Finance, Japan	Tokyo
R. Saleh	Bank Indonesia	Jakarta
Samali	Bank Indonesia	Jakarta
Sanyoto	*Business News*	Jakarta
D. Scott	IMF	Jakarta
A. Shakow	USAID	Washington
A. Sirigar	Bank Indonesia	Jakarta
Soejatmoko	BAPPENAS	Jakarta
J. Sudarsono	University of Indonesia	Jakarta

M. Suhadi	University of Indonesia	Jakarta
I. Sumedi	Min. of Industry, GOI	Jakarta
I. Tanjung	Min. of Finance, COI	Jakarta
A. Tokinoya	Embassy of Japan	Jakarta

Ghana: Hidden Disarray

The criterion of judgment in history is not some principle claiming universal validity, but that which works best.
Isaiah Berlin, 1957

Ghana When the Cheering Stopped

At 2 A.M. on January 13, 1972, troops and armor of the Ghanaian First Brigade began moving out of quarters north of Accra. In classic style, the brigade soon occupied the capital's airport, main roads, radio station, communications facilities, and key government buildings. By 6 A.M. Colonel I. K. Acheampong, commander of the First Brigade and chief plotter of the coup, had announced Ghana's third change of government in six years. Ghana, which had first been "decolonized," then "liberated," and then "democratized," was now to be "redeemed."[1]

Acheampong's maiden nationwide speech was candid. Although he started with charges of corruption and poor economic policy during the Busia regime he was replacing, he quickly came to the issues that had deeply concerned him and other military men:

The first people which Busia put his eyes on were the armed forces and the policy. Some army and police officers were dismissed under the pretext of retirement.... Then he started taking from us the few amenities and facilities which we in the armed forces and police enjoyed even under the Nkrumah regime.[2]

Acheampong rounded out his speech by calling for a review of the major controversial policies initiated by Busia but clearly showed that he and his colleagues had decided to rule without any burning ideological convictions.[3]

What made this drama of interests? How did Ghana's "redemption" differ from other coups where the military has intervened to protect its corporate interests?[4] What role did the December 27, 1971, devaluation of the cedi play in the coup decision seventeen days later? If Busia's party held an overwhelming majority in the Parliament (105 of 140 seats), why was there so little civilian displeasure over the use of force to change leadership?[5] Were there feasible alternative measures that Prime Minister Busia could have taken to minimize public discontent and thwart the coup?

In answering these questions, this chapter will follow the format of the India and Indonesia cases. In addition, we will be able to draw on a unique resource: a critique Dr. Busia wrote of an earlier version of this chapter. Although the former prime minister challenged several of my interpretations, and was particularly resentful of his aides and officials for disclosing information about his decision making in late 1971, his letter is a detailed justification of his actions and will be quoted here as part of the historical record. Apparently before his death, Busia planned to write his memoirs, but they have not yet been published. So unlike the India and Indonesia cases where we had to view Prime Minister Gandhi's and President Suharto's actions solely through the eyes of close observers, here we can judge a prime minister's own view.

The Aftereffects of Nkrumah

At independence, Ghana's economy reflected its colonial past. Ghana exported agricultural goods and raw materials, relying on Europe for consumer and capital goods. Many members of Ghana's elite resented this dependence, and the coherent aspects of Nkrumah's economic policies can be viewed primarily as an attempt to develop new trade and production patterns.[6] The hope was that Ghana could manufacture domestically much of what it had been importing and that this would reduce the country's external dependence and serve to create new jobs domestically. Thus it was a basic import-substituting industries strategy.

Nkrumah's economic record was an unmitigated failure. Table 4.1 shows that there was a surge in gross capital formation, yet this was accomplished to a great extent by a $1 billion splurge on imports and led to an inefficient use of the newly acquired machinery and intermediate goods.[7] With this massive buildup in capital goods went a rapid shift in resources from the private to public sector. State corporations soon grew in such varied operations as gold mining, farming, cocoa processing, and laundries.[8] The results of this attempt at African socialism followed quickly. Although capital was available, its misuse led to a decline in per capita GNP, while

Table 4.1
Basic economic data in constant (1960) prices (millions of cedis)

	1958	1959	1960	1961	1962	1963	1964	1965	1966	1967	1968	1969	Growth rate, 1958–1959 to 1968–1969 percentage (per annum)
Terms of trade effect[a]	+36	+20	0	−36	−73	−52	−35	−110	−106	−69	−24	+27	
Net fixed capital formation	76	120	141	137	112	139	133	154	65	15	4	4	
Private consumption per capita	92.3	99.1	103.2	108.8	100.1	102.5	95.9	94.3	88.3	90.2	85.7	86.6	−1.0
GNP per capita	126.7	137.3	140.6	136.0	134.9	138.2	140.6	127.4	117.6	115.3	119.9	124.5	−0.8
Gross domestic savings/GDP	17.7	19.0	17.4	10.3	14.7	14.9	19.9	10.8	10.8	8.3	15.8	17.8	

Source: Tony Killick, *Development Economics in Action: A Study of Economic Policies in Ghana* (New York: St. Martin's Press, 1978), chap. 4.
a. Difference between exports minus imports in constant prices and in current prices.

the growth of the state sector led to a decline in private consumption, and the eventual exhaustion of foreign exchange reserves brought net national savings to a halt. (See table 4.1 for the year-to-year changes in these indexes.)

To Nkrumah's credit, there were substantial increases in educational, health, and housing services during the early 1960s. Yet there was no valid election during the period. It is thus impossible to know whether this increase in public consumption (services plus government industries) linked with decreases in private availabilities was what the citizenry wanted.

Although numerous countries have failed to achieve rapid growth rates, it was Nkrumah's extravagance while the economic growth rate was stagnating that caused the greatest problems for his successors. The exhaustion of the country's foreign exchange reserves, lavish borrowing abroad, and maintenance of consumption at an unsustainable level made the inevitable subsequent retrenchments even more difficult.

In simplified terms, Nkrumah's political strategy was to split the Ashanti chiefs, maintain the loyalty of the relatively modernized urban groups (especially organized labor), divide the military by favoring an elite presidential guard, and achieve what unity he could through his charisma and appeals to pan-Africanism. This meant using the public sector as an employment sponge. In the early 1960s this could be financed by using foreign exchange to satisfy excess internal needs. Yet as even the opportunity to borrow overseas shrank with Ghana's fading credit rating, Nkrumah turned to internal deficit financing.[9] With rampant inflation accelerating, the economic strategy in obvious disarray, and Nkrumah off in Peking discussing solutions to the Vietnam war, the first military coup took place.[10]

National Liberation Council

When the National Liberation Council (NLC) ousted Nkrumah in February 1966, it did not have an articulated set of desired economic policies.[11] The military men who led the NLC were basically pragmatists, though, and they chose Ghana's leading economist, E. N. Omaboe, as their economic adviser and minister of finance. Omaboe recognized the seriousness of the situation and immediately began to look for new resources. The cocoa price was low at the time, the tax base was difficult to expand on short notice, and the situation was too tenuous to attract large amounts of private foreign capital. The NLC thus announced its inability to meet its debt payments and sought assistance from the IMF.

The IMF was willing to provide standby credit on the condition that the NLC launch a stabilization program, including steps to balance the budget, and exercise monetary restraint. The IMF sent a resident representative, M. Qureshi, specifically charged with monitoring Ghanaian economic policy. Qureshi turned out to be not only an economic adviser but a skilled political analyst; he soon became a confidant of Omaboe.

By mid-1967 the basic elements of the NLC economic strategy had become clear, and it followed not surprisingly classic IMF recommendations. The cedi was devalued by 30 percent in July, and the budget was stringent.[12] For the NLC's heirs, however, the most significant decision concerned the composition of government expenditures. Since budget balance had been a prerequisite for obtaining IMF support, the NLC had to decide where to cut. It was decided not to make any large-scale cuts in the bureaucracy or to shut down all unprofitable government enterprises.[13] Instead the NLC chose to cut government capital investment funds and to reduce credit availabilities through the banking system. The results of this course were immediately felt: private consumption per capita continued to decline, net fixed capital formation plummeted, and net national savings turned significantly negative. See table 4.1.

So, although the NLC brought economic stability, it was achieved at the price of recession and running down the country's capital stock. Also there was no fundamental attack on Ghana's structural economic problems. The external debt remained at over $550 million, the bulk of the civil servants were unproductive, government industries had high import requirements (aggravating balance of payments difficulties), about 70 percent of foreign exchange still came from cocoa, which subjected the country to the vicissitudes of the international commodities market, and the colonial pattern of food consumption remained (imports of cubed sugar, tinned milk, canned sardines, and corned beef were eaten in large quantities even at the village level). The essential point in this review of Ghana's problems is that any successor government to Nkrumah and the NLC would have been extremely vulnerable to small changes in its balance of payments position.

Ghana's Predicament

Could the difficulties Busia faced in October 1969 have been avoided? To respond to this question, it is useful to divide Ghanaian economic policy performance into its domestic and external components and then show the relationship between the two.

Even a quick glance at export statistics (table 4.2) shows the overwhelm-

Table 4.2
Composition of exports, 1962–1970 (in millions of postdevaluation new cedis)

	1962–1965 (average)	1965	1966	1967	1968	1969	1970
Cocoa beans and products	204.5	212.5	165.4	222.3	214.1	247.6	327.7
Timber	39.6	35.2	29.7	26.5	28.6	39.1	38.8
Gold	29.7	27.3	24.3	25.1	29.0	29.8	29.3
Bauxite	1.7	1.9	2.0	1.9	1.5	1.4	1.0
Manganese	13.1	13.7	17.4	11.2	10.5	7.0	5.9
Diamonds	16.7	19.3	15.4	15.1	17.4	13.9	13.9
Aluminum				9.6	26.7	43.9	35.0
Other exports	7.9	8.6	13.2	11.5	9.4	9.8	10.1
Reexports	6.3	4.9	5.7	6.9	4.7	6.8	6.3
Total	319.5	323.5	273.1	330.1	341.9	399.3	468.0

Source: Central Bureau of Statistics and Bank of Ghana.

ing importance of cocoa in Ghana's foreign exchange earnings. During the 1960s not only did cocoa bring in between 60 and 70 percent of export receipts, but duties on cocoa commonly yielded 25 percent or more of the government of Ghana's tax take.[14] This meant that cocoa became the critical factor in determining the level of feasible imports and domestic expenditure policy. Thus Ghanaian political economy was and remains in a very real sense dependent on the fortunes of the cocoa market.

If we now introduce the other aspect of cocoa's significance—the great fluctuations in its world market price—we see the complexity of the policy management task. Between 1958 and 1965 the cocoa price declined from $840 to $204 per ton, then rose to an average of $790 per ton in 1970, and was followed by a sharp drop to $470 in 1971 and $360 per ton in early 1972.

Many analysts have argued that Ghana's economic woes were primarily due to this dependence on cocoa and thus were beyond control.[15] This is an oversimplification. Although it is undeniable that the commodity terms of trade moved against Ghana during most of the 1960s (see table 4.1), neither Nkrumah nor the NLC did much to restrain local cocoa production or to provide sufficient incentives for the other nations to make the Cocoa Marketing Agreement effective. Moreover, little was done to diversify exports or increase the value added through domestic processing.[16] In fact, export promotion was not a principal goal.

Additionally, through most of the 1960s, Ghana was operating with an overvalued exchange rate, which meant that imports were subsidized and exports taxed. This gave little incentive for private firms to attempt new exporting ventures. When we combine this mediocre record on the policy variables that the Ghanaian government could control with important flows of net aid, we see that the situation Busia inherited need not have been as bleak on the export side as it actually was.[17]

In domestic economic performance, we see not only the importance of the balance of payments constraint but a consistent pattern of choices that led to inefficient use of investable resources and compounded the dependence on import availabilities.

Nkrumah's economic policies were an odd amalgam of Soviet and Western development strategies. The panoply of state corporations clearly drew on Marxist conceptions, but the attempt at import substitution and a big push on industrialization were taken directly from Latin American predecessors and the prevailing development economics literature of the late 1950s.[18] Regrettably the amalgam produced projects that were so poorly managed that they had neither the advantages of Soviet-style central control nor the individual plant efficiency favored by Western analysts. As an illustration of how wastefully capital was used, the incremental capital output ratio for Ghana between 1960 and 1960 was 8.0.[19] This meant that Nkrumah's investments took eight units of new capital to produce one unit of new product. This is four times the rate in Japan in the same period and three times the rate in many other developing countries.

This wasteful approach to capital utilization had several important implications. Since all the equipment was imported, this led to higher rates of foreign exchange use than was necessary. Also most of the plants were capital intensive, and this did little to generate jobs. Moreover, the use of capital for low-productivity public enterprises prevented its use in the private sector and thus lowered the overall growth rate. This syndrome of an errant industrial sector dragging rather than leading the economy was similar to the patterns observed in India and Indonesia where import-substituting-industries strategies were also pursued. Nkrumah's approach caused a particularly difficult set of problems for Ghana because its exchange reserves left from British times were so large that it was a substantial period before the seriousness of the mistakes become obvious. Also once large numbers of workers had been drawn to the state enterprises, they felt they had a right to continued employment. This meant that after Nkrumah's banishment, the country was left not only with debts but with an industrial infrastructure demanding to be supported as well.

Although the NLC ended the flamboyance of the Nkrumah era and was successful at imposing monetary and fiscal restraint, it did remarkably little on restructuring the economy and creating the conditions for a more efficient future pattern of growth. Tax collections declined, unemployment remained high, and with net national savings actually negative, there was little investment in any new productive fields.[20] Although the creditors were in essence providing aid by accepting the debt moratoria in 1966 and 1968, it was clear that the debts would have to be paid at some point. (See the Chronology for details on debt moratoria and rescheduling.) The NLC was thus mostly a holding operation, not a curative one.

One area where the NLC made some important innovations was in trade liberalization. An announcement was made in October 1966 that the government wanted to phase out import controls, and the method the NLC chose was to expand the range of items that could be imported under open general licensing (OGL).[21] The OGL list for 1967 was enlarged to include fertilizer, certain farm tools, pharmaceuticals, and some intermediate goods. Although the OGL imports amounted to only 3.2 percent of total imports in 1967, the NLC began a trend that the Busia government accelerated. The devaluation of the cedi in July 1967 complemented the trade liberalization as a means of using price rather than quantitative restrictions for import control.

Nevertheless, the NLC steps were modest, and, after a decade of import substitution, Ghana was more vulnerable to the balance of payments constraint than at the time of independence. It was also clear that a reduction in foreign exchange availabilities could affect several vital interest groups: creditors who were insuring new commodity flows only on the condition that recent debts be paid under the 180-day credit scheme; the military, which had come to have a substantial appetite for its imported perquisites; workers in government industries that depended on imported intermediate goods; and the large bulk of the population, which relied on various imported foods.[22] As we examine the attempts of the Busia regime to deal with the 1971 foreign exchange crisis, we therefore need to be alert to the seriousness of problems bequeathed and the political dangers in cutting imports.

The Busia Setting

When Dr. Kofi Busia came to power in October 1969, he had a coherent political philosophy, a large popular following, the ability to attract some very talented men into his government, and an optimistic nation. By the time he was overthrown twenty-eight months later, he was reviled as incompetent, and there was little public chagrin when the First Brigade commander decided that he would rule instead. How did this major change of opinion come about in such a short period of time? Before turning to the series of economic decisions that soured the Ghanaian public, it is useful to be familiar with the background of the Progress party and the key actors who advised Busia as the economic crisis mounted.

When the NLC withdrew from power, it was replaced by a newly minted parliamentary democracy.[23] The dominant Progress party was based on an interesting coalition: its leadership was almost entirely middle class though ethnically Akan, which meant that it could appeal on tribal grounds to the majority of the people in Ghana.[24] The only significant formal opposition came from Gbdemah's Justice party representing the rival Ewe tribes. Busia knew that he could count on Akan support because of ethnic ties, so he campaigned on a remarkably intellectual plane. He stressed the need to dismantle the corrupt controls system, widen the scope for the private sector, and improve rural development programs. This enabled him to enter office as a good government candidate favored by the civil servants, students, and the military while simultaneously holding the cocoa farmers.

Dr. Busia had a prominent intellect and considerable perseverance. Although elected to the Parliament at the time of independence, he chose to accept a visiting professorship at the Institute of Social Studies in Holland. Because Busia was a critic of Nkrumah, the Speaker of the Ghanaian Parliament used the absence in Holland as the stated rationale for declaring Busia's seat vacant. Busia subsequently took the chair of sociology and culture of Africa at Leiden University, directed a project on the church and urban society, and became a visiting professor at St. Antony's College, Oxford. During this period, he wrote four books while maintaining his active opposition to Nkrumah and interest in Ghanaian politics.[25]

The style of the Progress party leadership also warrants attention. What appeared to be intellectual precision and self-assurance in 1969 was perceived by 1971 as arrogant aloofness. The finance minister's brilliant speech at Legon University in June 1971, "The Wealth of the Nation," concisely stated the strategy of the Busia administration's economic policies.[26] J. H. Mensah argued that the real poor in Ghana were the farmers (not urban workers) and that strenuous efforts would be made to hold down urban incomes while raising those in rural areas. This naturally appealed to the Progress party's largest group of constituents. Yet the approach was seen correctly by the students, lower-paid civil servants, and the military as a barrier to their gains. Even in a parliamentary system where there had been no history of military intervention, this would have been a risky strategy because it implied a blatant challenge to the mobilized elites. Taking such a course, however, fit with the personalities of Mensah and Busia, the chief designers of the doctrine.

Busia had long been a political maverick. His views were similar to aspects of the neoconservative movement in the 1970s.[27] It would be hard to find a man who had more completely accepted the British parliamentary tradition. In writing off the urban workers and modernized leftists, he apparently thought they would recognize the legitimacy of his moves.[28] Busia was not adverse to having his finance minister lecture unionists on the necessity of their accepting lower real wages.[29]

Mensah has been variously described as "brilliant," "rigid," "insufferable," "caught in his own illusions," and "the one proud man who resisted the plethora of foreign advisors and donors."[30] A socialist by conviction, Mensah had nevertheless become disillusioned with Nkrumah's extravagance and economic mismanagement. From 1965 to 1969, Mensah was with the Economic Commission for Africa in Addis Ababa. During his time in Addis, he developed a more pragmatic set of policy views, gradually shifting toward accepting the usefulness of the market and competition. Busia's strategy of trying to aid the rural sector meshed with Mensah's own perspectives. Sadly, Mensah's peculiar work habits,[31] his imperious self-confidence, and his contempt for his peers in the cabinet[32] created problems during the period of crisis decision making, which culminated in the December devaluation.

The only other people who had a major influence on the Busia government's economic policies were the foreign advisers, and their part was significant only after October 1971 when the full extent of the payments crisis was recognized. T. Killick and J. Stern, economists with the Harvard Development Advisory Service team, had substantial work experience in developing countries, and both believed in applying market-oriented approaches to Ghana's resource allocation problems.[33] They had no direct access to Busia but developed close ties to J. Frimpong-Ansah, governor of the Central Bank, and by this route were able to get their work to the prime minister once Mensah's hold on economic policymaking had been weakened. John Odling-Smee, an Englishman, was actually hired as a personal assistant to Busia in the prime minister's office. Although Odling-Smee had no previous overseas experience, his approach was similar to that of Killick and Stern, and he cooperated closely with them.

The most enigmatic of the foreign advisers was Barbu Niculescu. His tie to Busia was close because the prime minister had considerable confidence in him. Niculescu did not inspire confidence in the other foreign advisers, however; he had no background in macroeconomics, was prone to making sweeping statements about complex problems, and appeared to oppose the 1971 devaluation. His influence on the prime minister was extensive as Dr. Busia's words indicate:

When Prof. Niculescu was on the staff of the Dept. of Economics at Legon in the 1950s, he was frequently consulted by the Nkrumah government. He had been closely involved during his twelve years in Ghana with a number of planning issues, organized the first high level discussion for the 10-year development plan, and put forward specific proposals concerning regional and sectoral developments.... In New Zealand, where he was Prof. of Economics at Victoria University in Wellington, he had been a member of the Central Planning Committee for the New Zealand economy.

I made a special request to the Prime Minister of New Zealand for him to be seconded to advise me on the economic problems facing us.... His position was official.

Prof. Niculescu's first visit was at the end of December in 1970. By January he had discussion with me, the Minister of Finance, and the Minister of Trade, pointing out that what was needed was:

a) A drastic structural reorganization of the economy, involving both the budget on the expenditure side as well as the tax side, and the internal credit situation.

b) An immediate declaration of moratorium on the external debts.

c) When both of these were in hand, but as quickly as possible, a devaluation of the Cedi of around 20%.

To deal with short-term problems, he advised, and I accepted, the setting up of the Economic Review Committee with a system of monthly reports and suggested Tony Killick as editor. To deal with the medium-term debt, I accepted his proposal to set up the Cabinet Standing Development Committee, with its system of sectoral planning reporting directly to it.[34]

The Busia government thus had two forceful figures at the top with strong opinions about policy and a lively competition among its foreign advisers.

Stage 1: The Arena Takes Shape

Although Prime Minister Busia's rigidity and determination to alter radically the direction of policy set by Nkrumah was bound to have created resentment, if there had been a more realistic economic agenda, public support would not have declined as rapidly as it did.[35]

The Progress party's initial strategy was to take the large revenues from cocoa and spend them on increased imports and rural development programs.[36] It was hoped that the rural works would yield benefits quickly enough to raise incomes and solidify these areas as a political base. On the import side, the risk was taken that there would be sufficient resources to continue the flow of desired consumer goods and allow further decontrol of the allocation process. The intent was to deal with the inefficient state industries, the large bureaucracy, and the military by gradually squeezing their budgets and going around them by using the market rather than licenses for distribution. The budget for fiscal year 1970–1971 became the first full expression of the regime's strategy and is thus the first major turning point leading to the crisis a year later.

The 1970–1971 Budget

Mensah designed, wrote, and personally oversaw the implementation of the 1970–1971 budget.[37] It was a bold, blunt statement that put into practice many of the Progress party's campaign promises. The package of measures included further liberalization of imports, a 53 percent increase in development budget expenditures, a continuation of various export subsidies, and the raising of import surcharges. It was a curious combination of steps. The development budget expenditures were strongly stimulative and targeted mostly for the agricultural areas. The export subsidies, though appearing substantial, posed so many administrative complications that they had little effect. The major move was the import liberalization where the OGL was increased to 60 percent of import commodities. The import surcharges were a scattered lot, varying from 5 to 150 percent, and were evidently intended to protect certain industries, raise revenue for the government, and serve as a price-rationing device on imports.

At the time Mensah was the czar of Ghanaian economic policy. No one even Busia, openly contradicted him. A cabinet meeting was called for 6:00 A.M. on the morning that Mensah was scheduled to give the budget message to the Parliament. Mensah rode roughshod over his colleagues in the three hours that he let them discuss his proposals. His strength in economics, his haughty attitude, and the short period of time that he gave the other ministers to review his work contributed to the endorsement he received.

It is not clear whether Busia was awed by Mensah or if he felt his finance minister was doing approximately what he wanted anyway and there was thus no need to bring him under stricter control. It is obvious, however, that Mensah got his way and that he planned the final moves without consulting the IMF, IBRD, major donors, or foreign economic advisers.[38]

The fundamental technical flaw in the budget was that the new cedi remained overvalued, thus keeping an artifically low price on imports and reducing much-needed incentives for export development.[39] Nevertheless from Mensah's personal standpoint, the moves were a success: by reducing controls he weakened one of his main rivals (Trade Minister Qureshi who handled much of the controls regulation), the switch to import duties gave him discretion over which goods should be most favorably treated, and his personal stature was enhanced by the broad acquiescence to his will.

The Constraints

The market-oriented strategy articulated in the 1970 budget was premised on large and continuing flows of imports. There was some controversy over it during the fall of 1970, but the real problems became painfully clear with the drop in cocoa earnings in 1971.[40] The Busia government was caught in the classic Ghanaian bind with an added complication: not only were import availabilities and general tax revenues pinched, but the Progress party was committed to maintaining the internal producer's price to its constituency, the cocoa farmers.[41] This meant that the growing shortfall in export earnings would be immediately felt on the domestic side through pressure on the nonagricultural expenditures. In the external sector, the gap had to be handled through increased aid, a decline in imports, or borrowing from private sources overseas.[42]

Some analysts have argued that Ghana was getting small amounts of foreign aid.[43] Although net inflows were modest due to payments for debt servicing, Ghana's donors cannot be blamed for the country's past profligacy.[44] In fact, as table 4.3 shows, the gross levels were quite substantial, with receipts ranging from $7 to $8 per capita during 1970 and 1971. (See Appendix 4A for details on yearly repayments, new aid, and international organization payment.)

Table 4.3
Ghana's aid and debts (millions of dollars)

Year	Gross aid Receipts	Debt servicing	Net inflow
1970	54.9	23.5	31.4
1971	63.3	36.3	27.0

There were obviously upper limits, however, to the donor generosity, and Busia was soon to find that maintaining new aid was dependent on careful management of Ghana's debt obligations.

What can we infer about the arena in which Ghanaian economic policy evolved? It appears that although the donors were consistently interested in Ghana's economic well-being, the country was never sufficiently attractive to warrant an intense commitment. Mensah was left to initiate and persist with a seriously overvalued exchange rate without serious criticism from either the creditor or donor groups, something that clearly did not happen in India or Indonesia. Since the donors were under no compunction to ensure the survival of the Busia regime, the worsening economic difficulties of 1971 stiffened rather than weakened their demands for rational stabilization policies. Unless it chose to follow the donor regimen, the Ghanaian government was left with efforts at private borrowing or cutting imports. Private borrowing was of limited promise for a country with its credit rating, and cutting imports was politically dangerous. Busia's ship was free to wander.

Stage 2: Maneuvering for Resources

The decision making that led to the December 1971 devaluation moved through three main stages: (1) a period when balance of payments problems were viewed as essentially short run and solvable through internal adjustments, (2) a phase where Busia began to break with Mensah, recognizing that the problem required foreign assistance but where it was still viewed as one necessitating only minor policy changes, and (3) the final month where Busia recognized that the crisis impelled both foreign resources and major changes in policy. The Chronology reviews the step-by-step decisions of the period; this section concentrates on the major turning points.

The Crisis Mounts

The August 1970 import liberalization was predictably followed by a massive upsurge in imports. Since the price of foreign goods was too low and Ghanaian consumption had been limited by various forms of import control throughout the previous decade, there was every incentive to import as much as possible while the liberalization lasted. The debate between Mensah and his critics then began to focus on whether the rise in imports was a temporary speculative reaction or a sign of a need for a major policy change (devaluation or much higher import duties).

Throughout the fall of 1970 and the spring of 1971, Mensah repeatedly claimed that the surge in imports would end once the speculative demands were met. He argued vigorously against a devaluation or increased tariffs, asserting that this would lead to a decline in imported intermediate goods and a subsequent slowing of the country's growth rate. Mensah's critics countered by saying that the overvalued exchange rate was merely subsidizing consumption at the expense of exports generated by the cocoa farmers.

The domestic effects of the 1970 budget took longer to identify but were felt by the spring of 1971 when the effects of the rural development expenditures began working their way through the economy. Although the influx of relatively inexpensive foreign goods was a price-depressing force, the sharply expansionary budget contributed to a spurt in inflation. Because urban workers were under a wage freeze and were not favorably inclined toward the Progress party anyway, the price rises created political tensions.

Busia sensed the need for some alternative economic advice. He took Niculescu's suggestion and set up the Cabinet Standing Development Committee (CSDC) to coordinate those ministries with major inputs to economic policy and the Economic Review Committee to facilitate interministerial discussion at the staff level. In January 1971 Busia also took the planning portfolio away from Mensah and decided to handle it himself.[45] Busia was not sufficiently adept in his new role to draw out of his staff a comprehensive alternative set of policies. Nevertheless, throughout the spring of 1971 there were numerous indicators that a crisis was building. The CSDC reviewed monthly statistics on the balance of payments and by June had estimates that 1971 imports might exceed exports by an enormous gap of $160 million.[46] The consensus of the CSDC was that the next budget should be much less expansionary and import surcharges were needed to dampen the demand for foreign consumer goods.

The 1971–1972 Budget

The drafting of the 1971–1972 budget marked the beginning of the second phase of the government of Ghana's response to its payments problems. Mensah was unquestionably under pressure to devise a less inflationary budget. The World Bank had a major review team in the field, which was waiting to release its report until the details of the budget were known, and USAID was slowing the discussion of a new program loan until the new policies were clear.

Mensah unfurled his 1971 effort with a flourish. Controversial policy changes were scattered throughout the document. The official interest rate was raised to encourage deposits in savings banks, and the Central Bank raised its loan rate; free education was ended at the university level, and students were offered a variant of the income-contingency loan plan;[47] government agencies were required to pay duties on the goods they imported; a profits and remittances tax was initiated to raise revenue from foreign firms; export bonuses were expanded; the incomes of all civil servants and military personnel were cut as numerous perquisites were abolished; the military budget was given a straight 12 percent cut; a national development levy (5 percent for low incomes and slightly progressive for higher incomes) was announced; and the import liberalization was extended—but still nothing was done about the exchange rate.

Mensah justified this wide-ranging series of changes by saying that it was an austerity budget and that all had to sacrifice if Ghana was going to accelerate its growth rate. Other members of the cabinet were again presented with the budget on the morning of Mensah's announced speech to Parliament. Although the budget cuts had been rather thoroughly discussed with the relevant ministries in advance, the revenue side, particularly the development levy, was a surprising jolt.

Mensah's budgetary secrecy before the 1970 presentation had been annoying but accepted. The 1971 replay, however, was more serious. Although Busia and the other ministers did not see the implications in time to stop the speech, they soon realized that the series of moves (1) would antagonize every major interest group except the farmers; (2) required deficit financing of 129 million new cedis in 1971–1972 and was thus inflationary; and (3) was likely to exacerbate the balance of payments problem, the most pressing issue. Busia quite rightly felt that if he was going to impose an austerity budget, he should at least have measures that would alleviate the crisis.

The most startling aspect of Mensah's budget was his dogged determination to proceed with import liberalization despite the growing trade deficit. Table 4.4 indicates the percentage of goods that were allowed in under open general licensing; it shows how the modest freeing of the market begun under the NLC expanded to almost three-fourths imports by the time of the devaluation. To have proceeded with this type of import liberalization when the exchange rate was overvalued was a positive inducement for importing.

Table 4.4
Percentage of imports under open general Licensing

1967	3.5
1968	18.5
1969	27.8
1970	47.0
1971	76.0

Source: J. C. Leith, *Ghana*, (New York: National Bureau of Economic Research, 1974), pp. 141–148.

Because there was such a diversity of measures, some of the cabinet members thought the trade gap would be narrowed. The prime minister's comments are interesting:

I would draw your attention to the fact that in this budget steps were taken to moderate the effect of OGL and related policies on the balance of payments. To reduce import demand, we:
1) taxed government imports. . . .
2) invisibles were taxed between 10 and 25% . . . ,
3) Car imports were restricted . . . ,
4) Luxury goods were restricted . . . ,

As the basic solution to Ghana's balance of payments problem lay in stimulating exports, a number of measures were taken to improve the competitive position of Ghanaian exporters. These measures in the 1971/72 budget included:
1) a 25% bonus on cocoa and non-mineral exports;
2) improvements in the administrative procedures relating to duty and sales tax rebates for exporters,
3) a 100% subsidy on railway freight costs for secondary species of timber;
4) establishment of the Export Promotion Council and company

It was recognized that these measures would have an impact in the medium-term rather than the short-term. . . .

You may also have noticed that measures were taken in this budget. Interest rates were raised on time deposits to 7.5% and a 1% interest rate was to be charged on demand deposits. Lending rates were to be raised. . . . Thus, the monetary measures were expected to reduce inflationary pressure in the economy and ease the strain that domestic price increases imposed on the external sector.[48]

Busia's summary of steps taken is revealing in its comprehensiveness but shows that he underestimated the likely problems that would come from expanding the OGL list and still thought in 1977 that his government could afford to focus on medium-term measures.

By late summer 1971, Busia had decided to take an even more personal role in the handling of economic policy. He made a personal visit to Prime Minister Edward Heath in Great Britain, dispatched his Central Bank governor, J. Frimpong-Ansah, to look for private overseas sources of borrowed capital, had the IMF contacted about Ghana's need for short-term assistance, and then made a personal swing through the major Western donor capitals to try to line up quick sources of new aid. For a man who had let Mensah dominate economic affairs for almost two years, this was a virtual whirlwind of activity. Yet although he had begun to diverge from Mensah, Busia was still uncertain about how to proceed. It was only after October 10 when he received a curt note from Prime Minister Heath that he realized the gravity of the situation. In the letter, Heath took an astringent line, arguing that Ghana must solve its short-term balance of payments problems before any increases in long-term British aid could be expected. This was essentially the same position as the other creditors and donors had taken. Heath's message meant that Ghana faced a unified front. This led to an increased tempo.

The Final Choices

The British decision to join with the other creditors forced the government of Ghana to deal with the IMF. Although Busia's foreign economic advisers had some reservations about taking the steps the IMF was likely to prescribe, they felt there was no alternative way to get the $43 million that came as the inducement for the standby provisions. The Bank of Ghana was running out of foreign exchange and would soon have to default on its 180-day credit payments. Mensah saw the IMF not only as a threat to his personal power but as a challenge to his whole expansionary program. He thus continued to play down the importance of the crisis and rejected the analysis of the foreign economic advisers who argued in their paper to the CSDC on November 30 that Ghana needed a return to licensing, radically increased import tariffs, or a devaluation.[49]

Busia, however, was receptive. Frimpong-Ansah, who had become the prime minister's chief economic confidant, reviewed the conclusions of the CSDC meeting with Busia and got approval to proceed with the final devaluation planning. Busia concurred with the ministers in the CSDC that a return to licensing would go against Progress party principles and felt that increased tariffs might not be sufficient. Frimpong-Ansah set up a twelve-member working group to provide confidential staff work for the devaluation.

An additional point of interest is the process by which the size of the devaluation was chosen. When the advisers did their estimates, they concluded that a devaluation of 35 percent in dollar terms would make a sizable improvement in the balance of payments. They noted, in addition, that an even larger devaluation would permit providing sweeteners to certain affected groups[50] Before leaving for Europe on a last-minute attempt to raise private capital, Frimpong-Ansah turned to the advisers and said he favored a devaluation of 50 percent. The advisers were not sure if he meant a 50 percent parity change in dollar or cedi terms, so they did calculations of several levels of devaluation.

With the Bank of Ghana branch in London cabling information on its dire condition and the IMF's consultation mission recommending a devaluation as part of stabilization package, the Ghanaian cabinet met on December 22, 1971, to consider its alternatives. (The Chronology discusses Bhatia's presentation to the CSDC.) The working group supervised by Frimpong-Ansah proposed a 75 percent devaluation in cedi terms; the elimination of import surcharges, the export bonuses, and the development levy; a 25 percent increase in the cocoa producer price, a 14 percent rise in the minimum wage; and expenditure cuts of 48 million new cedis.[51] The working group also prepared a note warning that there would be gainers and losers from the devaluation but did not mention the military (the group most capable of thwarting the Progress party's plans).

As the cabinet discussion proceeded, it was clear that there would be a devaluation. The surprise of the day was Mensah, who shifted from his past position of vigorous opposition to support of the devaluation. Not only did he begin favoring the devaluation, but he urged making it even larger than the Frimpong-Ansah group had recommended. He also favored keeping the import surcharges and the export bonuses. Mensah apparently switched his position because he wanted to avoid further expenditure cuts in the budget. The cabinet thus agreed to a 78 percent devaluation, with at least temporary retention of the import surcharge and export subsidies. Preliminary thinking was to publicize the decision before Christmas, but the cabinet decided to meet again on December 27 to reconfirm its decision. It was that day that the devaluation was announced. The real impact of the devaluation was even greater than this because the cedi was tied to the dollar, and the United States had just devalued the dollar by 10 percent, so the ultimate trade-weighted devaluation was about 90 percent.

Stage 3: Busia's Decision

Why was the devaluation made in such haste? Did the key decision makers understand the issues? Were there alternative or supplementary moves that could have been taken to ease the transition to a new set of policies?

On purely economic grounds, it is clear that some form of devaluation or return to import controls was inevitable unless the cocoa price took a sharp climb or some consortium of private lenders chose to advance the Ghanaian government credit. Since neither of these last resorts developed and the Bank of Ghana could not meet its obligations for the 180-day credits, something had to be done or suppliers would have cut off imports. To avoid the panic that would have followed an import ban, any regime would have had to devise a means for, at least temporarily, restraining imports and reversing the trade balance.

Busia viewed the devaluation as the first step in a four-part process. To a great extent, he saw the parity change as a gesture of good faith to be followed consecutively by a creditors' meeting to handle short-term obligations, a consultative group meeting to arrange the exact amounts of promised long-term aid, and negotiations to handle the Nkrumah debt issue. So despite his recognition that some unpopular domestic steps were necessary, he was still looking outward for resources. His was also a remarkably trusting approach: he was devising a major plan assuming that each part would work without fail and that the donors and creditors would be speedily accommodating.[52] Neither the Indonesian nor Indian government was likely to have taken such risks without having a carefully orchestrated series of donor pledges.

The IMF is not a donor organization, yet the Ghanaian approach to the fund was in the same vein as its reliance on other foreigners. Although Frimpong-Ansah had been successful at raising the amount of the planned IMF standby from $43 million to $53 million, the devaluation was announced sooner than even the IMF had expected, and the fund executive directors had not even approved the standby. (The Chronology discusses the December and January letters of intent to the IMF.) We thus see a pattern of almost cavalier decision making when the stakes were exceedingly high.

Busia pointed to three main reasons for the devaluation:

Although we found the devaluation unpalatable, there were several reasons why we accepted the IMF insistence on devaluation.... (1) the variation between the official exchange rate and the real exchange rate was large because of high import duties, taxes on foreign currency and export subsidies ... so one aspect was a tidying-up of our trade sector ... (2) the second purpose was an effective lowering of the value of the N₵ to reduce the capacity of groups within the economy to purchase goods which were in short supply ... and (3) the Minister of Finance insisted on cutting the budget by the smallest amount feasible and letting most of the burden be taken by the private sector—for, the more the public sector took of the cuts, the greater would be the danger of high unemployment to follow. For example, the IMF was arguing that they wanted a greater diversion of funds from current to capital. But the Cabinet decided to cut capital items, whereas the current items were retained for such things as employment workers to build dams in the Northern region.[53]

One of the most disturbing aspects of Busia's decision process was the failure to evaluate the outcomes that could be expected once the devaluation was announced. There is ample evidence that many of the cabinet members failed to understand the difference between the 47 percent devaluation in dollar terms and the 78 percent increase in import prices for those goods bought with cedis. In fact, some cabinet members informed their constituents that the devaluation was 15 percent when this was the number estimated for the rise in the total consumer price index as a result of the parity change.

Not only was there confusion over the extent of the imposed import price increases, but some ministers apparently thought that a shock to the public was necessary and felt this would be accepted without any special precautions. Although drastic measures were indeed called for those responsible failed to probe behind the technical memoranda presented. This pattern of approach might have been excusable in a country with no domestic opposition, but the fragility of the Ghanaian political system warranted prudence in assessing the political implifications of such a major decision.

There thus appear to be two main conclusions about the final decision process (1) At each stage of the crisis, the technical nature of economic analysis allowed economists (first Mensah, then the foreign economic advisers and the IMF) to shape the alternatives, dominate discussion, and ultimately extract decisions from politicians who had little appreciation of the likely results. (2) In his gradual transition from seeing the problem as an internally manageable, short-term issue to one requiring not only foreign assistance but major changes in policy, Busia was following a reasonably predictable search process.[54] The counterintuitive point, though, is that despite his seeming rationality, Busia lacked the technical background to make a balanced decision at any one of the stages. His minimal training in modern economics made him first overcautious and then a great risk taker, all because he could not adequately anticipate the probable outcomes.

Stage 4: Implementation

Because the coup occurred only seventeen days after the devaluation announcement and the NRC chose to revalue the cedi on February 5, 1972, it is impossible to evaluate what the long-term effects of the Busia decision would have been.[55] Nevertheless, we can comment on three areas: the interim political choices, the tactical economic steps, and the measures for dealing with the military.

Given that the cabinet was not overly worried about the public's reaction, it is not surprising that the government's political moves were uncoordinated and rudimentary. No government wishes to fuel speculative activity by mentioning a foreign exchange crisis to its citizens. Moreover, Busia was concerned that word of the devaluation would get to the public:

Before the decision had been taken, while the papers were being prepared, there had already been leaks, and I knew from information given me that transfers, exchanges, and stockpiling had already begun. The decision about devaluation was even leaked before Cabinet rose. That was the kind of situation in which I was operating.[56]

These worries about leaks were legitimate, but there had been few public warnings earlier in the fall about the need to restrain imports. It is hard to know if this failure to prepare the public reflected self-confidence or oversight.

Even after the sharp rise in prices and the complaints of other ministers at the December 30, 1971, cabinet meeting, Busia chose not to call in the leaders of the major interest groups most adversely affected to rally their support.[57] Although the cutting of imports would not have been relished under any circumstances, giving both Progress party and opposition figures a candid review of the problem and asking for their forbearance might have stalled some of the outrage the military was so carefully watching. It is thus not unfair to characterize Busia's postdevaluation political stance as insensitive.

Although the prime minister tried to explain the rationale for the devaluation twice, neither exposition was entirely candid. The initial radio address blamed the devaluation on the earlier U.S. decision to lower the value of the dollar; few found that believable. The second talk was a radio and television address to the nation on New Year's Eve 1971.[58] It explained the need to sacrifice and covered the risks in a devaluation but did not acknowledge that the Progress party cabinet had counted on higher cocoa revenues and did not want to slow the import liberalization. Thus both opinion leaders and the public were unprepared for the sharp drop in their living standard implicit in a 78 percent increase in import prices.

Two principal mistakes were made in economic tactics, and each accentuated the problems of the Busia government in getting acceptance of the devaluation. First, new price ceilings were not immediately announced for controlled strategic goods. Since merchants were sure that there would be some upward adjustments in price controls, they took their goods off the shelves until they found out in early January 1972 what the new price ceilings would be.

This problem with the price-controlled goods was compounded by a similar situation with goods imported under the 180-day credit scheme. The usual practice with imported goods was for the merchants to purchase their foreign currency for repayment only at the end of the 180-day period. Thus many items either in inventory or already sold had not yet been paid for. Merchants were uncertain if they would have to pay their debts at the new, higher exchange rate, but to cover their risks, they started raising prices dramatically on all their stocks. Only in January did the government announce that pre-December 27, 1971, letters of credit could be paid at the old exchange rate. This led to some readjustment of prices downward, but the public was already upset by the apparent scarcity.

Both mistakes exhibited a carelessness and lack of planning for the public response, which made the legitimate reductions in real income harder for the public to accept.

How inevitable was the coup? The obvious first statement is that nothing is inevitable until it happens. On the other hand, after seeing the Busia administration's relaxed style of handling its relations with the donors, economic choices, and political tactics, it is not startling that the military was able to unseat such a tenuous government. Nevertheless, to understand the coup fully, we need both necessary and sufficient explanations.

It has been argued that the coup was a straightforward affair with few ideological issues and few personality clashes involved; the military was just defending its corporate interests, which it correctly perceived as being threatened by Busia and Mensah's choices. The sharp cuts in military appropriations and perquisites coupled with the increased cost of imports after the devaluation provided ample evidence that the armed forces needed to move quickly to protect themselves.[59] If we add to this the common rumor in Accra that Colonel Acheampong had been planning a coup for over a year, we certainly have a sufficient explanation of the January 1972 takeover.

Yet in numerous other countries where the military has held a dominant coercive position and where assorted soldiers wished to govern, coups have been avoided. We thus need additional factors: those explaining the civilian disillusionment with the elected government, which led Acheampong to believe that he could govern after a takeover, and the lack of any major group within the military opposing a return to power.

Civilian discontent was high after the 1971 budget decision. Rocketing prices triggered by the December devaluation accentuated public unhappiness among the mobilized, urban groups. Although the Progress party could count on electoral support from the rural areas, it was the elite displeasure that was the key barometer for Acheampong's calculations.

The absence of a restraining force within the military can be explained by the military's judgment of Busia's naiveté and his faith in parliamentary government. Rather than acknowledging that he had been remiss in failing to place loyal officers in key positions, Busia admitted that there had been rumors of coup planning but said:

There was no appointment for counter-coup activities. As a result of promotions to the office of Chief of Defense Staff and to the office of head of the army, there was a vacancy as head of the first battalion which provided guards for the Castle, Broadcasting House, the residence of the President and Prime Minister. Recommendation for filling this spot came to the National Security Council from the Minister of Defense. Acheampong was recommended for this office and the Security Council, of which I was a member, accepted it. The appointment was made mainly on the recommendation of those who knew him. The appointment was not made by me personally, nor was it for countercoup activities.[60]

With a prime minister who took so little interest in his own security, it would not be hard to plan a coup. In sum, with the military's interests being threatened, with few civilian restraints, and with only minor internal opposition, the probability of a successful coup became high.

Conclusions: Ghana—The Brittle Polity

We can draw two main types of conclusions from this examination of economic policymaking in Accra: comments on the donor-recipient relationship and perspectives on the political economy of Ghana.

As we moved from the factors that shaped the aid arena in Ghana to the events leading up to the devaluation, it was striking how few manipulable variables the prime minister had under his control. Busia moved in a predictable manner: initially hoping that the problem could be solved internally, then seeing the issue as one needing short-term external palliatives, and finally recognizing that difficult internal choices had to be made. Not only was the situation becoming increasingly grave, but Busia was forced to give up what little maneuverability he had in his attempt to induce the maximum amount of assistance from the creditors and donors. An interesting twist was added as well when we see that much of the influence of the outsiders was indirect; their power was reflected in their ability to force Ghana to meet the conditions of the IMF.

Second, the events of the devaluation sequence fit one of the central arguments of this book. The technical specialists were capable of identifying the crisis and suggesting alternatives that fit their training in economics, but they overlooked a number of crucial details in carrying out the devaluation. Also they succeeded in getting the prime minister to view the crisis primarily in economic terms. In reality the economics was the least complex part of the problem. Clearly Ghana could not continue its import splurge without facing a balance of payments crisis.

The most difficult, and more fundamental, question was political: who should bear the burden of the necessary decline in resource availabilities? By failing to address this question at the beginning, the Busia government sequentially alienated enough key interest groups that the NRC could intervene with minimal public dissent.

Third, this review gives some insight into the inherently asymmetrical nature of aid relationships. Aid, and the concomitant policy changes required, appeared as an attractive option when there were few alternatives. Yet the process increased the recipient government's vulnerability. The donors could press for a settlement of Ghana's short-term problems before they would commit new aid. They did this knowing that events in Ghana would have little impact on their own domestic political fortunes. The Ghanaian government may well have fallen because it could not extract enough aid at the crucial moment.

In viewing the internal situation Busia faced, we see that Ghana was and remains a brittle polity. The ability of interest groups to make demands on the government had grown faster than institutional capacity.[61] Nkrumah encouraged this pattern. He wanted to appeal to the urban elite and urban laborers as part of his strategy to break the power of the Ashanti chiefs. To cement the relationship, Nkrumah used the state corporations to provide patronage for the Convention People's party and kept the exchange rate low to subsidize consumption of the urban groups.

The first military government, the NLC, introduced stabilization measures and conscientiously prepared the country for a return to parliamentary government, but it was a holding operation with no inclination for institution building. And although the Progress party had a nationwide organizational structure that could have served as a continuing reservoir of support and might even have been capable of winning the 1974 elections, it was not strong enough to limit the military. In his genteel way, Busia not only preferred to avoid polarizing the electorate but even felt the urban groups would recognize the justice in redistributing income to the farmers. The recent varegated history of the Linman government and the two Rawlings coups makes the Busia vision appear even more idealistic.

Appendix 4A   Chronology of the 1971 Ghanaian Devaluation and Related Subsequent Events

1966

February 24
Nkrumah was overthrown by the National Liberation Council (NLC). In the seven years of his rule, Nkrumah moved Ghana from $450 million in sterling reserves to net long- and medium-term debts of over $550 million. Much of the foreign purchasing had gone for lavish projects, but the most indelible imprint was from the establishment of inefficient government-owned manufacturing establishments.

March
The NLC declared a unilateral moratorium of debt for six months but opened negotiations with the IMF. After sending a visiting team, the IMF agreed to post a permanent representative, M. Qureshi. Qureshi began to play an increasingly important role in the design of the ensuing stabilization program. The IMF extended credits through standby agreements on the condition that Ghana balance its national budget and move toward a balance of payments equilibrium.

December
Ghana's creditors agreed to a substantial postponement of medium-term debt. The 180 million new cedis due between July 1, 1966, and December 31, 1968, and the arrears accumulated prior to July 1, 1966, were consolidated. The government of Ghana (GOG) agreed to pay 20 percent of the amount due before December 31, 1968, and the remaining 80 percent was postponed until the 1972–1979 period. Ghana still had a sizable problem, however, for a large amount of debt was due in 1969. The creditors thus put pressure on Ghana by making it clear that they wanted to see improved economic performance during 1967–1968 before they made a decision on the 1969 obligations.

The NLC experimented with a conservative program of slowing government expenditures and reducing the rate of money supply growth. This helped moderate inflation and laid the basis for the full-scale stabilization program initiated in mid-1967.

1967

July
The GOG devalued the cedi by 30 percent, began an import liberalization program for a few commodities, and tightened monetary policy. Before the devaluation was decided on, there were extensive discussions within the NLC about the likely political implications of the move. The NLC chairman, A. A. Afrifa, subsequently gave an extended and balanced explanation of the reasons for the decision on local radio. The import liberalization program had to be modified because as import demand had been built up (due to Nkrumah's banning of many kinds of imports) and the government's foreign exchange reserves were insufficient to meet the internal requests for foreign goods.

1968

October
The GOG again met with its creditors to request reschedulings. The medium-term payments due between January 1, 1969, and June 30, 1972, were delayed until the 1974–1981 period, but interest was maintained. This meant that Ghana had gotten some dramatic relief in the 1966–1968 period but received only a 47 percent cut in payments due for the years 1969–1972. The creditors also made no explicit link between the debt arrangements and new aid.

At the creditors' meeting, the British, who had the largest percentage of defaulted debt, chaired the group and clearly set policy.

1969

The World Bank was selected to chair a new consultative group to monitor aid. The IBRD showed willingness to consider increased lending if Ghana developed a coherent domestic economic plan.

The IMF representative, R. Bhatia (replacement for M. Qureshi), took a cautionary position as Ghana's outstanding drawings from the fund total $69 million (almost 100 percent of the GOG's quota).

February
The import liberalization program was expanded as pharmaceuticals and spare parts were put on open general licensing (OGL), but to dampen demand a small import surcharge of 5 percent was imposed.

July
The last NLC budget presented to the country announced several programs designed to spur exports: rebates on tax liabilities, granting of new import licenses for exporters, and a lowering of duties for materials that were intermediate goods in the export process.

August
In general elections, K. Busia's Progress party soundly defeated its main rival, K. Gbedemah's Justice party. The Progress party had stressed the need to reduce government controls and the advantages of moving toward greater use of the market.

October
Busia's government took office and the military men of the NLC stepped aside. J. H. Mensah, commissioner of finance under the NLC, became minister for both finance and planning. These posts and the paucity of other trained economists in other ministries gave Mensah an unchallenged position as the designer and director of Ghanaian economic policy.

1970

March
Mensah expanded the import liberalization program in line with his party's promises of decontrol.

A briefing paper prepared for Mensah analyzed the costs and benefits of Ghana's repudiating its external debt. Although the GOG did not favor such a stance, Mensah took a much harder line at the creditors' meeting than his predecessors had, arguing that "no debts are sacrosanct" and that there should be a link between new aid and debt rescheduling.

The creditors did not accept Mensah's position but agreed to another two-and-a-half-year moratorium on the Nkrumah medium-term debt, a provision for the incorporation of moratorium interest in the final settlement, and a commitment from the GOG on a final, long-term settlement in 1972.

August
The GOG expanded the OGL list again; 39.4 percent of the goods im-

ported to Ghana between January and September were under OGL. For the last four months of the year, almost 60 percent of imports were under OGL. Yet the exchange rate was left unchanged. Although some import duties were increased and varied from 5 to 150 percent, the exchange rate was overvalued, thus subsidizing those who imported. Given the severe controls of the Nkrumah and NLC periods, this led immediately to a splurge of importing by merchants who were unsure how long the policy would last.

There was some attempt to stimulate savings, however, with a modest scheme of increasing the interest rate on postal savings deposits from 2.5 to 5 percent.

Mensah announced an expansionary budget, with development expenses planned as 53 percent greater than the previous annual budget. As well as being late in the presentation of the budget, Mensah treated his cabinet colleagues in a high-handed manner by showing them the figures only on the day he presented the budget to Parliament.

September
The Ghana Aid Consultative Group met, with the World Bank president's special assistant, El Emairy, chairing the session. The donors continued the pretext that new aid was separate from debt rescheduling. The group, however, agreed that an IBRD mission should go to Ghana to do a thorough evaluation to serve as the basis for the 1972 Consultative Group Meeting. The French government representatives took the position that rescheduling was an exceptional procedure and multilateral organizations should not bail out countries that had gotten into financial troubles when the issues could be settled through private discussions.

October
Writers in the *Legon Observer*, Ghana's leading intellectual magazine for the social sciences, began to criticize the government's import liberalization program. Critics claimed that the program was primarily benefiting the wealthy because luxury goods were no longer banned.

December
The Berne Union of Export Finance guarantee organizations took the position that there was no precedent for extending debt payments due under the type of 180-day credit scheme instituted in Ghana in 1965. Under this system, a merchant or end user could import an item by putting up 20 percent and having the remaining 80 percent guaranteed by the

export insurance agency of the exporting country. Final payment for the goods was to be received within six months of the opening of the letter of credit. In essence, this was a means for having the exporting country finance the goods during shipping, warehousing, and shelf time before the items were sold. With the OGL list expanding and Ghanaians only having to put up 20 percent of the cost, it was a significant incentive to import.

1971

January
Prime Minister Busia announced that urban wages would not be raised and that civil servants had to begin to pay 15 percent of their salaries for the privilege of using government housing.

Busia also decided to take over the Planning Ministry himself. Although this formally reduced Mensah's responsibilities, Busia was not an economist and initially did not challenge the substance of Mensah's recommendations. Nevertheless, the Cabinet Standing Development Committee (CSDC) was established to look at long-run economic matters, and the Economic Review Committee (ERC) was set up to coordinate the work of the senior civil servants and advisers concerned with economic policy. The ERC was responsible for publishing a monthly summary of economic events, *Economic Indicators*.

February
The surge of imports initiated by the August 1970 import liberalization continued. Mensah argued that the sharp rise was temporary and that the rapid loss of foreign exchange was necessary to accommodate initial pent-up demand for foreign goods.

March
Frimpong-Ansah, governor of the Bank of Ghana, tried to convince Busia that Mensah's trade liberalization without greater tariffs and duties would produce a balance of payments crisis.

April
An IBRD evaluation mission led by James McGibbon and consisting of thirteen people was well into its study and finding consistent patterns in Ghanaian economic policy mismanagement: the overinvestment in industry during the Nkrumah years was hard to rectify because so many jobs were at stake; the neglect of noncocoa agriculture continued, and only 20 percent of the government investment projects were earning even enough

to cover their own borrowing (much less even considering making a profit). The IRBD staff nevertheless remained optimistic about the Busia regime and continued to talk of an IBRD program loan if "economic policy is rationalized." The bank's report was held from release awaiting details of the 1971–1972 budget, which Mensah was preparing in secrecy. Bank staff members hoped that if the new budget was reasonable, it would serve as a basis for arguing "Ghana's need and evolving pragmatism." This was seen as important to convince skeptics within the IBRD and among the bilateral donors.

June
In the June issue of *Economic Indicators*, ERC members estimated that a balance of payments deficit of $160 million would develop for 1971 if imports continued for the remainder of the year at the rate of the first five months.

The donors' Consultative Group was operating but loosely organized and took no formal position on Mensah's trade liberalization efforts. USAID as a single organization also took no formal position on GOG economic policy. Yet privately USAID staff members encouraged the steps toward decontrol, and the U.S. program loan and additional PL 480 agreement were interpreted as support of Busia.

July
The balance of payments position worsened as cocoa prices dropped and the growth of imports continued. John Odling-Smee, personal assistant to Busia, presented to the CSDC a paper arguing that import duties and surcharges were needed to avert an impending balance of payments crisis. Mensah rejected this argument saying that slowing imports would impair the country's growth prospects.

Mensah presented the budget for 1971–1972 labeling it a series of austerity moves. The provisions entailed a 12 percent direct cut in military allocations, as well as substantial cuts in such benefits as free water, electricity, subsidized automobiles, and "table allowances" for both civilians and military men. The reductions in expenditures were accepted by the military chiefs of staff, but Mensah kept secret his plans for covering the GOG's taxes. In a fashion identical to his performance the year before, Mensah kept the final draft secret until the morning of his parliamentary presentation. His manner and the political costs of his style of decision making became evident when he acknowledged that the government would impose two new taxes: fees for university students and a development levy of 5 percent on all wage incomes. The irony was that, while antagonizing the civil servants, military, students, and urban workers, Mensah still had not cut back on government expenditures that were causing inflation and had refused to revalue the currency to halt the deepening balance of payments crisis. The import liberalization was continued, and over 76 percent of imports were free of direct control. Some changes were extended to government imports and invisibles.

Hollis Chenery, newly appointed top economic adviser to IBRD President R. McNamara, visited Ghana and made it clear that the World Bank was still seriously considering a program loan.

Mensah's budget announcement contained a ban on the import of foreign automobiles. Nevertheless, despite the fact that there was no local production or assembly of cars, the number of new license plates issued continued to grow.

August 17
At a cabinet session, the GOG decided to continue pegging the new cedi to the dollar. Two days before, President Nixon had announced what amounted to a 7 percent devaluation. This meant that the cedi was also devalued against the main European currencies and the Japanese yen. Mensah strongly opposed a proposal by the Development Planning Secretariat to use the U.S. parity change as an occasion for an even more substantial cedi realignment. Busia conceded to Mensah's wishes but became increasingly worried over the situation and started to seek out other sources of advice, chiefly Frimpong-Ansah.

Busia privately visited British Prime Minister Edward Heath in the hope of getting British support. Busia wanted some type of stretch-out of short-term payments and some longer-term promises on the Nkrumah debt and new aid. He specifically requested that Britain help mobilize $360 million for Ghana: $200 to fund the 180-day credits outstanding, $60 million for profits and dividend payments in arrears, and the remaining $100 million to help refurbish the GOG's foreign exchange reserves. Although Heath did not promise anything, he left Busia with the impression that the proposed package was not unreasonable and the British would try to be accommodating.

September
Riots broke out over the initiation of the development levy. The Busia

government used the situation as an opportunity to announce that it would no longer collect union dues for members of the Ghanaian Trades Union Council (TUC). The TUC had been a consistent opponent of the Progress party and of plans to hold down urban workers' wages.

Two weeks after his return to Accra, Busia asked Frimpong-Ansah, governor of the Central Bank, and Alex Achiabor of the Planning Ministry to visit London and Washington to ascertain what Britain and the United States would offer.

Despite the severity of the impending balance of payments crisis, Mensah did not have the Finance Ministry prepare the report necessary to receive compensatory financing from the IMF. This special facility for producers of raw materials whose prices fluctuate greatly had been a source of $20.7 million for Ghana during the previous four years. In the search for new sources of financing, this virtually guaranteed source was neglected.

The GOG contacted the IMF at the IBRD-IMF annual meeting and requested assistance to cope with the worsening foreign exchange crisis. The IMF agreed to send an evaluation mission to consider a standby agreement.

Busia went to the British Commonwealth meeting and sided with Heath on Rhodesia, antagonizing other black African countries and surprising Heath. Busia pressed Heath again for special support, particularly on the short-term debt problem.

October 10
Busia received a stern note from Heath dated September 30 saying that Ghana needed to reach agreement with the IMF on a stabilization program before there would be any substantial new commitment of funds. Busia was annoyed because he had been building his strategy around assistance from the British and left his meetings with Heath believing that this would be forthcoming.

October 29
The CSDC considered a paper, *Debt Relief and the Management of the Economy*, which strongly urged major changes in foreign exchange policy and possibly having the GOG take steps that would make it possible for an IMF standby to be negotiated swiftly. Mensah strongly opposed this. He stated this was not a desirable direction for policy, would reduce the GOG's flexibility, and give the IMF substantial influence over economic policy.

November 1
Busia began a trip to Italy, France, the United Kingdom, and the United States to explore potential sources of aid.

Bhatia, the former IMF representative who had left a rather harsh impression by the end of his stay in 1969, led the IMF evaluation mission. He took a much more conciliatory stance than previously and had broad-ranging discussions with top GOG economic policymakers.

Mensah followed Busia to London and Washington, where he stressed different policy objectives from his prime minister. He emphasized the need to maintain imports to accelerate economic growth, while Busia concentrated on finding solutions to the short-term debt problem.

Frimpong-Ansah, governor of the Bank of Ghana, also made a trip to Europe to evaluate private financing that could help the GOG in its short-term payments difficulties. Because the interest rates for these arrangements were high, these leads were not pushed aggressively.

While Busia was in New York visiting the UN, he asked to see President Nixon. He later told acquaintances that he thought he made a good impression on Nixon and that, if there was a reasonable settlement of the short-term debt question and a prudent general economic plan drawn up, the United States would provide substantial aid.

Busia returned to Accra asserting that Ghana was likely to get a large amount of new aid from the British and the Americans. In the meantime, however, local representatives of the other creditor nations had taken the position that Ghana should solve its short-term debt problems before there was any discussion of the medium-term Nkrumah debt or of new aid and the IMF was the logical place to get help before coming back to the creditor-donor missions.

The British hardened their position and agreed with the other creditors that the short-term problems with the 180-day credit scheme had to be solved before new aid could be realistically considered. Busia was deeply aggravated because he felt that Heath had twice undercut his position. Busia then ordered a CSDC review of the remaining economic options.

November 30
Four foreign advisers—Tony Killick, Michael Roemer, Joseph Stern (of the Harvard Development Advisory Service, all contracted to assist in the Ministry of Planning) and John Odling-Smee (contracted to work directly

on Busia's staff)—completed a paper, *Alternative Methods of Dealing with the Economic Situation*, for CSDC discussion. The paper pointed out the severity of the balance of payments crisis facing the Busia government. The authors recommended narrowing the future economic options to three main approaches: increasing import duties, returning to licensing, or devaluation. In the CSDC discussion, there was no attempt to reach a final decision on the precise policy mix, but there was a consensus that a return to licensing should be avoided.

December 1
J. Frimpong-Ansah asked the authors of the CSDC paper to begin to work out the quantitative aspects of the necessary changes in economic policy. The four foreign advisers agreed to do this only if Ghanaians were included. Frimpong-Ansah thus established a technical committee of twelve members who were to work in secret. The committee was chaired by Dr. A. O. Adu, deputy governor of the Bank of Ghana. The group was told that Busia had decided against both the import surcharges and the return to licensing and that they were to concentrate on various devaluation options. They took the name Technical Committee.

December 8
Busia presented a detailed report to the full cabinet, stating how serious the economic situation was. He openly addressed the issues and for the first time acknowledged that the problem was broader than just financing for the short-term debts and included the need to restructure the balance of payments; the 1971–1972 budget had contributed to the crisis; and Ghana might have to take corrective action before outside assistance would be forthcoming.

Busia and his top personal assistants realized that the severity of the moves necessary to handle the balance of payments meant further stringency for domestic interest groups and further military dissatisfaction with the government.

Neither the Donor Consultative Group nor the Creditors' Group took a formal position on how the GOG should handle its economic problems, so the statements by individual governments became the basis for Busia's decisions.

December 11
Mensah wrote a personal letter to Busia but circulated a copy to the CSDC, arguing that the devaluation was not necessary and that the situation was

not as serious as other economists had claimed. He urged a 7 to 10 percent reduction in imports but feared the growth effects if more substantial cuts in imports took place.

December 12
J. Odling-Smee drafted an outline for work assignments necessary for the Technical Committee to synthesize the options under consideration.

December 14
The Technical Committee presented a working paper to Frimpong-Ansah, *Further Examination of Measures for Dealing with the Economic Situation: A Provisional Report to the Governor of the Bank of Ghana.* The paper concluded that a 45 percent increase in the price of imports would lead to a significant improvement in the balance of payments but that this level of devaluation would still require a large cutback in government capital and current expenditures (making layoffs inevitable). The paper also included estimates (or "sweeteners") if the devaluation were even greater. Frimpong-Ansah quickly noticed that a larger devaluation would yield greater tax revenue from the cocoa tax. Before leaving for Europe he thus instructed the Technical Committee to consider a 50 percent devaluation, but he never made clear whether he meant a 50 percent devaluation in dollar or cedi terms. The economists chose a middle ground: they based most of their calculations on a 45 percent devaluation in dollar terms (moving from 1 $.98 to 1 N₵ = $.55), which meant an increase of 78 percent in the price of foreign exchange.

December 15
Busia responded to Mensah's letter by replying in an letter and making it clear that he thought the economic situation was grave. The prime minister suggested that the finance minister present constructive proposals rather than calls to inaction and urged that Mensah put his proposed program in writing.

December 16
Several members of the Technical Committee wrote a revised working paper, *Impact of Alternative Exchange Rate Adjustments.* They quantified in more detail the sweeteners that would be possible with a large devaluation though they used a 42 percent devaluation (in dollar terms) to 1 new cedi per = $.57 U.S. as the basis of their estimates.

December 17
The December 16 working paper was presented to the cabinet members

attending the CSDC meeting, and there was discussion of how to deal with the IMF mission, which had returned to Ghana. Mensah still opposed a devaluation. The group agreed to meet on December 20 to make a final decision on what to recommend to the full cabinet.

December 18
Busia was informed that the Ghana Commercial Bank in London would have to suspend payments unless new sources of foreign exchange were immediately available. He became even more disillusioned with Mensah's interpretation of the mounting crisis.

In his informal discussion with top GOG officials, Bhatia said that the IMF was anxious to provide assistance, and he offered a draft letter of intent for the GOG to send to the IMF if the government was willing to accept fund terms for a standby Agreement. The letter sketched out the moves necessary for a major liberalization of trade, a balancing of the budget, and restriction of credit. The suggested figure for the total amount of standby credit was $43 million. The specific policy targets were left blank or to be completed later to enable the GOG to decide on which steps it preferred and how it intended to meet the IMF's stringent requirements.

December 19
The terms of the Smithsonian international monetary agreement were cabled to Accra, with the news that countries would be allowed to float their currencies within ± 4 percent of the official parity and that the United States had officially devalued the dollar.

December 20
The CSDC met. Bhatia made a polished presentation carefully starting by saying that it was not his position to tell the group what to do but there were severe bottlenecks in the economy that a new set of policies could ameliorate. He said that he was not pressing for any specific course but saw several advantages to the devaluation option. He was evidently convincing because many of the Ghanaians present concluded that a devaluation was a necessary first step in resolving the crisis. After considering a revised and extended letter of intent for the IMF with a request for a higher level of standby credit ($53 million), the CSDC agreed to recommend a devaluation to the full cabinet. The IMF's letter of intent suggested a credit ceiling on the banking system of $137.2 million, and a commitment to: increase operating expenses of the GOG by no more than 5 percent, eliminate the 180-day arrearages, and reduce by $25 million the other short-term obligations.

December 22
The full cabinet met and was given a detailed summary of the position papers prepared by the Technical Committee. The memo and the oral presentation to explain it were so abstract that few of the cabinet members understood the issues. Mensah claimed that he could have prepared an alternative solution, but devaluations appeared to be the only way to restore IMF and creditor confidence. The overwhelming majority of the ministers voted for the devaluation. The only vociferous opponent, V. Owusu, the attorney general, was not present. It was agreed to delay the devaluation until after Christmas but to meet on December 27 to confirm the decision.

The full cabinet also agreed to the sweeteners: a 25 percent increase in the price of cocoa to the farmers, a 33.3 percent rise in urban worker and lower-level civil servant wages, and abolition of the 5 percent development levy and the service payments allocation tax.

Upon hearing that Busia intended to go ahead with the devaluation on December 27, several of his top economic advisers urged him to delay it to provide adequate time for drafting a detailed statement of the problem and prepare the public for the major changes in prices. In addition, some suggested that by delaying, the GOG could find out the likely response of the IMF and the main creditors. Busia decided to go ahead with the devaluation as planned.

December 27
The full cabinet met to reconfirm the December 22 decision. The new cedi was to be devalued from 1 N₵ = $.98 U.S. to 1 N₵ = $.55 U.S. or 45 percent in dollar terms. This implied a 78 percent increase in cedi costs of imported goods.

Busia made a radio address to the nation in which he claimed that the recent U.S. devaluations (of August and December 1971) necessitated the Ghanaian depreciation. This argument generated immediate cynicism; few listeners believed that the U.S. parity changes (totaling 15 percent) was the real explanation for the 45 percent cedi devaluation.

The devaluation announcement was made with no plans for subsidizing shop owners with goods already in their stocks but imported under the 180-day credit scheme. Also, no announcement was made of the price ceilings for those goods considered strategic and thus previously subsidized. To keep from depleting stocks before these goods were raised in prices, merchants took these items off the shelves.

December 28

Mensah sent a detailed memo to all cabinet ministers announcing there would have to be an across-the-board budget cut of 3 percent (shared equally by departments) and asking them to reply by January 15, 1972, on which items they preferred to cut. He included a new salary schedule for workers getting 33.3 percent raises.

December 30

The full cabinet met again, and it became obvious that neither Busia nor the great bulk of the ministers had understood the necessary price effects of the devaluation. In the briefing paper used on December 22, the Technical Committee's estimate that the average of all consumer prices would rise immediately by 15 percent was misinterpreted because many ministers had told others that imports would go up by this figure (not the 78 percent that actually took place on most price-inelastic goods).

Staff members of the Bank of Ghana reworked the letter of intent to the IMF and presented their latest version to Bhatia.

December 31

Busia made a New Year's Eve address to the nation in which he gave a much more accurate, understandable account of the reasons for the devaluation. Nevertheless prices had already risen sharply, and discontent among consumers was evident.

1972

January 5

A new maximum price list was announced, but its effect was limited because the speculative fever was underway and retailers were hesitant to put goods back on the shelves because they did not know at what price level the speculative fever would abate.

Mrs. Nixon visited Accra, and dealing with her and her entourage took almost a week of Busia's time.

January 8

The CSCD met to work out the final wording of the IMF letter of intent after receiving the latest comments from Bhatia.

Preliminary indications from the creditors were that they had been impressed with the devaluation. Informal word passed that they would be willing to negotiate the medium-term Nkrumah debt as soon as the GOG handled the problem of arrears in its short-term obligations.

January 11
The final letter of intent was agreed on between the IMF and the GOG. The announcement of the standby credit of $53 million merely awaited approval by the IMF executive directors.

During a luncheon meeting in Accra, Mensah acknowledged his own vulnerability within the Busia cabinet and also said, "Some or all of us may not be around very long."

January 13
While Prime Minister Busia was in London for medical treatment, a group of military officers led by Colonel I. K. Acheampong carried out a coup d'état and announced the formation of a new government, the National Redemption Council. Busia and his ministers were vilified as being corrupt, incompetent, and having failed to negotiate favorable terms with Ghana's creditors and donors. In his first speech about the takeover, Acheampong reflected the views of his fellow military officers and quite openly acknowledged that the Busia government appeared to be threatening the corporate self-interest of the armed forces.

January 14
Busia stayed in England. Many of his fellow ministers were put in jail. The NRC immediately began to call on economists who were not close to Busia to help formulate new policies.

The civil servants who had participated on the Technical Committee recognized their tenuous position. They and other government officials who had close contacts with foreigners began a studied attempt to separate themselves from the foreign advisers and economists.

January 21
In a press conference open to all reporters in London, Busia said that the colonels' coup was a precipitate action, with a very narrow interest predominating. He claimed that his regime had faced a difficult crisis but was on the verge of a fundamentally different period because the IMF standby had been negotiated and there was a reasonable prospect of $140 million in new aid in the near future. (Other estimates were that the aid talked about

informally might have been apportioned roughly as follows: United States, $40 million; Britain, $20 million; IBRD, $40 million; all others, $20 million.)

February 5
The NRC announced a revaluation by raising the parity from the December 27, 1971, level of 1 new cedi per $.55 U.S. to a new rate of 1 new cedi per $.78. The NRC listed its debts as $230 of long-term, $320 million of medium-term, and $280 million of short-term obligations.

The NRC announced a clearly nationalistic package of new economic policies by

refusing to deal with the creditor nations as a group and demanding separate bilateral negotiations and refusing to pay all short-term obligations;

agreeing to pay the legitimate suppliers' credits for the post-1966 period only on IDA terms;

demanding a ten-year grace period before payment would begin on the Nkrumah debt;

selectively repudiating the Nkrumah contracts that were "corruptly" handled and stating its willingness to have the "legitimate" contracts arbitrated (but not specifying which contracts belonged in each category);

maintaining price subsidies on consumer goods imports, which were primarily consumed by the urban groups.

March
The World Bank released its seven-volume study started in April 1971 but delayed due to the change in government. The study was extremely critical of Ghanaian economic policy management.

May
Despite the NRC's adamant public position of intransigence toward the creditors, off-the-record discussions began in Accra between the Bank of Ghana and embassy officials of the creditor countries. Most of the aid donors had decided not to cancel ongoing aid but did hold on new commitments until it was clear how the Nkrumah debt and arrears on the short-term credits were being handled.

June 20
The governor of the Bank of Ghana called in representatives of key private foreign firms and announced that the GOG had decided to begin a program of participation (nationalization) by immediately acquiring up to 58 percent of the equity of foreign firms in assorted industries. It was not

clear from the governor's presentation whether there was to be a negotiated payment process or whether this was just a straight confiscation of assets phrased in vague terms.

July
The British formed a position on debt and invited other creditors to meet informally in London to form a unified position.

October
Through a variety of informal contacts, the GOG made it clear that it intended to remain independent of pressure from the major creditors, investors, and donors. To emphasize this position, the NRC assigned Colonel Enninful, a man with virtually no comprehension of international finance or diplomatic procedure, to represent Ghana in debt discussions and at the IMF-IBRD annual meeting. Enninful not only immediately showed his naiveté in the field but antagonized representatives of donor organizations.

November 9
The creditors sent their terms for the repayment of the Nkrumah debts: a five-year grace period, a ten-year amortization period, 2.5 percent interest on the principal during the amortization phase, and dropping the previous request that the GOG pay interest on the principal for the defaulted and moratorium years.

The GOG followed up its previous informal briefings on participation by making a formal announcement of its plan to nationalize certain foreign firms.

December
By the end of the year, the Ghanaian balance of payments position had substantially improved. Prices were up sharply on world markets for cocoa, gold, and lumber; the Bank of Ghana had withheld payment on the country's medium-term and short-term debt obligations; $40 million in previously agreed USAID program and PL 480 credits were drawn down; and the shops were running down in the excess inventories built up during the 1971 import splurge.

1973

February
The IMF tried to reestablish its role in advising the Ghanaian government and, despite the GOG's flaunting IMF rules, released a sympathetic situation report.

March

The GOG responded to the creditors' proposal of November 1972 by saying that the proposed terms were "a step in the right direction" but that it wanted even better terms. The Ghanaian response was vague, however, and did not specifically accept any of the points suggested in the creditors' plan.

The GOG announced the reduction of subsidies on certain strategic consumer goods and changed the names for the imported goods in this category to "foreign" items.

April

The creditors replied to the March GOG note by saying that they needed specific points of agreement or disagreement so that the final process of formal negotiations could be started.

May

A formal letter from the Ghanaian Ministry of Finance arrived at the USAID office in Accra requesting a continuation of aid after the current PL 480 and program loan credits were exhausted. This was the first formal acknowledgment in sixteen months that there was any GOG intention to continue with aid.

The request to USAID was significant because the U.S. government had made it clear that "there would be no new aid agreements unless satisfactory progress was in evidence toward a settlement of the short-term arrears and the Nkrumah Debt." The United States had also taken several steps during 1972 that could have been viewed as hostile by the GOG: refusing to sign the Cocoa Marketing Agreement, prohibiting the sale of grey cloth to Ghana under a PL 480 credit, and invoking the Long-Term Textile Agreement to limit Ghanaian exports of finished cloth to the United States. Given these widely know U.S. actions and the U.S. position on initiating new aid, the GOG request was also interpreted by other donors as a sign of decreasing intransigence by the NRC leaders.

July 3

Acheampong thanked the creditors for their willingness to consider modifications of the terms offered on November 9, 1972. He said that the GOG was willing to meet the creditors in July.

July 11

Because many of the creditor nation staff were on vacation and it was obvious that a full-scale meeting could not be set up quickly, Martin LeQuesne head of the British delegation and thus informal chairman of the creditors, offered to come to Accra accompanied by representatives of the United States and IBRD. After initial resentment that the British were trying to dominate the negotiations, the GOG accepted the offer.

July 23
M. LeQuesne, Chaufornier (IBRD vice-president for West Africa), and Smith (director of economic affairs for the U.S. State Department's Africa Bureau) arrived in Ghana. Discussions began the next day, and it was immediately obvious that there was disagreement and dissension among the GOG negotiators. Dr. A. A. Agama (head of the GOG's Debt Review Committee since February 1972 and concurrent member of the GOG Cocoa Board) had replaced Enninful as the chief representative, which improved the tenor of discussions. Yet the Ghanaians could not agree on which contracts were legitimate, and they tried to get the creditors to prove which debts were bona fide. The creditor representatives refused, saying that there was no point in continuing the discussions unless the GOG had a precise list of which debts were being repudiated.

July 25
The debt discussions faltered and ended with Dr. Agama's claiming that the GOG would put out a White Paper summarizing the debt situation from the Ghanaian perspective. Agama estimated that the paper would be ready by October 1973 and that this should lead to a final round of discussion in February 1974.

August 31
The IBRD decided not to forward a GOG loan request to its board for approval. This delay was taken even though all the analytic work had been completed and the IBRD representative in Accra was pressing for approval to get road repair work underway. The reason for the delay apparently was British pressure on the IBRD to show dissatisfaction with the pace of Ghana's negotiating on the past debt.

September 17
The Ghana Donors Consultative Group met in London and agreed that within eighteen months of a debt settlement, it would pledge to provide $140 million in new aid.

September 18
The day following the donors' meeting, the creditors met with most of the

same staff handling both issues. Peter Reiter, the IBRD's representative in Accra, flew to the session with the one test GOG proposal for debt settlement. The GOG offered to meet anytime in the two months after October 31, 1973, to discuss both the short-term arrears and the Nkrumah debts. The GOG claimed that 80 percent of the debt review would be completed by that time but that five principal disputed contracts would not be considered by inclusion in the payment package. The creditors reluctantly accepted this formula and agreed to go to Accra.

October 24
The IBRD staff recommended that the proposed road repair loan be forwarded to its board for approval.

December 11
For the first time since the 1972 coup, the representatives of the GOG met with all the creditors (something the February 5, 1972, statement by the NRC said would not happen). The meeting was rather tense and there was considerable testing of the creditors' position by the Ghanaians present. N. Y. R. Ashley-Lassen had replaced Dr. Agama as the chief GOG negotiator, and this second change in personalities was a further improvement for the speed and decisiveness of discussions. The basic terms proposed were as follows:

	Creditor offer	GOG offer
Years' grace:	7	10
Years' repayment	25	35
Moratorium interest	2%	0.75%
Grant element	61%	79%

December 12
Although there was no final agreement on a consensus set of terms, several Ghanaians privately went to the creditor representatives and said that, for internal political reasons, they needed to keep at least the ten-year grace period from the February 5, 1972, NRC statement.

1974

January
Several Ghanaians involved with the debt negotiation process became worried that the momentum for a settlement would slow because

Le Quesne and Smith were being given new assignments by their respective governments. Le Quesne and Smith were considered to be about as sympathetic toward the Ghanaian position as any likely alternatives, so the GOG increased its activity on the issue, hoping to conclude the negotiations before the two men were reassigned.

January 20
Ashley-Lassen proposed a new meeting with a small group of the most influential creditors but claimed that the GOG wanted the equivalent of most favored nation treatment, giving it the right to renegotiate if the creditors gave any other nation more favorable treatment in a subsequent debt rescheduling. This was immediately rejected by the creditor representatives contacted.

February 1
The GOG cabled the IBRD and said that it would like to have Ashley-Lassen meet with the creditors for an attempt at a new variant of a settlement. The creditors agreed to go to London.

February 4
Ashley-Lassen proposed to the small number of creditors at the London meeting that they accept the ten-year grace period, but as a concession the GOG would accept a 2.5 percent interest charge during the moratorium period. Those present agreed to check with their respective organizations and to meet in Rome on March 6.

March 13
After a week of discussions, a final settlement was reached on the following terms: ten years' grace, 2.5 percent interest during the moratorium phase, and an eighteen-year repayment period beginning January 1, 1983. The agreement contained an unprecedented clause that allowed the GOG to repudiate tainted contracts from the Nkrumah period "as long as no single country" was adversely affected. The GOG was required to present whatever information it had to substantiate a claim of a corruptly negotiated contract and to have the discussions before June 30, 1974. The agreement was to be completed in phases: starting with the initialing at the Rome Conference, conducting the talks over the disputed contracts, and concluding the process with a series of individual bilateral treaties between the GOG and the creditor nations.

June
The GOG attempted to challenge five contracts from the pre-1966 period

but, surprisingly, not the five British contracts that had been anticipated by the creditors. None of the challenges had sufficient documentation to lead the creditor representatives to accept the GOG claims. The GOG dropped the subject.

Signing of the bilateral debt agreements proceeded swiftly. Then the signing of new aid agreements followed with a $20 million USAID program loan and a 70 million deutsche mark loan from the West German government.

Appendix 4B

Table 4B.1
Financial Assistance to Ghana, 1966–1971 (millions of cedis)

	1966	1967	1968	1969	1970	1971[i]
1. Contractual medium-term debt obligations $(p + 1)^a$	46	72	80	64	52	39
2. Negotiated medium-term debt obligations $(p + 1)^b$	5[f]	12	41	22	27	20
3. Debt relief $(1 - 2)$	41	60	39	42	25	19
4. Net credit from IMF[g]	58	26	15	−7	−32	−40
5. Gross long-term aid commitments[c]	28	69	89	79	73	n.a.
6. Gross long-term aid receipts[c]	14	14	61	71	75	54
7. Gross total assistance $(3 + 4 + 6)$	113	100	115	106	68	33
8. Actual debt service payments $(p + 1)^d$	24	19	36	30	30	35
9. Net total assistance $(7 - 8)$	89	81	79	76	38	−2
10. Net long-term aid $(6 - 8)$	−10	−5	25	41	45	19
11. External indebtedness[e]						
medium term	509				394[h]	
long term	130				338	
total	639				732	

Source: T. Killick, *Development Economics in Action: A Study of Economic Policy in Ghana* (New York: St. Martin's Press, 1978), p. 113.
Note: Figures calculated at 1.28 new cedis per U.S. dollar.
a. $p + 1$ signifies principal plus interest payments.
b. As negotiated at 1966, 1968, and 1970 debt conferences. Not all these payments were actual made, however, due to delays in completing bilateral agreements and various disputed items. Due to imperfect data, these are order-of-magnitude estimates only.

c. Receipts differ from "commitments" because of delays in disbursements.

d. These figures relate to servicing of medium- and long-term debts. They are derived from balance of payments data but because of various inconsistencies in the data are subject to substantial margins of error.

e. Excludes indebtedness to the IMF and various short-term debts. At the end of 1970 there were arrears on current payments of about 72 million new cedis and various other obligations (chiefly arrears on profit and dividend payments) amounting to about 60 million cedis. The 1966 figures refer to the position as at February 24, 1966. The 1970 statistics relate to the end of the year.

f. Estimated actual payments in 1966.

g. Excludes use of special drawing rights.

h. Certain disputed debts have been excluded, and arrears in certain other payments have been added.

i. Most of the estimates for this year are provisional.

Appendix 4C   Interviews Conducted

Interviewee	Organization*	Place
K. Anyemadu	GOG Ministry of Finance	Accra
Appiah	GOG Ministry of Finance	Accra
R. Baseoah	GOG Ministry of Finance	Accra
R. Bhattia	International Monetary Fund	Washington, D.C.
S. Botchway	Bank of Ghana	Accra
R. Bruce	U.S. Department of State	Accra
R. Cashin	USAID	Jakarta
M. Chinery-Hesse	GOG Ministry of Finance	Accra
W. Drew	U.S. Department of State	Accra
N. Hicks	IBRD	Washington, D.C.
J. Keane	USAID	Accra
T. Killick	University of Nairobi	Cambridge, Mass.
J. McGibbon	IBRD	Washington, D.C.
A. Nicoi	Bank of Ghana	Accra
H. Nissenbaum	IBRD	Washington, D.C.
J. Odling-Smee	London School of Economics	Cambridge, Mass.
M. Qureshi	International Finance Corp.	Washington, D.C.
G. Roane	USAID	Accra

M. Roemer	Harvard Institute of International Development	Cambridge, Mass.
L. Sailes	USAID	Accra
R. Selley	Legon University	Legon
W. Steele	Vanderbilt University	Legon
J. Stern	Harvard Institute for International Development	Cambridge, Mass.
M. Steuer	Legon University	Legon
D. Williams	*West Africa*	London

*Affiliation at time of interview.

5   Conclusions

Not all governments faced with pressure to devalue go ahead with the decision. One of the most widely debated and controversial decisions to avoid devaluation was made by British chancellor of the exchequer, Winston Churchill. On April 25, 1925, Churchill decided to persist with the overvalued sterling exchange rate, and reestablish the pre–World War I conversion to gold and the U.S. dollar.[1] This decision was made over the objections of economists like J. M. Keynes and K. Wicksell, who argued before the Chamberlain-Bradbury Commission that staying with the overvalued rate would hurt export potential, slow employment growth, and weaken chances for an economic recovery.[2]

Churchill made this decision after extensive analysis, however, and he (along with a majority of the British cabinet) was willing to incur the costs to obtain the benefits of price stability and confidence in sterling. The loss of prestige to the British financial community and criticism from overseas holders of sterling was more threatening than the risk of slower economic growth at home. Moreover, the United Kingdom had the good fortune of being able to rely on repatriated profits from overseas investments to maintain imports despite declines in its exports.[3] Churchill therefore had a cushion that few developing country finance ministers have today. Thus, in looking at the patterns in the three devaluation cases presented in this book, we need to decide how much maneuverability the governments had and how well they played the options available to them.

Patterns in Devaluation under Pressure

Arguments for and against Devaluation

The 1971 Ghanaian devaluation without question was brought on by a balance of payments crisis. With the Bank of Ghana representative in

London sending frantic cables to Accra requesting instructions on what to do about obligations that could not be met, Prime Minister Busia had to act. There were two immediate problems: how to delay some claimants on foreign exchange so that the 180-day credit scheme could continue to finance consumer imports and how to convince foreign donors that adequate steps were being taken to resolve more fundamental problems.

In retrospect, it appears that Busia had five major options: (1) some delay or relief from the creditors and a return to formal import controls: (2) a de facto devaluation through higher import tariffs and lower export duties; (3) a small devaluation with various internal income or consumption taxes to reduce aggregate demand; (4) the devaluation as implemented with a 14 percent rise in the minimum wage and a 25 percent increase in the price of cocoa; or (5) a default with a turning away from the Western donors and the hope of some possible aid from the Soviet Union and Eastern Europe.

Import controls and government intervention in the economy were an anathema to the Progress party, so a return to Nkrumah's methods would have been unacceptable. Similarly, with the strong positive sentiment toward the West and a formal attitude toward obligations, a default would have been even less likely to gain cabinet support.

Actual maneuverability was thus sharply limited. In tactical terms, the essential issue facing Busia was whether a de facto or small devaluation would have been adequate to please the donors and simultaneously been more acceptable internally. In fact, the cabinet did discuss this choice and preferred the larger devaluation (because cocoa taxes were denominated in cedis and this was a disguised form of taxation that could help balance internal budgets). Also the cabinet faced the trade-off between cutting capital expenditures or public works programs and chose the former rather than risk antagonizing workers who would be laid off. It appears that the Busia government chose devaluation and the mix of related policy changes because they seemed to be able to solve a number of problems simultaneously. Clearly neither the foreign advisers nor the cabinet adequately probed the potential costs.

Prime Minister Gandhi did not face the same type of incipient crisis that her Ghanaian counterpart did. Although the Reserve Bank's foreign exchange situation was worrisome, the Indian public had only minimal expectations about the supply of imported goods. Moreover, at the time she took the devaluation decision, the extent of the 1966 drought was not yet known, and the foreign exchange picture looked tight but manageable. Mrs. Gandhi's options were to tighten import controls, vary export subsidies, and delay any major changes until after the 1967 General Election;

proceed with the devaluation but maintain the structure of both trade and internal industrial controls; or devalue but simultaneously announce a dramatic reduction in controls.[4]

It is a credit to her boldness and the vision of the Bell mission team that Prime Minister Gandhi was persuaded to try the devaluation. Clearly the easiest option would have been to delay until after the upcoming general election; at the other extreme, the risks of complete decontrol were too daunting.

Devaluation had a number of important technical advantages for India at the time. With the overvalued rupee, imports were being subsidized. Although administrative controls were being used to minimize consumer imports, the low cost of foreign exchange was actually encouraging businessmen to buy foreign equipment and rely on foreign intermediate goods. The devaluation therefore was important as a means of changing business decision making and improving the efficiency of resource allocation.

The Indian decision came in three stages: the commitment to major policy changes (the Woods-Mehta agreement), the statement by the Indian representative to the IMF, Anjaria, that a realistic exchange rate would be established, and the final choices on the size and timing of the devaluation. Although the June 6, 1966, date was poor timing given the crop year, Mrs. Gandhi knew that the inducements would not be available indefinitely unless major policy changes were attempted.

The Indonesian devaluation, like the other two cases, was not just a parity change. The Indonesian economists had a long-term agenda, and, though it was linked with the military, it was in no sense a pure, conservative, free market view. In fact, in the April 1970 policy changes, the economic technocrats used their influence to increase central government control over resource allocation.

By late 1969 it was clear that the stabilization program had been basically successful, and there was a desire to shift the focus toward faster growth. To do this, Indonesia needed aid, foreign investment, and the continued blessing of foreign donor and advisory organizations. It was therefore very unlikely that the government would try to challenge a major doctrine of the IMF: the desirability of unified, realistic exchange rates.[5] Accordingly, as foreign exchange reserves declined and there was increasing pressure on the DP rate, the Indonesians had several alternatives: letting the spread between the BE and DP rates grow and not requesting a standby from the IMF, trying to negotiate with the IMF for the standby without major policy changes, or proceeding with the devaluation and making other changes that they favored.

Letting the DP rate depreciate would have been a partial devaluation anyway, and not getting the standby credit would have forced the government to operate on very limited foreign exchange reserves. There was some possibility that the IMF might have agreed to a less sweeping package of policy changes in return for the standby, but the Indonesians knew that the IMF would keep pressing. It thus seemed prudent to go ahead with the devaluation and get the standby as a reserve while the overall stabilization program seemed to be in good shape.

In addition, given that the Indonesian economists wanted better central control over taxes and export duties, the time was propitious for an amalgam of regulatory changes. From the standpoint of pure allocative efficiency, Indonesia might have grown more quickly if there had been less central control over export receipts. Yet although the outer islands generated most of the exports, the Javanese-dominated bureaucracy and military had no intention of allowing the regional governments more autonomy in spending foreign exchange.

Hence the economists advising President Suharto saw the 1970 devaluation and rate consolidation as inevitable. If they could get a substantial standby credit and tighten their control over export earnings, the move was worth the risk of creating some inflationary pressures.

Choices by the Decision Makers: Maneuverability Exercised

What triggered these devaluations? For Indonesia, it was the growing spread between the exchange rate for essential and nonessential goods and the desire to have the balance of payments situation in hand before presenting the economic program to the IGGI aid consortium. In Ghana, Prime Minister Busia knew by November 30, 1971, that drastic action was necessary; it was only after he was unsuccessful at raising new aid, however, that he knew the IMF and devaluation were his last resort.

In Prime Minister Gandhi's case, it is rumored that an astrologer selected the actual devaluation day (6/6/66); yet two other factors precipitated the event: a growing concern that news of the devaluation would leak, causing a further drain on foreign exchange reserves and allowing opposition to mobilize, and, like Indonesia, a desire to complete the major policy actions several months before the aid consortium meetings. It is interesting that each leader had a trusted adviser urging acceptance of the parity change: Busia relied on Niculescu, Gandhi was influenced by Asoka Mehta, and Suharto consistently followed Widjojo's advice.

Here it is worth commenting on the issue of timing. Because governments have often exacerbated or created the problems that necessitate measures like devaluation, it is not surprising that these governments are loathe to recognize and acknowledge the problem. When India's commerce minister argued that a store does not hold a bargain sale when its shelves are empty, he made an important point. Unfortunately it was precisely because of the types of controls and overvalued exchange rate that he favored that Indian businessmen focused on the internal market rather than on rapidly developing exports. Thus, in cases where devaluation is linked with decontrol and a shift in investment behavior, the accompanying changes are often dreaded as much as the devaluation itself. To launch such an effort requires fortitude and conviction.

Given the natural tendency to avoid difficult choices, devaluations are frequently delayed longer than is wise; however, it is curious to note that after they had actually made the decision to devalue, two of the three governments in this study rushed the actual announcement so much that the timing was wrong. Ghana would have benefited from the assurance of a standby from the IMF obtainable within a month), and India might have postponed or changed the scope of the devaluation if the effects of the second drought were anticipated (which could have been known within two months of the June announcement). Additionally, in India's case a host of regulations on importing and exporting needed to be abolished or modified and were not completed by the time of Sachin Chaudhuri's speech. In looking at other devaluation cases, it may therefore be useful to see if there was a pattern of delaying the basic decision and then rushing the implementation.

How systematic were these national leaders in searching for new resources? Each had a distinctive style and different cards to play. Upon recognizing the severity of the situation, Prime Minister Busia made personal trips to Italy, France, Britain, and the United States. He returned to Accra relatively optimistic about support from Britain and the United States but found there was virtual unanimity among the donors that Ghana should get its short-term debt (180-day credits) under control before new aid and a resolution of the medium-term (Nkrumah) debt would be negotiated. This meant that Ghana had limited alternatives: try to raise loans from commercial banks or go to the IMF for a standby. Because the private bankers were aware of Ghana's problems covering its short-term debt obligations, they probably would have refused or imposed onerous terms, and many would agree to be involved only if the IMF was supervising a stabilization plan. In sum, Busia's search was carefully thought out and quite rational. Yet the circumstances left him with one option: to negotiate a standby agreement with the IMF.

Mrs. Gandhi had more options but appears not to have pursued them as systematically. The success of her visit to Washington and the appeal of increased bilateral and World Bank aid made a market-oriented shift in policy the focus of her attention. The devaluation was her first major economic policy decision. Given the complexity, it is not surprising that she left the details to her planning and finance ministers; however, it is odd that she seemed not to have thought through the implications of linking devaluation with the politically volatile process of decontrol.

Although we do not know Mrs. Gandhi's personal calculations on this decision, the fact that she denied foreign pressure (which was an integral part of the Woods-Mehta agreement) and so quickly flew to Moscow after she was criticized is an indication that she thought she could continue playing her father's game of getting support from East and West. That approach may have been technically feasible, but it rested on a major miscalculation of President Johnson's reaction. It also demonstrated that she was not fully committed to the industrial decontrol inside India necessary to make the overall economic policy package effective. Prime Minister Gandhi's search therefore seems to have been skillful at eliciting new resource commitments yet shortsighted since it was not designed to maintain her new constellation of supporters.

President Suharto had the luxury of keeping his distance from the embarrassing process of eliciting aid. As long as Indonesia's stabilization program was proceeding satisfactorily, there was little doubt that adequate aid would be forthcoming. This meant that internal macroeconomic performance variables were probably more important than any particular meeting, trip, or argument that Suharto might make. It also allowed the enormous advantage of freeing the chief executive to stay clear of the wrangling that inevitably accompanies a major policy decision.

What steps were taken to minimize adverse reaction to the devaluations? Prime Minister Gandhi's approach was the boldest: she claimed there had not been any concessions to the foreigners and attempted to downplay the decision by delaying on the administrative changes that were originally planned to accompany the parity change. In essence, she let the decision stand but immediately began backing away from it. Her foreign travel and then the second drought began to occupy the media. Little effort was made to mobilize support for the decision among groups that would benefit, like agricultural and industrial firms with sizable exports. It is also an interesting reflection on Indian economists that only three (Shenoy, Raj, and Bhagwati) were willing to support the devaluation strongly and publicly. The strategy for dealing with criticism was avoidance; Mrs. Gandhi may have surmised that support was so limited it did not warrant any further expenditure of her political capital.

Prime Minister Busia took exactly the opposite tack. Not only was he convinced that the devaluation was the right move, but he was willing to stake his national reputation on justifying it. He gave two nationwide radio addresses explaining the decision and met the mobilized, urban groups (labor, students, civil servants and the military) head on, saying that they had to accept a reduction in their living standards.

This hardly enhanced his standing among these groups and unfortunately seemed to obscure the fact that several concessions had been made with the devaluation package: lower-level worker and civil servant incomes were raised, the 5 percent development levy was abolished, and the excise tax on services ended. In terms of domestic politics, however, the urban groups would not forgive the reductions in their real incomes, and the rise in the Cocoa Board's payments to farmers was clearly seen as a sweetener for the Progress party's principal constituency. Although Busia deserves high marks for intellectual honesty, his boldness generated a resentful coalition of opponents.

President Suharto minimized his difficulties by attempting to distance himself from the fray. His planning minister, Widjojo, tried to explain the devaluation on a television broadcast, but the discussion was so technical that the general public was unable to follow the complex set of measures he reviewed. Moreover, the Indonesian strategy was to proceed with the stabilization program but never violate the cardinal rule of maintaining a cheap rice, cheap cloth policy. The Indonesian technocrats favored efficiency, yet they were not so wedded to consistency that they would do away with production subsidies for rice and textiles. This meant that the lowest-income groups hardly noticed the devaluation. The more cognizant urban elites were benefiting from other aspects of the stabilization program and were not inclined to mobilize opposition over so technical an issue. Consequently the Indonesian government was able to rely on an expanding economy and considerable public confidence as a reservoir of support when their devaluation was announced. In contrast, although the Ghanaian cabinet took several explicit steps to soften the effects of the devaluation, the choices were limited in a setting where incomes were being reduced.

Did the results warrant the risks? We can answer this question for these three cases but must be cautious about generalizing because the devaluations were never fully implemented in two of the cases. The National

Redemption Council decision in February 1972 to raise the value of the cedi reduced the effects of the Busia devaluation approximately by half. Similarly Mrs. Gandhi's failure to proceed with substantial liberalization of production and investment controls seriously inhibited the resource reallocation effects intended in the devaluation planning.

To decide if the risks were warranted, one needs to ask the related question: what were the alternatives? Prime Minister Busia had virtually no alternatives. Assuming that he intended to stay in power in a democratic system, he needed to find a new source of external funds to maintain consumer imports. If he had a means of coercing the public, they might have been forced into placidly accepting their lowered incomes. As it was, he had to play to the majority (rural agricultural exporters) and hope that the benefits for the lowest-income laborers and civil servants would prevent the formation of an opposing coalition of all urban groups.

Since the bilateral donors were conditioning their future assistance on a Ghanaian agreement with the IMF, this was virtually certain to entail a devaluation. What is still unexplained, however, is why Busia chose to go ahead with the parity change before securing the ability to draw on the $43 million IMF standby, which was under negotiation. Moreover, since we know that he was concerned about unrest in the military, it is especially odd that he took the additional risk of such a major change without cushioning the impact on his likely opponents. Hence, taking the risk of devaluation was probably unavoidable. Yet in restrospect, taking the second risk of acting without a ready pool of resources to pay off the 180-day credits and cover new imports seems foolhardy.

Prime Minister Gandhi also took significant risks. Given the strong tradition of civilian control of the military in India, a coup was probably not her worry, but establishing firm control of the Congress party definitely was. Because she was a compromise choice for prime minister and deeply indebted to several regional political leaders, she could ill afford to incur massive criticism without giving her patrons second thoughts. Also because the Congress party relied on continuing contributions from businessmen protected by the import and investment controls, the threat of greater competition in their industries was not likely to increase her support in a vital Congress constituency.

Although Mrs. Gandhi wanted the new resources to come from the bilateral donors and the World Bank and was willing to take a substantial risk in negotiating a secret agreement to get those resources, unlike Prime Minister Busia, she was not prepared to stake her political fortunes on it. She took the risk but appeared to have no strong convictions about preferred directions for economic policy. When the venomous attacks on her decision went public, threatening her hold on the leadership, she rapidly backtracked and began to focus on other issues. Because devaluation and decontrol are extremely complex technical issues, it is unfortunate that she faced the decision so early in her tenure, when her hold on power and knowledge of the system were less secure.

President Suharto's personal investment in the Indonesian devaluation was so minor that it is tempting to conclude he made a riskless decision, but that would be an overstatement. The Indonesian economy was still in a rather fragile condition in April 1970. Had there been an unforeseen drop in commodity prices, a bad harvest, or sharp increases in the prices of imported goods (all of which occurred in the 1970s), the devaluation could have appeared poorly timed and ill conceived. Had these circumstances occurred together, there could easily have been a resurgence of inflation and a loss of confidence in the stabilization program. Although Planning Minister Widjojo would certainly have received the most direct criticism, the president would doubtless have borne part of the burden. That the decision was taken in a period of calm is another indication of President Suharto's good fortune.

How did the three economies subsequently perform? Was further trade liberalization possible? The Indonesian performance was the most spectacular. In the three years after the devaluation, gross domestic product (GDP) grew at 6.0 percent, 9.4 percent, and 11.3 percent, respectively.[6] This spurt in growth was obviously not due to the devaluation alone, but it was a sign that both Indonesians and foreigners had substantial confidence in the economic program and were making major investment commitments. It was also an indication that resources, which had been under-utilized in the 1960s, were being more effectively employed.

These impressive results were achieved before the 1973–1980 increases in oil prices, which caused a further boom for the Indonesian economy. In addition, the immediate objectives were attained. The IGGI pledging session was oversubscribed, trade continued to be liberalized, and inflation slowed further.[7] The Indonesians also developed sufficient confidence in their own economic policy management that in August 1971 they chose to devalue the rupiah again. This subsequent devaluation was 6 percent more than the parity change for the dollar at that time.[8] Interestingly, the decision was taken without consultation with the IMF resident representative in Jakarta. The 1970 decision therefore represents an interesting turning point: the stabilization program was reaffirmed, the donors increased their aid, and the Indonesian economic team made the transition to a more autonomous style of decision making.

The Ghanaian case is at the other extreme. Although unit prices for cocoa quadrupled between 1971 and 1977 and "this was enough to improve Ghana's terms of trade by 25 percent despite the first oil price increase," overall economic performance was very poor.[9] There was essentially no growth in GDP between 1970 and 1977, and there was a steady decline in gross domestic investment. This means that, despite a favorable setting for exports, Ghana did not capitalize on it. This sad record, however, could by no means be blamed on the devaluation of 1971. The erratic governments that followed Busia's created a setting in which policy was in constant flux, the future uncertain, and the environment unconducive to economic growth. Although sporadic attempts were made to tighten or loosen various controls, the trauma surrounding the 1971 devaluation clearly made it harder rather than easier for subsequent regimes to consider reinitiating steps toward trade liberalization.

The Indian case was also disappointing, for a variety of reasons. Total exports fell in the first two years after the devaluation. Far from producing an era of decontrol as the World Bank mission and bilateral donors had hoped, the episode was followed by a relapse into elaborate controls. "Differential export subsidies emerged at significant levels; quantitative restrictions continued with high premia on [imported] items; the principle of automatic protection was not abandoned; and, industrial licensing continued in substance."[10]

The intricate relationship among the Indian business community, the Congress party, and the ministers created a setting in which none of these power centers had an incentive to press for decontrol and greater efficiency. Because this is the type of iron triangle often spoken about in U.S. political settings, the coalition for inaction should not be surprising; however, it is curious that in India, the intellectual community and the political Left supported precisely those controls that strengthened the hand of the large, established businesses and reinforced corruption in government. Instead of attacking the system as an example of an exploitative business-government arrangement, the Indian Left vituperously criticized any attempts at decontrol.[11]

This strange set of circumstances came about because devaluation and greater flexibility in the private sector were seen as yielding to imperialist pressure. This meant that virtually all the prominent forces in the Indian political system leaned toward controls, and it would have required more than the minimal efforts of a new prime minister to undo the mosaic of the controls system.

The devaluation episode in India had some chilling after-effects because it ruined rather than helped the chances of a significantly greater liberalization. The 1966 drought caused a major industrial recession, and exports fell not because foreigners paid less for Indian goods (relative price effects) but because more than half of India's exports were agricultural (and low yields led to supply constraints). These are complex issues that require some technical background to evaluate. To the Indian public and most of its politicians, there were few economic policy measures as uninviting as currency devaluation. Thus the timing and execution of the 1966 decision had an impairing effect because it reduced the range of future options.

Role of the Foreign Advisers

How well did the foreigners perform in these episodes? The Ghana case provides the most provocative example for discussion because of the unusual variety of foreign organizations and individuals involved. The most important foreign economist was Professor Niculescu, and his influence derived not from technical sophistication but from his personal tie to Prime Minister Busia. Having taught at Legon University during the Nkrumah period and kept up his ties through periodic visits, he was a familiar figure and a nonthreatening one to Busia. There is conflicting information about Niculescu's views during the first eleven months of 1971, but all participants agree that during December 1971 he favored the devaluation and urged Busia to proceed with the planning.[12] This assist was important to add legitimacy to the technical preparations that the other economists had underway.

One of the most fundamental problems, however, was that there was no clear system by which economic analysis was to reach Prime Minister Busia. The finance minister, J. H. Mensah, saw all others as competitors and excluded them to the extent that he could. This meant that the prime minister relied on personal confidants like Niculescu and Odling-Smee, while the Harvard Development Advisory Service (HDAS) group (Killick, Roemer, and Stern) ended up cultivating Frimpong-Ansah, governor of the Central Bank, as a route for their work.[13] In addition, although the World Bank's role was modest,[14] the IMF's Rattan Bhatia was pivotal in convincing the CSDC that devaluation was necessary.[15]

Each of the principal foreigners can thus claim, with substantial credibility, that his advice was only partially followed. Niculescu never wrote

out a detailed prescription; the devaluation was larger than the Harvard
DAS group recommended and done without fully consulting them. The
World Bank never took a formal position, and the IMF certainly did not
anticipate that Ghana would devalue before arranging the details of the
standby credit. Hence, the foreign analytic resources were poorly co-
ordinated and ineffectively used. Had any of the principals of the foreign
organizations known the course that events would take, they would almost
certainly have suggested delay and further technical work. Nevertheless,
having planted the idea and reinforced the need for a devaluation, the
foreign organizations were ultimately excluded from the most critical and
sensitive stages of the decision.

In India, where the senior levels of the civil service have outstanding
personnel and there is considerable sentiment for minimizing foreign involvement in governmental decision making, there was never any question that the foreign organizations would play a role in the details of the
devaluation planning. What the foreigners did was to provide an analytic
critique of Indian economic performance and offer the inducement of a
large increase in aid and a shift toward more program lending.

Various prickly issues of sovereignty arose, however. The World Bank
staff intended to present the Bell mission volumes as the 1965 situation
report, thus making them available to all aid donors. India's senior economists vehemently objected, and the World Bank staff relented, even agreeing to keeping the volumes classified (as they remain today). A similar
pattern emerged in the negotiations between George Woods, president of
the World Bank, and Asoka Mehta, Indian planning minister. Although
Mehta made specific commitments to change Indian policy and Woods
committed himself to try to raise the additional aid, Mehta did not want
the understandings included in a formal document he signed. The Woods-
Mehta agreement was classified and, to this day, even Indian government
officials working for the World Bank are not permitted to see the
document.

This type of extreme sensitivity to foreign involvement may be particularly pronounced in India but is indicative of a concern that all LDC
governments have. The irony of this situation is that most of the principal
foreigners resident in New Delhi who took part in the preparations leading
up to the devaluation were very positive toward India.[16] In sum, although
the foreigners were primarily involved in providing a broad alternative
vision of how economic policy might be organized (decontrol and greater
use of the market) and specific attempts to increase aid flows, the devaluation discussions were conducted in secrecy at the IMF in Washington, and

the Indian government clearly wanted to give the appearance of acting on its own.

In Indonesia the foreign role was not as sensitive or contentious an issue. The IMF resident representative handled the mechanics of the exchange rate consolidation and devaluation with the Ministry of Finance; the World Bank representative was consulted but made no major suggestions; the Harvard DAS team was helpful on some of the preparations but did not play the kind of instrumental role that their colleagues had in Ghana; and the donor nation embassies were not even notified in advance. Hence the Indonesian sequence was a low-profile, technocratic one. The role of the foreigners was carefully balanced: those providing analysis were specialists with limited leverage, while the donors with influence stayed at a measured distance. Therefore unlike India and Ghana, the Indonesians were able to avoid a situation in which the aid donors provided both prescription and resources.

The Hypotheses and Political Dynamics

The short-run adjustments necessary for a successful devaluation are adequate incentives to exporters and producers of import substitutes; government macroeconomic policy that makes changes in investment, consumption, and trade behavior rational; the avoidance of capital flight; and sufficient public acceptance of the move so that the devaluation is not blocked by other steps.

Although the three case studies are not meant to be statistically representative of all LDC devaluations, in both the Ghana and India cases, even the minimal, short-run criteria for success were never met. In India Prime Minister Gandhi initially avoided pushing ahead with the decontrol of industry that would have been necessary to encourage a more export-oriented growth policy. Although in the late 1960s and 1970s steps were taken to stimulate exports, Mrs. Gandhi should have moved in June 1966 to gain the full benefits of the devaluation.

In the Ghanaian case the Acheampong regime reversed the thrust of the Busia devaluation by formally appreciating the currency. The Acheampong decision permitted a net devaluation, but it gave off confusing signals and failed to reassure either the IMF or private lenders. The appreciation of the cedi thus violated another condition of a successful devaluation: it aggravated rather than improved the picture for capital flows.

Only in the Indonesia case were the essential short-run criteria met.

Buoyant raw material prices provided a favorable environment for expanding exports, the basic stabilization program continued to work so domestic investors were reassured, the IMF standby credit was obtained, which was seen as an imprimatur encouraging the continued inflow of private capital, and the public accepted the rise in import prices because it was a minor irritant in an overall setting where real per capital incomes were growing rapidly.

For longer-run success a devaluation must lead to basic shifts in resource allocation. Here again, of these three cases, the Indonesians moved the furthest to provide a policy climate conducive to exporting. The government of Indonesia proceeded on two separate tracks: encouraging foreign investment in new labor-intensive industries (like textiles and electronics assembly plants) while proceeding with incentives to expand investment and productivity in the traditional export sectors of cash crops (coffee, rubber, and spices) and minerals (tin and copper).

The Indian resentment of and resistance to foreign investment limited that option, and the recession caused by the droughts of 1965 and 1966 produced such excess industrial capacity that there was little incentive for new investment. Although growth in India resumed in 1968 and many of the recommendations of the Bell mission report were finally introduced, the long delay meant that the devaluation provided price incentives, but the structural environment limited resource reallocation. In Ghana the Acheampong regime had the good fortune to be in office during a dramatic rise in the international price of cocoa. This provided major increases in foreign exchange earnings, which masked the continuing need for diversification of exports away from the reliance on cocoa.

A government's maneuverability during a devaluation episode is determined by the composite of its internal economic and politial constraints and the character of the external trade and financial scene. For Prime Minister Busia in Ghana, maneuverability was sharply limited. Private loans, aid, and the IMF standby were all conditioned on a devaluation. The irony was that Busia concentrated so much on the economic constraints and saw devaluation as helping the rural majority of the population that he failed to deal with a far more threatening constraint, dissatisfaction within the military.

Prime Minister Gandhi's political maneuverability was also severely constrained as long as she pursued a middle-of-the-road strategy of trying to avoid criticism from the Left. Had she been willing to move the Congress party in demonstrably more conservative directions, she might have been able to create a coalition that provided greater incentives for exporting and efficient use of capital. But by attempting to placate the Left and being unwilling to challenge the protected domestic firms, Mrs. Gandhi ended up with the costs of a devaluation and few of the benefits. President Suharto did not have those concerns. Domestic industry was benefiting from the overall economic recovery and so favored him over the legacy of the Sukarno period that the increased cost of imported goods was an acceptable price to pay.

In these three cases, external macroeconomic conditions were relatively favorable. High cocoa prices helped Prime Minister Busia's successors, high commodity prices aided Indonesia in the early 1970s, and Mrs. Gandhi could not legitimately claim that external economic conditions were a key constraint. Resource reallocation was thwarted, however, by the political power of domestic industry, which saw devaluation and decontrol as threatening its protected position. In the Ghanaian situation retailers were upset by the devaluation and clearly would have joined with the civil servants, students, and union members to oppose the moves of the Busia government, but the coup by the military made long-term opposition building unnecessary.

The complexity of planning the devaluations was a problem in all three cases. Since the Indonesian government was in basic agreement with the policy direction favored by the IMF, there was only minimal debate about the details, and to a large extent the Indonesian technocrats relied on staff work by the IMF. The Indian government was unwilling to give either the World Bank or the IMF staff access to its internal planning, so the small, secret working group under S. Bhootilingham was left with the monumental task of deciding which parts of the vast Delhi bureaucracy to attack first. Not surprisingly, much of the planning remained undone on the day agreed for the announcement of the devaluation, and the Indian business community was not given a clear picture of how the new steps at decontrol would work. This gave all the protectionist forces time to rally behind the commerce minister and press for exceptions in their areas.

In Accra the planning proved an even bigger albatross. By failing to explain that import prices would go up by 94 percent, the cabinet members did not originally know what they were voting for, and there was considerable misinformation spread about the likely effects of the devaluation. It is also striking that in both the Indian and Ghanaian cases the top political leadership lacked a clear idea of which groups would be the gainers and losers as the impact of the devaluation worked its way through the respective economies.

Political Dynamics

From the standpoint of implementing a devaluation, the Indonesia case represented almost an ideal set of conditions. Real per capita income was growing (and did not have to be constrained), vocal opposition was immobilized, and the public had given the Suharto regime a basis of support that could easily tolerate occasional shocks like the April 1970 devaluation.

The Indian case provides a pointed example of how diverse opposition groups can join together to limit a government's options. Although the ideological Left and the businessmen who wanted protection would rarely agree on other matters of social policy, neither wanted decontrol or greater competition in the marketplace. Prime Minister Gandhi thus faced a strong coalition for inaction. When the intensity of the opposition became known and the strains of a second massive drought besieged the government, it became far easier to let the devaluation and decontrol initiative fade in prominence.

For Ghana, it can be argued that Prime Minister Busia's basic strategy was rational. If the only issue was maintaining popular support from a majority of the population, Busia was proceeding logically. The entire country faced austerity, but the most numerous group (small-holder cocoa farmers) would have been relatively better off than the urbanized groups, which absorbed the bulk of consumer imports. This strategy was clearly flawed, however, because actual influence was not distributed evenly in the Ghanaian political arena.

In all three cases, the devaluation created its own dynamic effects. In Indonesia the continued inflow of private capital, the cushion of the IMF standby, and the fortuitous high demand for export products supplemented the Suharto government's basic goals. At the other extreme, the dynamic in Ghana was adverse for the Busia cabinet; it received a hailstorm of criticism and did not have a standby to use for financing new imports. As the resistance mounted, Busia had nothing new to offer as a palliative.

In India the devaluation announcement on June 6 created a shock, and, by the time the opposition was fully mobilized, Mrs. Gandhi had decided that the venture was not worth the political capital it would cost. To make a political analogy, in Indonesia the devaluation created some turbulence but was overwhelmed by a favorable tide; in Ghana the move started a wave that hit a barrier and engulfed the creators; and in India, the effort sank unceremoniously until it was cleansed of its foreign imprint and raised at a later stage in a different guise.

How Do Circumstances Differ Today from These Three Historical Cases?

Structure of the System

There have been some fundamental changes in the structure of the international economic system in the 1970s. The most striking change was the initiation of the fluctuating exchange rate system.[17] At the time there were three principal arguments in favor of fluctuating rates: (1) by allowing a country's exchange rate to follow its internal inflation rate, adjustment could be continuous rather than in large shocks;[18] (2) the system would insulate countries from the transmission of business cycles;[19] and (3) by permitting more national autonomy, fluctuating rates would allow a government to pursue more independent economic strategies and reduce the need for maintaing large foreign exchange reserves.[20]

For the industrial countries, it does appear that the system has permitted more gradual adjustments in currency alignments and somewhat reduced the trauma associated with devaluation. Yet the LDCs have generally chosen to peg their currencies to one of the major reserve currencies. This introduces the double problem of daily fluctuations in the major currency and determining whether the ratio between the LDC currency and the reserve currency is correct.

There is also evidence that counters each of the original claims in favor of flexible rates. In the past decade, exchange rate movements have not been closely correlated with inflation rates,[21] rapid movements of capital have often complicated rather than simplified national economic policy management,[22] and for a variety of reasons, governments more than doubled their holdings of foreign exchange reserves between 1972 and 1982.[23] There are additional concerns that the system may achieve short-run equilibria but produce long-run movements that are not reflective of the true value of the respective currencies,[24] that national differences in real interest rates can lead to large capital flows that inhibit rather than facilitate necessary trade adjustments,[25] and even rational expectations advocates admit that instability can be transmitted by fluctuating rates.[26]

Thus it appears that there is less enthusiasm about fluctuating rates among analysts than there was a decade ago. Nevertheless, there is no consensus about what should be done to mitigate the system's weaknesses, and it seems reasonable to assume that the LDCs will have to cope with the current level of exchange rate volatility for the foreseeable future.

Increases in Private and Public Lending

Another dramatic change in the 1970s was the surge in private bank lending to LDCs. This was partially a result of greater creditworthiness in the developing countries as their export earnings grew significantly, but it was also a reflection of large OPEC country payments surpluses being recycled by money center banks to oil importers. The magnitude of these loans is stunning. By the end of 1982 the gross external debt of the twenty-one largest LDC borrowers was $501.2 billion. This has both positive and negative features. The advantages are that LDCs have been able to tap a vast source of capital and are no longer constrained to use predominantly internal savings and public resources as they were in the 1950s and 1960s[27] Under the right circumstances, many LDCs have considerably more flexibility in financing payment deficits than they had in previous decades. Harsh measures like devaluation and austerity programs can often be postponed.

But eventually debt must be repaid, and if foreign exchange earnings have not grown adequately, a country's future options can be sharply limited. The twenty-one largest LDC borrowers had current account deficits that grew from 12 percent to 23 percent of exports between 1974 and 1983, and much of this was financed with external borrowing, so the same countries had total debt service ratios that soared from 42 percent to 73 percent of exports.[28]

Although the largest absolute and percentage gains in lending to the LDCs came from the private sector, there was a major increase in public sector lending as well. Between 1974 and 1981 the World Bank expanded its loans from $30.4 billion to $92.2 billion, and the IMF added two oil facilities and the Supplementary Finance Facility (totaling $19 billion) and completed a new quota increase (adding an additional $40 billion to lending capacity).[29] Moreover, the IMF has significantly broadened its terms for lending. Under the enlarged access policy LDCs can borrow up to four and a half times their quota if they are following a fund-approved structural adjustment program.[30] India has taken advantage of this new IMF flexibility to arrange for a $5 billion loan, many orders of magnitude larger than Mrs. Gandhi could have negotiated in 1966 at the time of her devaluation decision.[31]

Yet the burden of repaying substantial debts when real interest rates are at all-time highs and when the U.S. dollar has appreciated in relation to other currencies should not be minimized. This has forced several countries to compress their imports dramatically, which has slowed economic growth and investment rates and cut real per capita incomes as well.[32] So although the combination of increased private and public lending capacity has enhanced LDC maneuverability, it has led to major jolts for societies trying to meet debt obligations. Faced with a debt crisis, most governments have chosen adjustment programs that cause substantial losses in output and employment.[33]

Protectionism

Some other structural changes in the international economic scene have been less positive. The growth during the 1970s of an increasingly mercantilist attitude toward trade policy has constrained the rapid growth of exports in certain sectors. This is by no means a problem specific to LDCs, but it does pose special difficulties if there are already quotas in an industry and the LDC is trying to develop its markets.[34] It should be noted, however, that the LDCs have particularly high tariff and nontariff barriers themselves, and they could get major gains from trade if they would reduce their own impediments to trade.[35]

This mercantilist tendency is not limited to import protection. The French and Japanese have aggressive export financing programs, and Brazil, South Korea, and Taiwan are following their lead.[36] Although export finance is generally straightforward to identify, many countries have direct and indirect export subsidies, and these distort efficient trade patterns.[37] It is difficult to quantify the global effect of these mercantilist steps, but they limit the extent to which devaluations and macroeconomic policies can correct trade imbalances. Although suasion may be useful at limiting the most flagrant forms of protection, the problem is likely to be a permanent part of the international trade scene, and it adds both a barrier and greater complexity to the planning process for LDCs.[38]

Heightened East-West Tension

An additional complicating factor has been the heightened tension between the United States and the Soviet Union, particularly since the overthrow of the shah in Iran and the Soviet invasion of Afghanistan in 1979.[39] This tension and the related competition has led to an increased focus on bilateral assistance. The Soviet Union has sharply expanded aid to Vietnam, Ethiopia, Syria, Cuba, Angola, and Nicaragua, while the United States has increased its support to Pakistan, Turkey, Somalia, Zaire, Egypt, and Israel. Even the Japanese have begun to devote more attention to security questions and have decided to broaden their regular aid program while making a highly visible commitment to South Korea of $4 billion.[40] It is difficult to know whether this security orientation in foreign assistance will ultimately raise or lower the total amount being transferred to LDCs, but it definitely changes the pattern of distribution by focusing on those countries that are strategically important rather than those with the greatest economic needs.

World Macroeconomic Conditions

Variations in world macroeconomic performance also affect the options open to LDCs facing current account deficits. If the deficit is significant, countries have three main alternatives: (1) slowing growth to reduce imports, (2) stimulating exports or import substitutes through external borrowing or domestic incentives, and (3) borrowing abroad to avoid making structural adjustments, anticipating that an expansion of world trade will eventually help exports.

During the 1950s and 1960s most LDCs could count on a reasonably steady expansion of world trade as a means of increasing foreign exchange earnings. The most recent decade has produced unanticipated shocks and major dislocations.[41] The extensive droughts in the 1972–1974 period forced most of the Sahelian African countries to concentrate on survival rather than economic growth, and the two dramatic periods of oil price increases created worldwide recessions.

The 1973–1974 recession was sharp but short-lived, and most LDCs dealt with their increased oil import bills by external borrowing. In the mid-1970s, when LDC debt levels were modest, private banks were willing to increase their exposure, and their loans helped cushion the effects of the 1974–1975 recession. Yet by the time of the second recession in 1980–1983, world trade had declined, real interest rates had soared, and debt reached unprecedented levels. This process of servicing debt while attempting to maintain economic growth thus became significantly more complex. It was also becoming clear that, despite their high debt burdens, the middle-income LDCs were more capable of adjusting than the poorest countries, which had low internal savings rates and small amounts of foreign capital available.

By 1983 the world macroeconomic picture had begun to look more optimistic. Real output in the industrial countries increased by 2.5 percent in 1983 and expanded by 4.5 percent in 1984. This had a stimulative effect on the LDCs. Economic growth in the nonoil LDCs was down to 1.75

percent in 1982 but rose to 2 percent in 1983 and to 3.75 percent in 1984.[42] If these positive trends continue for several years, it could provide an encouraging setting for LDC export prospects.

In trying to reach a balanced judgment on the difficulties facing the economic policy managers in the three case studies versus those faced today, it seems fair to conclude that the structural changes in the system have generally improved flexibility and made adaptation somewhat easier. Nevertheless the growing pattern of mercantilism, heightened security problems, and less certainty about the expansion of world trade constrain LDC options.

Increasing the Likelihood of a Devaluation's Success

There appear to be two broad ways in which the probability of designing and implementing a successful devaluation can be improved: further structural changes in the international financial system and more adept choices by individual countries.

Modifications in the International Financial System

Given the demonstrated resilience of the fluctuating exchange rate system during the shocks of the past decade, there is only limited support among the developed countries for a return to the gold standard and fixed exchange rates.[43] Although the LDCs are inconvenienced by fluctuating rates, these nations' influence on the design of the system is limited, and it is not realistic for LDC governments to expect a return to fixed rates. Similarly, after the $40 billion increase in IMF quotas in the fall of 1983, it is not plausible to expect major near-term increases in public lending authority.

In the distant future, it is possible that there could be agreement among the major monetary authorities to intervene more extensively to moderate fluctuations in exchange rates[44] or moves to achieve better macroeconomic coordination.[45] Either step would make adjustment easier for LDC governments. Yet the U.S. government strongly opposes greater intervention in the exchange markets, and closer integration of macropolicies of member countries of the Organization for Economic Cooperation and Development would entail giving up substantial national autonomy, which few political leaders find appealing.

Hence, it appears prudent for LDC governments to anticipate only minor structural changes in the system that would ease their problems during balance of payments crises. In a number of areas, skillful choices by individual nations can improve the likelihood of a devaluation's success.

Analytic Work

Economists working on the planning for a devaluation typically operate under severe time pressure and face a fundamental problem: how should they convey to generalist political leaders the likely ramifications of different policy options? Part of the problem is the exceptional complexity of the devaluation process. One could do hundreds of regressions estimating supply and demand elasticities for principal traded goods and still not have an accurate forecast unless monetary balance and aggregate demand effects were also analyzed. The principal technical problem is how to integrate these diverse factors. Moreover, even if this integration can be done with a large staff of quantitatively trained economists, few LDC governments have sufficiently broad in-house staffs to do this work on a confidential basis.

The situation can be less formidable if it is approached in discrete stages: first, making crude estimates of the likely effects from different sizes of devaluation, then comparing parity changes to other options (quotas, tariffs and controls), and finally identifying the eventual gainers and losers from the alternative choices. Ideally the options should attempt to increase government maneuverability, and the political leaders should be brought in at this point to give their judgment on which groups they are willing to antagonize and reward. Once the political constraints are clearly specified, it is feasible to go back to the technical options and estimate their impact with greater precision.

In addition to knowing which sectors are likely to expand and contract, what the employment effects will be, and whether there will be significant disparities among regions, it is also important to develop a feasible timing sequence. Many LDCs are able to launch a devaluation and decontrol effort but find that they are immediately struggling with the inflationary effects of import price increases, complaints from displaced workers, and a slow response in the exporting sectors.[46] If there is a high probability that the devaluation will fail, interim or delaying measures may be preferable.

In the India case, Prime Minister Gandhi substantially lowered her future chances for success with liberalization by trying devaluation at the wrong time. Patience can thus be a critical element in policy choice. Clearly the most vexing situation is knowing that the timing is inappropriate but facing overwhelming pressure to act nonetheless.

Analytic work alone cannot create optimal maneuverability for an LDC, but it can identify risks and opportunities. One of the key requirements therefore is linking the technical economic estimation process with the political calculus of which constituencies the government needs the most.

Devaluation as One Part of Adjustment

There is growing recognition in both the academic literature and in the advisory staffs of the multilateral agencies that devaluations are generally most effective when they are part of a broader adjustment process. Both the World Bank in its structural adjustment lending and the IMF in its enlarged access policy have recognized the need of many LDCs for extended transitional support.

Adjustment is a broad term.[47] It can mean moving away from a long legacy of controls, protection, and subsidies; it can be the distinctive problem of fuel-importing countries trying to change their capital stock to greater energy efficiency; it may be dealing with the effects of costly external borrowing; or it can have the narrower meaning of a country that was proceeding satisfactorily and encountered an unexpectedly adverse situation (like a bad crop year or a drop in the price of a key export).

If devaluation is being designed only to correct a trade imbalance, then deciding on its size and timing is vastly simplified. Yet if any of the adjustment problems are severe, then the link to internal macropolicy and micropolicy changes is essential for an adequate transition. For making these kinds of adjustments, it is clearly preferable for world economic stability for LDCs to experience a smooth change in policy.

One of the unstated but firm rules of the IMF's operating style is that there will be no discussion of the political situation in countries that come to the IMF for assistance. This tradition has certain advantages: it stresses the technical aspects of a particular country's request and minimizes the incentives for ideological voting by the executive directors. But the political setting is vital for determining the success of a devaluation, and it is naive to focus only on the economic aspects of the decision. There is also the sensitive issue of dealing with a government that is trying to extract resources immediately while different individuals may be in power when the austerity measures are introduced and the loans repaid.

As part of viewing adjustment in its broadest context, it would thus seem advisable for lenders to consider more explicitly the political feasibility and timing sequence for the steps to be undertaken.

Generating Public Support

Few prominent figures in any society will step forward to defend a government that has taken unpopular measures. Without going public, however, a government can start building a coalition of likely supporters for devaluation: exporters, key businessmen in the sectors and regions that will benefit, and those who favor market-oriented policies over controls. If these groups know that they are not isolated, they can form a useful pool of support for the policy changes.

Given that devaluations are typically part of a series of policy changes, it is often feasible to design measures to cushion the impact for adversely affected industries and income groups. In LDCs it may not be realistic to expect trade adjustment assistance on the scale found in the developed countries, but some help in job relocation and retraining can be useful to those who are permanently displaced. It may also be manageable to allocate funds from government development banks to employers in expanding industries if they are in areas that have displaced workers.

On the import side, if devaluation is linked with decontrol, there may be good arguments for considering a phased introduction of liberalization. Adjustment is a costly process, and firms that will face increased import competition will be far more cooperative if they have a known planning horizon for pricing, retooling, and retraining. On the export side, though it is important to provide incentives to exporters immediately so they will expand production. If a country is a food exporter, it may be prudent to increase export volume gradually and thus avoid sharp price movements in politically sensitive items.

Finally, the explanation to the public about the devaluation should be forthright. There is a need to review in direct language the rationale for the decision. Accurately estimating the timing for the various benefits and burdens will increase the government's credibility. It also seems worthwhile to cover the role of foreign organizations in sufficient detail so that conspiracy theories do not arise or can be met directly.

Ultimately the essential criterion for a successful devaluation is adequate maneuverability. Much of the literature on devaluation concentrates on the economic conditions necessary for an improvement in the balance of trade. Although this is an essential part of the problem, most LDC governments face more complex difficulties. Inflation, a bind on debt servicing, domestic budget deficits, and a need for an overall stabilization program are frequently found concurrently.

The intent of this book has been to show that maneuverability for a devaluing government comes from a blend of three factors: the speed of internal economic adjustments, the external trade and financial environment, and the extent of domestic political constraints. Because an increasing percentage of currency devaluations is the result of external pressure, it is important to identify in advance how much flexibility a devaluing government really has. The Indian, Indonesian, and Ghanaian cases highlight the strikingly different results that can occur when devaluations are undertaken. To integrate these factors in a consistent theoretical manner, a framework has been presented that categorizes the likely gainers and losers from devaluation and identifies four key stages in most devaluation episodes. With these caveats in mind, future devaluations perhaps may be less wrenching experiences.

Notes

Chapter 1

1. *Wall Street Journal*, June 24, 1983, sec. 2, p. 25.

2. E. Tagaza, "Huge Payments Deficit Brings New Devaluation in the Philippines," *Christian Science Monitor*, October 6, 1983, pp. 17–18.

3. For two different views of the role of the external sector in the Philippines, see I. Otani, "Inflation in an Open Economy: A Case Study of the Philippines," *IMF Staff Papers* 22, no. 3 (November 1975): 721–774, and R. Lim, "The Philippines and the Dependency Debate," *Journal of Contemporary Asia* 8, no. 2 (1978): 196–207.

4. "Peru—Debtor in Disarray," *Economist*, July 30, 1977, p. 60.

5. N. Girvan, "Swallowing the IMF Medicine in the Seventies," *Development Dialogue*, no. 2 (1980): 55–74.

6. "IMF Deal—At Last," *Economist*, August 12, 1978, p. 73.

7. G. K. Helleiner, "The Less Developed Countries and the International Monetary System," *Journal of Development Studies* 10, nos. 3–4 (April–July 1974): 347–373.

8. For a discussion of the links between LDC and reserve currencies, see W. R. Cline, *International Monetary Reform and the Developing Countries* (Washington, D.C.: Brookings Institution, 1976).

9. M. Goldstein, *The Exchange Rate System: Lessons of the Past and Options for the Future*, IMF Occasional Paper, no. 30 (Washington, D.C.: IMF, July 1984).

10. The Marxist countries of the Community of Economic Co-operation (COMECON) have partially insulated themselves through their artificial price system and barter trade.

11. Secrecy is critical for several reasons: leaked information could allow speculators an easy profit in currency trading, traders might try importing large quant-

ities if they thought the exchange rate was going up, and foreign exchange could be wasted by the central bank if it tried to defend a parity that would subsequently be lowered.

12. For a detailed discussion of how particular groups are rewarded and the adversely affected ones try to recoup, see C. Diaz-Allejandro, *Exchange Rate Devaluation in Semi-Industrialized Countries* (Cambridge, Mass.: MIT Press, 1965).

13. For a review of the theoretical problems in selecting a currency regime, see Y. Ishiyama, "The Theory of Optimum Currency Areas: A Survey," *IMF Staff Papers*, 22, no. 2 (July 1975): 344–383.

14. These are not new problems. See the following work done over a period of three decades: J. H. Williams, *Postwar Monetary Plans and Other Essays* (New York: Knopf, 1944); Robert Triffin, *Gold and the Dollar Crisis: The Future of Convertibility* (New Haven: Yale University Press, 1960); Tibor Scitovsky, "A New Approach to International Liquidity," *American Economic Review* 56, no. 5 (1966): 1212–1220; Organization of American States, *Latin America and the Reform of the International Monetary Systems* (Washington, D.C.: OAS, 1972).

15. The conclusion is known as the Marshall-Lerner Condition, coming from: A. Marshall, *Money, Credit and Commerce* (London: Macmillan, 1924), and A. P. Lerner, *The Economics of Control* (New York: Macmillan, 1944).

16. A. O. Hirschman, "Devaluation and the Trade Balance," *Review of Economics and Statistics* 31, no. 1 (February 1949): 50–53.

17. S. Alexander, "The Effects of Devaluation on a Trade Balance," *IMF Staff Papers* 2, no. 2 (April 1952): 263–278.

18. P. Krugman and L. Taylor, "Contractionary Effects of Devaluation," *Journal of International Economics* 8, no. 3 (August 1978): 445–456.

19. For a comparison of the assumptions of these three schools, see R. N. Cooper, *Currency Devaluation in Developing Countries*, Essays in International Finance, no. 86 (Princeton, N.J.: Princeton University, 1971).

20. For a discussion of how rapid shifts in the capital markets can create instability in exchange rates, see R. Dornbusch, "Expectations and Exchange Rate Dynamics," *Journal of Political Economy* 84, no. 6 (December 1976): 1161–1176.

21. A. O. Hirschman, *National Power and the Structure of Foreign Trade* (Berkeley: University of California Press, 1980), revised edition of the original 1945 publication.

22. The classic statement of dependency theory appears in A. G. Frank, "The Development of Underdevelopment," *Monthly Review* 18, no. 4 (September 1966): 17–31.

23. Two very different approaches to this problem are presented in S. Krasner, *Defending the National Interest* (Princeton, N.J.: Princeton University Press, 1978), and R. T. Libby, "External Co-optation of an LDC's Policy Making: The Case of Ghana, 1969–1972," *World Politics* 29, no. 1 (October 1976): 67–89.

24. R. Keohane, *After Hegemony—Co-operation and Discord in the World Economy* (Princeton, N.J.: Princeton University Press, 1984).

25. The consolidation of the Indonesian dual exchange rate was not entirely completed in April 1970 because the government had tied aid available that it could not sell at the same rate as free foreign exchange. Accordingly the Indonesian government maintained a special low exchange rate for these program aid funds.

26. Cooper, *Currency Devaluation.*

27. In this multi-volume series, *Foreign Trade Regimes and Economic Development* (New York and Cambridge, Mass.: Columbia University and Ballinger Presses, 1974–1978), Bhagwati and Krueger propose a typology of government choices during foreign exchange crises and a detailed set of country case studies.

28. See T. Schelling, *The Strategy of Conflict* (New York: Oxford University Press, 1960), for a review of different bargaining strategies.

29. See, for example, the approach suggested by A. Krueger in *Liberalization Attempts and Consequences* (Cambridge, Mass.: Ballinger Press, 1978).

30. A study of this type is W. Cline's assessment of the Peruvian stabilization program during the 1975–1978 period, in W. Cline and S. Weintraub, eds., *Economic Stabilization and Developing Countries* (Washington D.C.: Brookings Institution, 1981).

31. An interesting review of recipients' ability to manipulate donors is R. Keohane, "The Big Influence of Small Allies," *Foreign Policy*, no. 2 (Spring 1971): 161–182. Keohane shows how the Portuguese and Israelis have skillfully extracted assorted concessions from the United States.

32. When India invaded East Pakistan during the civil war of 1971, the United States moved an aircraft carrier into the Bay of Bengal, presumably with the intention of making Mrs. Gandhi reconsider India's attempt to create an independent Bangladesh.

33. The term *bureaucratic politics* is being used as defined by G. Allison, *The Essence of Decision* (Boston: Little, Brown, 1971), chap. 2.

34. D. O. Beim, "Rescuing the LDCs," *Foreign Affairs* 55, no. 4 (July 1977): 717–731.

35. Prime Minister Busia consented to respond to written questions and provided a

detailed justification of the actions he had taken.

At the end of each case study, names and titles of those interviewed are listed.

36. For a detailed review of theories on how decision makers process information, see J. Steinbruner, *The Cybernetic Theory of Decision* (Princeton, N.J.: Princeton University Press, 1974).

37. See the discussion in D. Cole and P. Lyman, *Korean Development* (Cambridge, Mass.: Harvard University Press, 1970), p. 87.

38. There is an interesting parallel between Lopez Portilla's actions and those of Mrs. Gandhi, who nationalized the Indian banks in 1969. In both cases the chief executive used a crisis to accomplish an objective that was desirable for other (political) reasons.

39. G. G. Johnson and T. M. Reichman, *Stand-By Arrangements in the Upper Credit Tranches, 1973—75* (Washington, D.C.: International Monetary Fund, 1978), p.12.

40. See T. Hayter, *Aid as Imperialism* (London: Penguin Press, 1970).

41. R. Prebisch, "The Economic Development of Latin America and Its Principal Problems," *Economic Bulletin for Latin America* 7 (February 1962): 1—22.

42. A striking example of claimed certainty in predicting resource needs is presented in H. Chenery and A. Strout, "Foreign Assistance and Economic Development," *American Economic Review* 56, no. 4 (September 1966): 679—733.

43. C. Gullick and J. Nelson, "Promoting Economic Development Policies: AID Experience in Developing Countries," USAID Discussion Paper no. 9 (Washington, D.C., September 1965).

44. J. Grant, "Development: The End of Trickle-Down?" *Foreign Policy*, no. 12 (Fall 1973): 43—65.

45. M. D. Morris, *Measuring the Condition of the World's Poor: The Physical Quality of Life Index* (New York: Pergamon Press, 1979).

46. International Labor Organization, *Employment, Growth and Basic Human Needs: A One-World Problem* (New York: Praeger Publishers, 1977).

47. G. Brown, *Korean Pricing Policy and Economic Development in the 1960s* (Baltimore, Md.: Johns Hopkins University Press, 1973).

48. E. Sturc, "Stabilization Policy: Experience of Some European Countries in the 1950s," *IMF Staff Papers* 15, no. 2 (1968): 197—219.

49. T. Connors, "The Apparent Effects of Recent IMF Stabilization Programs," U.S. Federal Reserve Board, International Finance Discussion Paper, no. 135 (Washington, D.C., April 1979).

50. C. Payer, *The Debt Trap* (New York: Monthly Review Press, 1975).

51. A. O. Hirschman, *Journeys toward Progress* (Garden City, N.Y.: Anchor Books, Doubleday, 1965). See a discussion of this claim and the view of many Latin American governments about the IMF in the 1950s and 1960s in chapter 3.

52. R. H. Green, "Political Economic Adjustment and IMF Conditionality: Tanzania, 1974–81," mimeo. (presented at the Institute for International Economics, March 1982, Conference on the IMF).

53. R. Mikesell, "Appraising IMF Conditionality: Too Loose, Too Tight or Just Right?" mimeo. (IIE, March 1982 conference).

64. T. Killick, and M. Chapman, *Much Ado about Nothing: Testing the Impact of IMF Stabilization Programmes in Developing Countries* (London: Overseas Development Institute, 1982).

55. J. Williamson, *The Lending Policies of the IMF* (Washington, D.C.: IIE, 1982).

56. S. Dell, "The International Environment for Adjustment in the Developing Countries," *World Development* 8, no. 11 (November 1980): 833–842.

57. S. Khan and M. Knight, "Determinants of Current Account Balances of Non-oil Developing Countries in the 1970s—An Empirical Analysis," *IMF Staff Papers* 30, no. 4 (1983): 819–842.

58. See D. Donovan, "Macroeconomic Performance and Adjustment under Fund-Supported Programs: The Experience of the 1970s," *IMF Staff Papers* 29, no. 2 (1982): 171–203.

59. There is an elaboration of this argument in H. Eckstein, "Case Study and Theory in Macropolitics," mimeo. (Princeton, N.J., 1971).

60. George Woods was president of the International Bank for Reconstruction and Development (World Bank) at the time the Bell mission report was initiated.

61. The leader of the Indonesian economic team, Dr. Widjojo, had participated in the drafting of the 1963 Eight Year Plan, and there are some interesting similarities between the 1963 effort and the post-1967 program.

62. See W. Hollinger, "The Foreign Exchange Rate as a Policy Instrument, the Indonesian Case: 1966–70." Harvard Development Advisory Service Paper (June 1970), for a discussion of the gradual changes in the exchange rate system that led to the devaluation.

Chapter 2

1. At the end of each of the three country cases is a chronology that covers the key events before and after the respective devaluations. Although the discussion in

the text of the chapters is comparative and follows a similar format, the chronologies vary so that they provide extensive background for the specialist reader without making the main text overly detailed. The India and Indonesia chronologies emphasize the history of donor and recipient interaction. Because of the Acheampong coup and the subsequent revaluation, the Ghana chronology focuses more on events after the devaluation.

2. M. Brecher, *Nehru's Mantle* (London: Oxford University Press, 1966), contains a good discussion of the prime minister's political strategy.

3. In chapter 8 of Nehru's *The Discovery of India* (New Delhi: Asia Publishing House, 1961), there are premonitions of his desire for heavy industry, import substitution, and central government control. This is significant because the book first appeared in 1945. There is also strong evidence of Nehru's cultural pride and the ambivalence he felt about the social changes commonly accompanying industrialization.

4. See J. Bhagwati and P. Desai, *India: Planning for Industrialization* (London: Oxford University Press, 1970), for documentation of these trends.

5. The 1962 elections showed Nehru's enormous appeal, despite the growing ossification of the Congress party.

6. The Kamaraj plan (where key ministers were asked to resign in 1963 and return to their home states to rebuild the Congress) was an indication of the acknowledged Congress difficulties.

7. Baldev Nayar, *The Modernization Imperative and Indian Planning* (New Delhi: Vikas, 1972), claims that the one central belief that unites the overwhelming majority of the Indian policymaking elite is the need for India to be a world power and thus strong militarily.

8. See Durga Das, *From Curzon to Nehru and After* (London: Collins, 1969), for a discussion of Nehru's involvement in the Foreign Ministry. Not only did he personally hold the portfolio for a decade, but he often spent hours drafting even routine cables.

9. N. Maxwell, *India's China War* (Bombay: Jaico, 1970). After secretly being given access to GOI files, Maxwell concluded that Nehru was overconfident and provocative to the Chinese, who preferred a peaceful settlement to the Aksi-Chin dispute.

10. Throughout his political life, Nehru was resentful of the top members of the civil service. Most of the Indian Administrative Service (IAS) staff personnel who held important posts during his term of office had worked closely with the British as Indian civil service (ICS) members. Nehru knew that he had to depend on these civil servants to manage, but he tried to keep policymaking in the hands of those

who he felt shared his values. Shastri, on the other hand, bore fewer grudges and relied extensively on his IAS secretary, L. K. Jha.

11. TTK so strongly opposed devaluation that he virtually refused to listen to Bernard Bell and Ambassador C. Bowles when they called on him to discuss the findings of the IBRD Bell report. TTK also prevented the Bell report from being disseminated within the government of India. TTK delayed passing it up to Shastri, thus postponing the possibility of action on the recommendations.

12. See the discussion in the Chronology regarding the September 1964 Planning Commission meeting where V.K.R.V. Rao outmaneuvered T. T. Krishnamachari. The resulting decision to proceed with new investments as well as social expenditures forced a reduction of funds for precisely the raw materials and intermediate goods necessary for existing industry.

13. The national defense remittance scheme allowed Indian nationals living abroad to get import licenses equal to 60 percent of the foreign exchange they sent to India. Since import licenses were sold at a considerable premium, the GOI was acknowledging that the official exchange rate was overvalued.

14. IBRD, *Economic Situation and Prospects of India* (SA-32a, May 10, 1972), vol. 2. The consortium members were Australia, Belgium, Canada, Denmark, France, West Germany, Italy, Japan, Netherlands, Norway, Sweden, United Kingdom, United States, IBRD, and IDA. The nonconsortium donors were Bulgaria, Czechoslovakia, Hungary, Poland, the USSR, Yugoslavia, Switzerland, and Australia.

15. K. N. Raj, a scholarly socialist, was releasing his critical report on the Indian steel industry shortly after J. Bhagwati, who was more market oriented, was publishing his "More on Devaluation" in *Economic and Political Weekly*.

16. C. E. Lindblom, economic adviser to Ambassador Bowles from 1963 to 1965, later published his "The Rediscovery of the Market," *Public Interest*, no. 4 (Summer 1966): 89—101. Lindblom argued that the market could be just as effective a device in LDCs as in developed countries.

17. The IBRD initially expected to make the Bell report the annual situation report for 1965, but the report was so critical that the GOI did not want it to be available to the executive directors from other countries (as was the usual practice for situation reports). The GOI also took exception to the actual mention of devaluation in the summary volume, which it claimed needed to be kept secret.

18. Economic growth was a virtually sacrosanct goal at the time, which M. Millikan and W. W. Rostow's *A Proposal Key to an Effective Foreign Policy* (New York: Harper & Row, 1957), had helped to reify by arguing that increasing GNP would increase the probability of governments' choosing stable, democratic paths to development.

19. Performance conditioning was also a reigning doctrine. See H. Chenery and A. Strout, "Foreign Assistance and Economic Development," *American Economic Review* 56, no. 4 (1966): 679–733, and C. Gulick and J. Nelson, "Promoting Economic Development Policies: AID Experience in Developing Countries," USAID Discussion Paper, no. 9 (Washington, D.C., September 1965).

20. In C. Bowles, *Ambassador's Report* (New York: Harper, 1954), and J. P. Lewis, *The Quiet Crisis in India* (Washington, D.C.: Brookings, 1962), there is essentially the same argument: that India is of great strategic significance, that it is coping with enormous problems, and that its gradualist, democratic government should be rewarded.

21. For a review of the controls system, its operation, and effects on economic performance, see Bhagwati and Desai, *India*.

22. See M. Weiner, *Political Change in South Asia* (Calcutta, 1963), for a detailed discussion of the differences between the elite and mass cultures and the resulting tensions arising between top civil servants and top politicians.

23. For a discussion of Indian foreign policy goals, see B. Nayar, "Treat India Seriously," *Foreign Policy* no. 18 (Spring 1975): 133–154.

24. Girilal Jain argued in "Freezing the Status Quo: Consequences of the Nehru Model," *New Delhi Times of India*, March 7, 1974, that Nehru's decision to build a consensus system created the setting for political stability but also stagnation. By making the Congress party reflect local interests, it reduced dissent but also inhibited change.

25. It is important to remember that the inflation after 1962 was not characteristic of earlier GOI policy.

26. Using structural functionalist terminology, the primary goal of the Indian elite was system maintenance, and the civil service and Congress party leaders accepted the same basic approach.

27. See S. Kochanek, *Business and Politics in India* (Berkeley: University of California Press, 1974), chap. 2. See D. McClelland and D. Winter, *Motivating Economic Achievement* (New York: Free Press, 1969) for hypotheses on Indian businessmen.

28. See A. Krueger, "The Political Economy of the Rent-Seeking Society," *American Economic Review* 64, no. 3 (June 1974): 291–303, for a typical liberal argument that Indian controls will undermine their own legitimacy.

29. Although there were important steps toward decontrol in the 1975–1983 period, they were halting and in no sense a reflection of widespread elite confidence in the market.

30. A. D. Moddie, "Letter on 'The Sirkar Culture,'" *Times of India*, August 12, 1974.

31. As numerous commentators have shown, the British kept up India's war supplies despite the deaths of hundreds of thousands of people in the 1943 Bengal famine.

32. R. G. Agarwal, *Price Controls in India since 1947* (Delhi: FICCI, 1956).

33. Decontrol was tried on a selective basis. For example, in May 1966, the steel casting, cement, and pulp industries were given exceptions to license requirements. Nevertheless, the general pattern was for massive control and oversight by numerous ministries. In the mid-1970s, though the Ministry of Industry claimed to have reduced oversight, investment approvals took an average of 450 days for clearance.

34. A. O. Hirschman, "The Political Economy of Import Substituting Industries in Latin America," *Quarterly Journal of Economics* 82, no. 1 (February 1968): 1–32. J. Bhagwati and T. N. Srinivasan, *Foreign Trade Regimes and Economic Development: India* (New York: National Bureau of Economic Research, distributed by Columbia University Press, 1975).

35. The Monopolies Inquiries Commission of 1965, the Industrial Licensing Policy Inquiry of 1967, and the Wanchoo report of 1971 uncovered corruption and malfeasance in the GOI's licensing and control efforts.

36. *Program aid* is the term for general-purpose assistance not tied to a particular project. Program aid is sometimes called balance of payments supports. It can be tied to purchases from the donor country or not and can be limited to specific types of goods or simply provided to finance a specific quantity of the recipient country's imports.

37. In the 1971 general election, Mrs. Gandhi's move to the Left not only drew voters to her faction of the Congress for seats in the Lok Sabha but contributed to erosion of support for the parties of the Left in the state assemblies as well.

38. Although the GOI has been able to get its creditors to reschedule its debt many times, it has consistently met obligations. In contrast, the government of Pakistan postponed its debt payments in the middle of the 1971 war and did not reach an agreement on resuming payments until 1974.

39. See W. Ilchman and N. Uphoff's discussion of the search for resources that most national leaders face in *The Political Economy of Change* (Berkeley: University of California Press, 1971).

40. The secrecy surrounding the decision also affects research on the topic. Many of those involved are willing to talk about the decision, but few are willing to be quoted. Observations about individual positions are included here only if I was able to get corroboration from two independent sources.

41. M. Shah later directed the Indian Council of Applied Economic Research study

on the prospects for various Indian exports that reflected his view that government should (and could) pick the fields most likely to yield benefits. See *Export Strategy for India* (New Delhi: ICAER, 1969).

42. At the time, Bhootilingham was special secretary for the Department of Economic Affairs in the Ministry of Finance; Patel was the chief economic adviser in the Ministry of Finance; Jha was the secretary to the prime minister; Marathe was economic adviser to the Ministry of Industry; and Ramaswamy was one of the deputy economic advisers in the Ministry of Finance.

43. There are competing claims about I. G. Patel's views on devaluation. V. V. Bhatt, for example, states that Patel was never fully convinced that the devaluation was necessary and that Patel's ambivalence about the devaluation may have delayed the preparations for the parity change.

44. In 1966 literally thousands of foreign aid personnel were working in India. USAID alone had approximately 200 direct hire staff, over 200 contract hire related foreigners, and over 1,000 Indian staffers.

45. Those in the U.S. embassy who felt Lewis was too close to the Indians said the USAID motto became: "Tell us what we can do for India."

46. Bell did make at least one bureaucratic mistake, though: he put the devaluation recommendation in print. The GOI was thus given an easy excuse for suppressing the report, and this minimized the intended readership.

47. Bernard Bell, like David Bell, administrator of USAID at the time, was considered to have a critical perspective. David Bell and Bernard Bell were often confused by the Indians.

48. The first formal consortium-GOI consultation was held in New Delhi in October 1965, with B. Bell and A. De Lattre representing the donors.

49. The significance of the Subramaniam-Freeman agreement was threefold: it committed the GOI to adequate incentives for farmers and decontrolling the distribution of fertilizer, it was clearly an example of foreign pressure on the GOI, and it created a further demand for imports because imported fertilizer was necessary for the higher-yielding varieties of seed. The subsequent $50 million U.S. fertilizer loan of December 1965 also carried conditions. The GOI was vulnerable at this point because its own fertilizer plants had not yet been completed and India imported $280 million worth of fertilizer in the 1965–1966 period.

50. Mrs. Gandhi was later criticized for not sending "more skeptical negotiators" to Washington to meet with Woods, but she knew this would foil the basic objective of getting the most attractive possible offer from the consortium.

51. John Lewis, USAID director at the time, argued that the main purpose of the devaluation was to provide an opportunity for rationalizing the import scheme.

52. Rao said, "Devaluation is like rearranging a lady's handbag: too complex to be worth the effort unless the situation is grave."

53. Although both the Bell mission report and the Woods-Mehta agreement are kept highly classified at the World Bank, a senior staff member of the IBRD who had access to the documents allowed me to review them and take notes. It is unfortunate for the purposes of full historical discussion that these documents are not released. Given that Mrs. Gandhi denied that she agreed to the devaluation because of foreign pressure, it appears unlikely that the material will soon be available to the public.

54. The target for program aid and fertilizer combined was $795.4 million. The actual pledge on November 8, 1966, was $901.2 million although $250 million of the U.S. pledge had already been signed in May and July 1966. Source: IBRD (India, no. 18, 12/27/66).

55. Some staff members—rather disingenuously—argued that a float would not need to be labeled a devaluation and that the decision could be termed "letting the market set the price."

56. These estimates are from Bhagwati and Scrinivasan, Foreign Trade Regimes, p. 97. This meant that the previous level of export subsidization had been on the average equal to 35.2 percent, while import duties had averaged 12.7 percent.

57. For goods with a low elasticity of demand (like tea and jute), export taxes were imposed to prevent windfall profits or having exporters agree to lower sale prices more than necessary.

58. Lok Sabha debates July 26, 1966.

59. See the Chronology for a list of the newspapers taking favorable and opposing positions. See "The Political Response to the 1966 Devaluation," Economic and Political Weekly (September 1972) by J. Bhagwati, T. Srinivasan, and K. Sundaram, for a detailed review of the positions taken by various interest groups.

60. New Delhi Blitz, July 23, 1966.

61. Lok Sabha debates, col. 219, July 26, 1966.

62. New Delhi Blitz, October 15, 1966.

63. Government of India, Ministry of Food and Agriculture Area, Production and Yield of Principal Crops in India 1949–50 to 1967–68 (New Delhi, 1969).

64. Government of India, Ministry of Finance, Economic Survey, 1967–68 (New Delhi, 1969).

65. Government of India, Department of Statistics, Central Statistic Organization Estimates of National Product, 1960–61 to 1969–70 (New Delhi, 1972).

66. See Bhagwati and Srinivasan, *Foreign Trade Regimes and Economic Development: India*, p. 114.

67. The GOI actually reduced the size of its deficit between 1965–1966 and 1966–1967 and slowed the rate of real money supply growth.

68. In 1967 the recession reduced import demand for raw materials, machinery, and spare parts. Because these were the goods to be financed from donor program loans, the actual drawdowns of the aid were less than anticipated. The donors thus felt that maintaining the program aid level was not necessary for the pledging made in the fall of 1967. By the fall of 1968, however, the GOI had used up its program aid backlog and wanted large pledges. By this time the donors felt the GOI had completely failed to implement the Woods-Mehta agreement, and there was no enthusiasm for increasing program aid levels.

69. Mrs Gandhi later claimed to Americans that the communiqué in Moscow had been a "mistake" made by a new, junior press aide. The credibility of this claim is subject to serious doubt because communiqués are generally reviewed with great care.

70. Mehta was moved to a less conspicuous ministry and later led the Congress (opposition). Subramaniam's resignation was taken after political complaints about the distribution of PL 480 food, which was under the aegis of the Agriculture Ministry.

71. By 1970 the Reverse Bank of India had foreign exchange or gold worth more than $1 billion substantially more than any other period since the late 1940s (when reserves were high due to the effects of World War II).

72. For a sophisticated version of the argument that aid is a duty to be handled without stipulations, see I. G. Patel, *Foreign Aid* (New Delhi: Institute for Public Enterprise, 1968).

Chapter 3

1. H. Feith and L. Castles, *Indonesian Political Thinking, 1945–1965* (Ithaca: Cornell University Press, 1970), p. 40.

2. F. LeBeau, June 1970 USAID memo based on Indonesian Department of Agriculture and Logistics Agency statistics, and A. Booth and P. McCauley, *The Indonesian Economy during the Suharto Era* (Kuala Lumpur: Oxford University Press, 1981), p. 4.

3. Examples of work sharply critical of Suharto's policies are R. Mortimer, ed., *Showcase State: Illusion of Indonesia's Accelerated Modernization* (Sydney: Angus & Robertson, 1973); K. J. Dorodjatun, "Economic Strategy and Social-Political

Costs," *Jakarta Tempo*, April 24, 1971; R. Shaplen, "Letter from Indonesia," *New Yorker*, April 1, 1974, pp. 57–90; I. Palmer, *The Indonesian Economy since 1965* (London: Frank Cass, 1978).

4. D. Dapice, "An Overview of the Indonesian Economy," in *The Indonesian Economy*, ed. G. Papanek (New York: Praeger, 1980), p. 14.

5. In G. Tomasson, "Indonesian Economic Stabilization 1966–69" *Finance and Development* 7, no. 4 (December 1970): 46–53, the former deputy IMF representative in Jakarta argues that the results were predictable once the "right" policies were followed.

6. J. Newmann, "Inflation in Indonesia" (Ph.D. diss., Tufts University, 1974), stresses the role of the authoritarian government in achieving compliance with desired economic policies.

7. For a discussion of stabilization programs that failed in democratic countries (which subsequently became authoritarian) see A. O. Hirschman's review of Chilean inflation in the 1950s, *Journeys toward Progress* (New York: Doubleday, 1965), chap. 3, and R. Baldwin's comments on Philippine policy in the 1960s, *The Philippines* (New York: National Bureau of Economic Research, distributed by Columbia University Press, 1975).

8. M. Gillis makes a related argument in "Episodes in Indonesian Economic Growth"(presented at the Conference on World Economic Growth, Mexico, April 28, 1983).

9. Except for one exception, Professor Sarbini. See the Chronology (March 1966) for a discussion of the split between Sarbini and the rest of the economic team.

10. In Jakarta in the early 1970s, it was said that "the other economists shine in Widjojo's reflected glory."

11. International Monetary Fund, *Recent Economic Developments* (Washington, D.C.: IMF, November 30, 1970), table 15. For a critical perspective on outside involvement, see F. Weinstein, *Indonesian Foreign Policy and the Dilemma of Dependence* (Ithaca, N.Y.: Cornell University Press, 1976).

12. The Chronology presents the details of Sumitro's lobbying to get the Brewster amendment introduced into the 1950 U.S. Foreign Assistance Act—and the resulting U.S. pressure on the Dutch.

13. For a discussion of the issues involved in the MSA treaty and the maneuvering both in the USG and GOI, see the Chronology.

14. The book is J. Hughes, *Indonesian Upheaval* (New York: McKay, 1967). The academic paper is in the Cornell series by R. McVey and G. Kahin, but it is not widely available.

15. East Java is the poorest province in Indonesia, the most favorable to Sukarno, and the scene of PKI organized uprisings in 1928 and 1948.

16. When the interim government was established on March 12, 1966, the formal structure was a troika: the sultan (economics), Malik (foreign affairs), and Suharto (acting president and defense and security).

17. Central government taxes, which were 23.4 percent of gross domestic product (GDP) in 1980, were only 3.9 percent of GDP in 1965. *Nota Keuangan* (Jakarta: Ministry of Finance, Government of Indonesia, 1969).

18. Although the GOI later recognized and exploited the advantages of having a consortium where the donors could be forced to compete, the consortium concept was initially favored by the United States partly to limit U.S. involvement and partly to put pressure on the Japanese to contribute a substantial amount of aid.

19. The creditors elected a French chairman, became known as the Paris Club, and met annually to roll over the debt until the final settlement was reached.

20. Herman Abs, a well-known West German banker, was asked to review the GOI debt and propose terms for rescheduling the capital and interest. He completed his review by 1969, and the negotiations with most of the Western creditors were completed by the end of 1970.

21. After 1967 there was assistance on statistical collection from the UNDP and substantial involvement by the IMF, IBRD, and Harvard Development Advisory Service in recommending the appropriate aid level.

22. The GOI and field mission of the IGGI donors also met periodically in Jakarta to discuss new projects likely to come up for future funding. These meetings evinced the donor competition over projects.

23. Once the debt negotiations were going smoothly, the stabilization program was well underway, and donor attention beginning to focus more on project rather than program aid, the IBRD report became the essential one.

24. In 1970 the consortium commitments from multilateral organizations were $85 million or 15 percent of the total; in 1971 they were $105 million, or 14 percent of the total. These figures exclude technical assistance (which many of the multilateral organizations give), but the dollar totals for technical assistance are small.

25. The Indonesian mission was the IBRD's first permanent field mission and carried special status with the World Bank; Bell reported directly to McNamara, rather than the usual pattern of reporting through the bank's regional vice-president for Asia and the Pacific.

26. The Indonesia word for such an individual is *perantara* or literally "go-between." The broker must have the full confidence of all parties, be imaginative at

suggesting alternatives to the impasses, and be sufficiently impartial and unegoistic to avoid being a threat to the status of those concerned. Many Asians feel at ease with this form of conflict resolution, and it doubtless made the coordination of the IGGI far smoother than it might otherwise have been.

27. A tangible sign of Dr. Bell's significance to the GOI was the formal Indonesian request to McNamara to extend Bell's tour after he had been recalled to Washington and promoted. Key GOI ministers realized immediately that Bell's departure would bring about an immediate change of relationship with the IBRD. They were right. See the Chronology for the list of members and observers.

28. Both the BE and DP rates were initially allowed to float in February 1966. In October 1968, the GOI decided to keep the BE rate stable through market interventions but without declaring a fixed parity. Then a similar fixing of the DP rate was agreed on in May 1969. The GOI thus had the flexibility of a floating rate for four years but gradually moved toward a fixed parity which began in April 1970.

29. Many of the moves by the GOI were modest and exploratory, designed to test what would work best. The Chronology presents a summary of these often intricate steps.

30. This initial working session was held at a bungalow in the Puncak. It is ironic that eight years later, the group returned to the Puncak for a crucial meeting with President Suharto to defend their program from attack by the president's other aides.

31. Employees were still kept in these sectors, but salaries were very low except for the payment in kind of food.

32. This was done by having the Bank of Indonesia rebate only part of the foreign exchange proceeds that the exporters were required to surrender.

33. Newmann, "Inflation in Indonesia."

34. When Sumitro returned in 1967 (from ten years of exile) he was treated cautiously by his former students. Widjojo was the leader of the economic team and having Sumitro around created a chance of being second-guessed. Once in the cabinet, Sumitro made several attempts to broaden his influence beyond trade but was consistently kept out of areas where Widjojo did not want him to operate.

35. For a discussion on the welfare effects of the multiple exchange rate system, see B. Glassburner, "Pricing of Foreign Exchange in Indonesia, 1966–67," *Economic Development and Cultural Change* 18, no. 2 (January 1970): 166–187.

36. The lower and middle levels of the civil service were dominated by PNI members whose initial loyalty was to Sukarno.

37. The Sumatrans, along with other outer-islanders, had revolted against Sukarno in the PRRI rebellion of 1958. The Sumatrans and other non-Javanese were looking

for signs of more favorable terms from the central government, and the BE system was a tangible indicator.

38. By 1973 the GOI had set up programs like the per capita grants to villages at the province and county (*Kabupaten*) level. These efforts were proposed as a means of developing the capabilities of local governments and also selecting projects of local interest that might not be thought of by a planner in Jakarta.

39. Although Suharto's Golkar party won 63.9 percent of the vote in the 1971 elections, the electoral process was not his main concern. Establishing his legitimacy was, and economic performance was the best indication of competence. See R. William Liddle, *Political Participation in Modern Indonesia* (New Haven, Conn.: Yale University Press, 1973).

40. In contrast, the principal donors in the Aid-India Consortium knew before June 1966 that India would devalue as part of the liberalization and decontrol package.

41. The GOI reduced the use of this escape valve when in May 1969 it decided to set up a fixed DP rate—even though the government was not formally committed to the level of 378 rupiah per U.S. dollar.

42. The quick decision to devalue even more than the dollar in 1971 showed how anxious the economic team was to avoid an overvalued rate, so it is unlikely that the 1970 situation would have continued indefinitely.

43. R. Sundarum, "The Equilibrium Exchange Rate: Some Considerations," *Bulletin of Indonesian Economic Studies* (March 1976).

44. IMF, Memo to the Executive Board, "Indonesia—Changes in the Exchange System" (Washington, D.C., April 13, 1970). Although Indonesia was allocated special drawing rights of 34.8 million, the GOI was relying on an IMF standby and a private bank loan of $50 million to augment its thin reserve position.

45. An indication that the IMF took its recommendations seriously was that P. P. Schweitzer, the managing director, raised the topic during his visit in August 1969. See the Chronology.

46. The decision to go ahead with marketing boards for export crops that would tie into the trading syndicates was the type of bold departure that the other economists resented.

47. To join the Suharto cabinet, Sumitro was forced to promise that he would not undertake any partisan political activity.

48. See *Business News*, April 22, 1970, for a summary of the talks made by Widjojo, Sumitro, Subroto, Wardhana, and Radius on this television panel show.

49. The regional governors were virtually all military men and appointed directly by the president, so they were naturally going to give only a muted response

unless the moves had so seriously affected key constituents that their positions were endangered.

50. Although the Suharto regime began a systematic repression of the press and intellectuals after the January 1974 Tanaka riots, in 1970 the press was still very free—possibly the least restrained in Southeast Asia.

51. There was no change in price for the less essential consumer goods which had previously been coming in at the DP rate of 378/$.

52. The United States informally devalued by 7 percent on August 15, 1971. Not only did the GOI have the rupiah follow the dollar down, but the rupiah was devalued an additional 10 percent against the dollar.

53. B. Glassburner, "Indonesia's New Economic Policy and its Socio-Political Implications," in K. Jackson and L. Pye, eds., *Political Power and Communication in Indonesia* (Berkeley: University of California Press, 1978).

54. Interestingly, the spinning industry was approximately 50 percent government owned, and a powerful general, Marjadi, was the director of the government enterprises—creating something of a military-technocratic conflict. Ending subsidies is a step that most governments in high- and low-income countries have trouble doing. The persistence of large subsidies for the shipbuilding and merchant marine industries is a good example of this problem in the United States.

55. Gillis, "Episodes," argues that the Indonesian economists have preferred "macro reform and micro dirigisme" (p. 9).

56. For a critique of the economic team that advocates moving even further away from use of the market, see S. Mubyarto and Boediono, eds., *Ekonomi Pancasila* (Yogyakarta: Faculty of Economics, 1981).

Chapter 4

1. On March 6, 1957, Britain granted the Gold Coast independence. In the process, the name was changed to Ghana, and the Nkrumah government stressed the need for decolonization until its overthrow on February 24, 1966. At that time, Nkrumah was replaced by a group of military officers who called themselves the National Liberation Council. The NLC supervised elections in August 1969, which led to K. Busia's Progress party's assuming office of a parliamentary government on October 1, 1969. One of Busia's main concerns was to have democracy function effectively. In implementing his coup against Busia, Acheampong called his group the National Redemption Council.

2. *West Africa*, January 28, 1972. See for a full account of the colonel's 6 A.M. speech and his follow-up talk several hours later.

3. Acheampong specifically referred to the need for reconsidering the development levy, the 1971 currency devaluation, various rural development efforts, and cocoa purchasing methods.

4. For case histories of various types of coups, see H. Bienen ed., *The Military Intervenes* (New York: Russell Sage, 1969).

5. Although the Parliament was dissolved, the Progress party banned, and some of Busia's ministers jailed, the NRC never conducted any systematic effort at repression. Apathy rather than public antagonism was the common reaction to the coup.

6. See W. Birmingham, I. Neustadt, and E. N. Omaboe, eds., *A Study in Contemporary Ghana*, vol. 1 of *The Economy of Ghana* (Evanston, Ill.: Northwestern University Press, 1966), for an overview of economic policy during the colonial and Nkrumah periods.

7. Foreign exchange reserves went from a surplus of $450 million when Nkrumah took over from the British to a net debt position of $550 million in 1966. See N. Uphoff, "Ghana's Experience in Using External Aid for Development 1957–66" (Ph.D. diss., University of California 1969), for a review of the aid component of capital goods imports.

8. See W. Steele, "Import Substitution Policy in Ghana in the 1960s" (Ph.D. diss., MIT, 1970), for a review of the costs of this effort.

9. See D. Scott, "Growth and Crisis: Economic Policy in Ghana 1945–65" (Ph.D. diss., Harvard University, 1967) for a review of the major changes in Ghanaian monetary and fiscal policy during the pre-independence and Nkrumah years.

10. The inflation rate for 1965 was 26.4 percent, an exceptionally rapid rate for a country that had previously known consistent price stability.

11. Colonel Afrifa, *The Ghana Coup* (London: Cass, 1966), chaps. 1, 4, shows that, like their successors in 1972, the NLC plotters had neglected to do any careful planning of future policy before they took power.

12. The NLC followed a strict stabilization regimen for sixteen months before devaluing. This meant that the devaluations took place when inflation was moderating, and the NLC was only trying to affect its trade position, not trying to boost export taxes as the Busia government did.

13. Although there were cuts in a few government enterprises (the meat factory, mango operation, and state laundries), there was no systematic across-the-board cut or an immediate program to phase out the inefficient operations, as was done during the Suharto government's initial stabilization efforts.

14. In the 1970–1971 budget, for example, cocoa export duties were 114.8 million new cedis out of a total revenue take of 426.6 million new cedis.

15. In E. Eshag and P. Richards, "A Comparison of Economic Development in Ghana and the Ivory Coast since 1960," *Bulletin of Oxford University Institute of Economics and Statistics* 29, no. 4 (November 1967): 353–372, this argument is elaborated.

16. Although there were plants set up for initial processing of gold, lumber planning, and making cocoa butter, they were poorly managed and not models for a successful export diversification plan.

17. T. Killick, *Development Economics in Action* (New York: St. Martins, 1978), table 5.5, estimates that net long-term aid between 1966 and 1972 was 110 million new cedis for an average of $14.0 million per year. Gross aid was five times this level, but repayment of previous debt obligations reduced the net inflow after the mid-1960s.

18. The "big push" concept is generally credited to Paul Rosenstein-Rodan, "Problems of Industrialisation of Eastern and Southeastern Europe," *Economic Journal* 53, nos. 210–211 (June–September 1943): 202–211.

19. N. Hicks, "Some Structural Problems in the Economy of Ghana" (Accra: USAID, January 1970).

20. In ibid., there is a summary of the major structural problems that persisted throughout the NLC period.

21. J. C. Leith, *Ghana: Foreign Trade Regimes and Economic Development*, (New York: National Bureau of Economic Research, 1974), p. 142.

22. See the Chronology for a description of the operation of the 180-day credit scheme guaranteed by the export promotion agencies in the exporting countries; 80 percent of the loan financing for this scheme came from exporting country banks.

23. The NLC members made a complete exit from power. On turning over the government, they resigned their military commissions as well.

24. J. Kraus, "Arms and Politics in Ghana," in C. Welch, ed., *Soldier and State in Africa* (Evanston: Northwestern University Press, 1970).

25. Dr. Busia's four books were *A Purposeful Education for Africa*, *The Challenge of Africa*, *Urban Churches in Britain*, and *Africa in Search of Democracy*.

26. J. H. Mensah, "The Wealth of the Nation," *Legon Observer*, July 2, 1971.

27. In certain areas, Busia's thinking was similar to P. T. Bauer's. See, for example, P. T. Bauer, *West African Trade* (London: Routledge and Kegan Paul, 1963), and P. T. Bauer and B. S. Yamey, *The Economics of Under-Developed Countries* (Cambridge: Cambridge University Press, 1957).

28. In the 1969 election, the Progress party won only two of the nine parliamentary seats from the Accra metropolitan area.

29. In July 1971 the new budget included a 5 percent tax on all wage income. Because this was uncollectible in the rural areas, it fell predominantly on the working poor as a burden. Given the 9 percent inflation rate for 1971, it meant a clear reduction in real incomes for 1971.

30. He studied economics at the London School of Economics and Stanford University.

31. Mensah quite often missed work for a long period and then showed up at his office at midnight, calling his staff to assemble for work.

32. In the summer of 1971 *Evening News*, a paper hostile to the Progress party, reported that Mensah was a director of a farm in his home district and that he had renovated his office at the ministry by putting in a bed and a small kitchen. Although the Ghanaian constitution forbade ministers to be in business, Mensah refused to resign from his director's post because, he said, it was a cooperative, not a business farm. Similarly he refused to apologize for the expenses on his office. Had he been willing to make these small gestures, he would have saved his party considerable criticism.

33. Both Killick and Stern were members of the Harvard Development Advisory Service (HDAS) team, which was providing analytic assistance to the Ministry of Planning. Another team member, Roemer, joined them in working on the balance of payments crisis in its later phases, but other members of the HDAS group remained mostly uninvolved.

34. K. Busia to D. Denoon, January 7, 1977, p. 11.

35. For example, besides his economic choices, Busia lost a great deal of internal popularity by initiating a dialogue with South Africa and supporting Prime Minister Heath's position on Rhodesia. It has been argued that these moves were made to line up British aid, yet there was also the element in Busia that "believed white racists could be won over if they only realized that Ghanaians were gentlemen too."

36. The cocoa price in early 1970 was high: $790 per ton.

37. The Ghanaian fiscal year runs from July 1 to June 30. In this case the actual presentation of the budget was delayed until August 25, 1970.

38. At the 1970 debt negotiations with the creditors, Mensah set the directions in which he expected the government to move but did not give details or indicate the extent of the inflationary budget he was planning.

39. It is common to view the price of foreign exchange as serving three functions: (1) determining the level of exchange earnings and reserves utilization, (2) a means to ration the distribution of imports, and (3) a means for raising or lowering the demand for domestic goods. It appears that Mensah was so concerned about

replacing controls with the market as a means for distributing imports that he was less worried about the exchange loss if cheap foreign goods were easily available. An alternative interpretation is that Mensah wanted to establish the principle of liberalized imports first and later add the more unpalatable part by increasing the price. It is also possible that he thought the cocoa price would hold up for a longer period, making the drain on reserves less of a problem.

40. The import liberalization was allowing in unnecessary luxuries, which Nkrumah and NLC controls had forbidden.

41. Cocoa farmers were being paid 8 new cedis for each 60 pound "head load" of beans presented to the Cocoa Marketing Board agents.

42. At this point the government of Ghana had drawn all of its gold tranche from the IMF and could not get any more credit without a review of its policies—which Mensah wished to avoid.

43. See V. P. Bennett, "The Motivation for Military Intervention," *Western Political Quarterly* 26, no. 4 (1973): 659–674.

44. Debt servicing included payments on past aid loans, medium-term Nkrumah credits, and an obligation under the 180-day credit scheme.

45. In "External Co-Optation of a LDC's Policy Making: The Case of Ghana, 1969–1972," *World Politics* 29, no. 1 (October 1976): 67–89, R. T. Libby claims that Busia was trying to humiliate Mensah by taking over the planning portfolio. Given Busia's spirited defense of Mensah and his decision to allow Mensah to prepare the 1971–1972 budget, Libby's claim seems overstated.

46. This estimate was done by T. Killick in his capacity as an adviser to the Economic Review Committee.

47. This decision caused the Progress party considerable criticism in the student and academic community. The planning for this step started under the NLC, and the basic idea was to get students to pay part of their educational expenses, which had been free under the Nkrumah regime. The university costs per year were about 2,000 new cedis, and the proposal was to have students pay 500 new cedis. If they could not afford it, they would get a loan repayable one year after they started full employment after graduation with an interest rate of 1 percent to cover the cost of administering the loan.

48. Busia to Denoon, p. 16.

49. The memo, *Alternative Methods of Dealing with Economic Situation*, was drafted mainly by Killick, Stern, Roemer, and Odling-Smee, with assistance from K. Pianim and S. Botchway.

50. These internal fiscal results came about in Ghana because the government is the sole purchaser of cocoa. A devaluation raises the number of cedis per unit of

foreign exchange, while the Cocoa Board could keep paying the farmers the old price. This is a disguised tax on the farmers, though the government can reduce the burden by redistributing part of the revenue collected. It is this new revenue that was used to cover the expenditures on assorted sweeteners. See the Chronology discussion for December 14, 1971.

51. M. Roemer, "Ghana 1950–1980: Missed Opportunities," Development Discussion Paper, no. 148 (Cambridge, Mass.: Harvard Institute for International Development, April 1983), p. 26.

52. Although the situation after February 5, 1972, was clearly quite different, the twenty-five months that it took to negotiate the final Nkrumah debt settlement is an indication of Busia's unrealistic schedules.

53. Busia to Denoon, p. 19.

54. In his search for both advice and revenue, Busia was probably more open to foreigners than is common in many other LDCs.

55. The National Redemption Council did not revalue the cedi all the way back to its pre-December 27, 1971, level of 1 new cedi per $.98 but instead chose a middle position of 1 new cedi per $.78.

56. Busia to Denoon, p. 7.

57. The prime minister did instruct the trade minister to meet with key businessmen, but this was a low-keyed information session, not an effective approach to rallying support.

58. See "Towards National Self-Reliance," radio and television broadcast to the nation, by K. A. Busia, December 31, 1971 (Accra, Republic of Ghana).

59. See Bennett, "Motivation," for an elaboration of this argument.

60. Busia to Denoon, p. 6.

61. In this sense, it is an example of praetorian society as described in S. P. Huntington, *Political Order in Changing Societies* (New Haven, Conn.: Yale University Press, 1963), chap. 4.

Chapter 5

1. R. Z. Aliber, "Speculation in the Foreign Exchanges: The European Experience, 1919–1926," *Yale Economic Essays* 2, no. 1 (Spring 1962): 171–246, contains calculations of the extent of overvaluation using various price indexes. The Churchill decision is sometimes referred to as the "Norman Conquest of $4.86" (the dollar-pound conversion rate). This a reference to Lord Norman, governor of the Bank of England, who strongly opposed a sterling devaluation. See H. Clay, *Lord Norman* (London: Macmillan, 1957).

2. D. E. Mogeridge, *British Monetary Policy, 1924–31* (Cambridge: Cambridge University Press, 1972), chap. 2.

3. A. C. Pigou, "1946 and 1919," *Lloyd's Bank Review* (July 1948).

4. As noted in chapter 2, there was a brief discussion of allowing the rupee to float (and thus avoid calling it a devaluation). This was not a serious option because it would have been harder to manage than a regular devaluation and would have vastly complicated the implementation of remaining controls.

5. In fact, the IMF proved relatively pragmatic in this case and approved keeping the cheaper exchange rate for aid goods when it was obvious that the aid would not be bought at the higher exchange rate.

6. A. Booth and P. McCawley, eds., *The Indonesian Economy during the Suharto Era* (Kuala Lumpur: Oxford University Press, 1981), p. 4.

7. The World Bank recommended $600 million for the 1970–1971 year, and the donors were so enthusiastic that they pledged $622 million.

8. In August 1971 President Nixon devalued the dollar by 7 percent and imposed a 10 percent surcharge on U.S. imports. In December 1971, after the Japanese, West Germans, and French had agreed to let their currencies appreciate, the United States devalued an additional 8 percent but removed the 10 percent import surcharge.

9. M. Roemer, "Ghana 1950–1980: Missed Opportunities," Development Discussion Paper, no. 148 (Cambridge, Mass.: Harvard Institute for International Development, April 1983).

10. J. Bhagwati and T. N. Srinivasan, *Foreign Trade Regimes and Economic Development: India* (New York: National Bureau of Economic Research, 1975), p. 170.

11. See, for example, the discussion of proposals for a second Indian devaluation in 1971 in *New Delhi Link*, December 8, 1971.

12. In his lengthy response to my letter, former Prime Minister Busia stated that Professor Niculescu had suggested a devaluation as early as December 1970. Apparently Niculescu favored a devaluation only after there was a "major restructuring of the economy and a debt moratorium." It is not clear how these two preconditions were to be achieved. Most of the other economists felt Niculescu opposed the devaluation until the November 30, 1971, CSDC memo demonstrated Ghana's limited alternatives.

13. The Harvard Development Advisory Service (HDAS) changed its name to the Harvard Institute for International Development (HIID).

14. The World Bank was not directly involved in the devaluation, but Vice-President Hollis Chenery did speak to the Ghanaian government about the possi-

bility of a loan program if a sound economic restructuring package could be agreed upon.

15. On December 20, 1971, when Bhatia spoke to the CSDC, he did not specifically recommend a devaluation but included it among the few viable options and noted that it would be easier to get an IMF standby if a devaluation was part of the stabilization package.

16. For example, Ambassador Bowles, AID director John Lewis, and economic adviser C. E. Lindblom were all Americans who wanted to see policy changes but who pushed extremely hard to increase aid levels.

17. Although the formal ratification of the fluctuating exchange rate system was not until January 1976 in the Jamaica Accords (*IMF Survey*, January 16, 1976), the United States had begun letting the dollar float by February 1973. For a discussion of how the system was envisaged to work, see George N. Halm, ed., *Approaches to Greater Flexibility in Exchange Rates* (Princeton, N.J.: Princeton University Press, 1970).

18. M. Friedman, "The Case for Flexible Exchange Rates," in R. Caves and H. Johnson, eds., *American Economic Association Readings in International Economics* (Homewood, Ill: Irwin, 1968), pp. 413–440.

19. E. Sohmen, *Flexible Exchange Rates*, 2d ed. (Chicago: University of Chicago Press, 1969).

20. R. Mundell, "The Monetary Dynamics of International Adjustment under Fixed and Flexible Exchange Rates," *Quarterly Journal of Economics* 74, no. 2 (May 1960): 227–257.

21. J. Frenkel, "The Collapse of the Purchasing Power Parities during the 1970s," *European Economic Review* 16, no. 1 (May 1981): 145–165.

22. M. Whitman, "Assessing Greater Variability of Exchange Rates: A Private Sector Perspective," *Papers and Proceedings of the American Economic Review* 74, no. 2 (May 1984).

23. IMF, *International Financial Statistics*, (from years 1979–1983), (Washington, D.C.: International Monetary Fund).

24. S. Islam, "Currency Misalignments: The Case of the Dollar and the Yen," *Federal Reserve Bank of New York Quarterly Review* 8, no. 4 (Winter 1983–1984): 49–60.

25. European complaints about high U.S. interest rates (and their adverse effects on the franc) at the 1983 Williamsburg Economic Summit are a good example of this sentiment. The issue is particularly difficult to resolve when the country choosing a tight monetary policy has its currency widely used as an international reserve currency and there is a conflict between domestic and international objectives.

26. N. Duck, "Prices, Output and the Balance of Payments in an Open Economy with Rational Expectations," *Journal of International Economics* 16, nos. 1–2 (February 1984): 59–77.

27. The poorest LDCs still are not sufficiently creditworthy to borrow much from commercial banks. However, India could borrow significantly more from the private banks in 1983 than it could in 1966, and Indonesia has borrowed $25 billion in private and public credits.

28. R. De Vries, "Global Debt: Assessment and Prospects," Testimony before the Senate Foreign Relations Committee, January 19, 1983. Total debt service ratios include interest and amortization on all trade credits, as well as short-, medium-, and long-term debts.

29. World Bank, *Annual Reports*, June 30, 1974, June 30, 1981. This total includes both IBRD and International Development Association lending.

30. M. Guitian, "Fund Conditionality: Evolution of Principles and Practices," Pamphlet Series, no. 38 (Washington, D.C.: International Monetary Fund, 1981).

31. For a discussion of the Indian loan, see C. Gwin, "Financing India's Structural Adjustment: The Role of the Fund," mimeo. (New York: Carnegie Foundation, 1982).

32. IMF, *World Economic Outlook*, Occasional Paper, no. 27, (Washington, D.C.: IMF, April 1984). In 1983, for example, the Central and South American countries' imports declined by 21 percent.

33. M. Khan and M. Knight, "Some Theoretical and Empirical Issues Relating to Economic Stabilization in Developing Countries," *World Development* 10, no. 9 (September 1982): 709–730.

34. R. Blackhurst et al., *Trade Liberalization, Protectionism and Interdependence* (Geneva: General Agreement on Tariffs and Trade, 1980).

35. For an interesting study simulating how trade would increase if there were reductions in trade barriers among LDCs, see J. Holsen and J. Waelbroeck, "LDC Balance of Payments Policy and the International Monetary System," mimeo. (Washington, D.C.: World Bank, February 1976).

36. *Report to the U.S. Congress on Export Credit Competitiveness and the Export-Import Bank of the U.S.* (Washington, D.C.: Eximbank, 1982).

37. G. Hufbauer and J. S. Erb, *Subsidies in International Trade* (Washington, D.C.: Institute for International Economics, 1984).

38. J. Zysman and S. Cohen, "Double or Nothing: Open Trade and Competitive Industry," *Foreign Affairs* 61, no. 5 (Summer 1983): 1113–1139.

39. S. Bialer and J. Afferica, "Reagan and Russia," *Foreign Affairs* 61, no. 2 (Winter 1982–1983): 249–271.

40. H. Okazaki, "Japanese Security Policy: A Time for Strategy," *International Security* 7, no. 2 (Fall 1982): 188–197.

41. See, for example, S. Brittan, "A Very Painful World Adjustment," *America and the World, 1982, Foreign Affairs* 61 no. 3 (1983): 541–568.

42. For an overview of recent world macroeconomic performance, see *World Economic Outlook Revised*, IMF Occasional Paper, no. 32 (Washington, D.C.: IMF, September 1984).

43. For an early discussion of the advantages of using gold and fixed exchange rates, see R. A. Mundell, "The Dollar and the Policy Mix: 1971," Essays in International Finance, no. 85 (Princeton, N.J.: Princeton University Press, May 1971).

44. For a discussion of the reaction by different OECD country governments to proposals for greater intervention in the currency markets, see "Hard Pounding This, Gentlemen: A Survey of the World Economy," *Economist*, September 24, 1983.

45. For a review of different views on the likelihood and efficacy of greater macroeconomic coordination, see *From Rambouillet to Versailles: A Symposium*, Essays in International Finance, no. 149 (Princeton, N.J.: International Finance Section, Princeton University, December 1982).

46. An example of a country that chose devaluation but was not able to follow through with the other steps necessary for success and then had to revert to controls is Egypt. See B. Hansen and K. Nashashibi, *Foreign Trade Regimes and Economic Development, Egypt* (New York: National Bureau of Economic Research, 1975), p. 129.

47. These problems are not limited to LDCs. See W. Diebold, "Adapting Economies to Structural Change: The International Aspect," *International Affairs* 54, no. 4 (October 1978): 573–588.

Bibliography

Afrifa, Col. *The Ghana Coup*. London: Cass, 1966.

Agarwal, R. G. *Price Controls in India since 1947*. Delhi: Federation of Indian Chambers of Commerce, 1956.

Alexander, S. "The Effects of Devaluation on a Trade Balance," *IMF Staff Papers* 2, no. 2 (1952): 263–278.

Aliber, R. Z. "Speculation in the Foreign Exchanges: The European Experience, 1919–1926." *Yale Economic Essays* 2, no. 1 (Spring 1962): 171–246.

Allison, G. *The Essence of Decision*. Boston: Little, Brown, 1971.

Area, Production and Yield of Principal Crops in India, 1949–50 to 1967–68. New Delhi: Government of India, Ministry of Food and Agriculture, 1969.

Bauer, P. T. *West African Trade*. London: Routledge and Kegan Paul, 1963.

———, and B. S. Yamey. *The Economics of Under-Developed Countries*. Cambridge: Cambridge University Press, 1957.

Beim, D. O. "Rescuing the LDCs." *Foreign Affairs* 55, no. 4 (1977): 717–731.

Bennett, V. P. "The Motivation for Military Intervention." *Western Political Quarterly* 26, no. 4 (1973): 659–674.

Bhagwati, J., and P. Desai. *India: Planning for Industrialization*. London: Oxford University Press, 1970.

Bhagwati, J., and A. Krueger. *Foreign Trade Regimes and Economic Development*. 10 vols. New York: Columbia University and Ballinger Presses, 1974–1978.

Bhagwati, J. and T. N. Srinivasan. *Foreign Trade Regimes and Economic Development: India*. New York: National Bureau of Economic Research, 1975.

Bialer, S., and J. Afferifa. "Reagan and Russia." *Foreign Affairs* 61, no. 2 (Winter 1982–1983): 249–271.

Bienen, H., ed. *The Military Intervenes*. New York: Russell Sage, 1969.

Birmingham, W., I. Neustadt, and E. N. Omaboe, eds. *A Study in Contemporary Ghana*. Vol. 1 of *The Economy of Ghana*. Evanston, Ill.: Northwestern University Press, 1966.

Blackhurst, R., et al. *Trade Liberalization, Protectionism and Interdependence*. Geneva: General Agreement on Tariffs and Trade, 1980.

Booth, A., and P. McCauley. *The Indonesian Economy during the Suharto Era*. Kuala Lumpur: Oxford University Press, 1981.

Bowles, C. *Ambassador's Report*. New York: Harper, 1954.

Brecher, M. *Nehru's Mantle*. London: Oxford University Press, 1966.

Brittan, S. "A Very Painful World Adjustment." *Foreign Affairs* 61, no. 3 (1983): 541–568.

Brown, G. *Korean Pricing Policy and Economic Development in the 1960s*. Baltimore, Md.: Johns Hopkins University Press, 1973.

Chenery, H., and A. Strout. "Foreign Assistance and Economic Development." *American Economic Review* 56, no. 4 (1966): 679–733.

Clay, H. *Lord Norman*. London: Macmillan, 1957.

Cline, W. R. *International Monetary Reform and the Developing Countries*. Washington, D.C.: Brookings Institution, 1976.

————, and S. Weintraub, eds. *Economic Stabilization and Developing Countries*. Washington, D.C.: Brookings Institution, 1981.

Cole, D., and P. Lyman. *Korean Development*. Cambridge, Mass.: Harvard University Press, 1970.

Connors, T. "The Apparent Effects of Recent IMF Stabilization Programs." International Finance Discussion Paper, no. 135. Washington, D.C.: U.S. Federal Reserve Board, April 1979.

Cooper, R. N. "Currency Devaluation in Developing Countries." Essays in International Finance, no. 86. Princeton, N.J.: Princeton University, 1971.

Dapice, D. "An Overview of the Indonesian Economy." In *The Indonesian Economy*. Edited by G. Papanek. New York: Praeger, 1980.

Das, D. *From Curzon to Nehru and After*. London: Collins, 1969.

Dell, S. "The International Environment for Adjustment in the Developing Countries." *World Development* 8, no. 11 (1980): 833–842.

Diaz-Allejandro, C. *Exchange-Rate Devaluation in Semi-Industrialized Countries*. Cambridge, Mass.: MIT Press, 1965.

Diebold, W. "Adapting Economies to Structural Change: The International Aspect." *International Affairs* 54, no. 4 (1978): 573–588.

Donovan, D. "Macroeconomic Performance and Adjustment under Fund-Supported Programs: The Experience of the 1970s." *IMF Staff Papers* 29, no. 2 (1982): 171–203.

Dornbusch, R. "Expectations and Exchange Rate Dynamics." *Journal of Political Economy* 84, no. 6 (1976): 1161–1176.

Duck, N. "Prices, Output and the Balance of Payments in an Open Economy with Rational Expectations." *Journal of International Economics* 16, nos. 1–2 (February 1984): 59–77.

Eshag, E., and P. Richards. "A Comparison of Economic Development in Ghana and the Ivory Coast since 1960." *Bulletin of Oxford University Institute of Economics and Statistics* 29, no. 4 (1967): 353–372.

Feith, H., and L. Castles. *Indonesian Political Thinking, 1945–1965.* Ithaca: Cornell University Press, 1970.

Frank, A. G. "The Development of Underdevelopment." *Monthly Review* 18, no. 4 (September 1966): 17–31.

Frenkel, J. "The Collapse of the Purchasing Power Parities during the 1970s." *European Economic Review* 16, no. 1 (May 1981): 145–165.

Friedman, M. "The Case for Flexible Exchange Rates." In *American Economic Association Readings in International Economics.* Edited by R. Caves and H. Johnson. Homewood, Ill.: Irwin, 1968.

"From Rambouillet to Versailles: A Symposium." Essays in International Finance, no. 149. Princeton, N.J.: International Finance Section, Princeton University, December 1982.

Gillis, M. "Episodes in Indonesian Economic Growth." Paper presented at the conference on World Economic Growth, Mexico, April 28, 1983.

Girvan, N. "Swallowing the IMF Medicine in the Seventies." *Development Dialogue,* no. 2 (1980): 55–74.

Glassbruner, B. "Indonesia's New Economic Policy and Its Socio-Political Implications." In *Political Power and Communication in Indonesia.* Edited by K. Jackson and L. Pye. Berkeley: University of California Press, 1978.

———. "Pricing of Foreign Exchange in Indonesia, 1966–67." *Economic Development and Cultural Change* 18, no. 2 (January 1970): 166–187.

Goldstein, M. *The Exchange Rate System: Lessons of the Past and Options for the Future.* IMF Occasional Paper, no. 30. Washington, D.C.: IMP, July 1984.

Grant, J. "Development: The End of Trickle-Down?" *Foreign Policy*, no. 12 (Fall 1973): 43–65.

Guitian, M. "Fund Conditionality: Evolution of Principles and Practices." Pamphlet Series, no. 38. Washington, D.C.: International Monetary Fund, 1981.

Gullick, C., and J. Nelson. "Promoting Economic Development Policies: AID Experience in Developing Countries." USAID Discussion Paper no., 9. Washington, D.C., September 1965.

Halm, G. N., ed. *Approaches to Greater Flexibility in Exchange Rates*. Princeton, N.J.: Princeton University Press, 1970.

Hansen, B., and K. Nashashibi. *Foreign Trade Regimes and Economic Developments, Egypt*. New York: National Bureau of Economic Research, 1975.

"Hard Pounding This, Gentlemen: A Survey of the World Economy." *Economist*, September 24, 1983.

Hayter, T. *Aid as Imperialism*. London: Penguin Press, 1970.

Helleiner, G. K. "The Less Developed Countries and the International Monetary System." *Journal of Development Studies* 10, nos. 3–4 (1974): 347–373.

Hicks, N. "Some Structural Problems in the Economy of Ghana." Accra: USAID, January 1970.

Hirschman, A. O. "Devaluation and the Trade Balance." *Review of Economics and Statistics* 31, no. 1 (February 1949): 50–53.

———. *Journeys toward Progress*. New York: Anchor Books, Doubleday, 1965.

———. *National Power and the Structure of Foreign Trade*. Berkeley: University of California Press, 1980.

———. "The Political Economy of Import Substituting Industries in Latin America." *Quarterly Journal of Economics* 82, no. 1 (February 1968): 1–32.

Hollinger, W. "The Foreign Exchange Rate as a Policy Instrument, the Indonesian Case: 1966–70." Harvard Development Advisory Service Paper. June 1970.

Holsen, J., and J. Waelbroeck. "LDC Balance of Payments Policy and the International Monetary System." Mimeo. Washington, D.C.: World Bank, February 1976.

Hufbauer, G., and J. S. Erb. *Subsidies in International Trade*. Washington, D.C.: Institute for International Economics, 1984.

Hughes, J. *Indonesian Upheaval*. New York: McKay, 1967.

Huntington, S. P. *Political Order in Changing Societies*. New Haven, Conn.: Yale University Press, 1963.

Ilchman, W., and N. Uphoff. *The Political Economy of Change*. Berkeley: University of California Press, 1971.

International Bank for Reconstruction and Development. *Economic Situation and Prospects of India*. SA-32a. Washington, D.C.: IBRD, May 10, 1972.

International Labor Organization. *Employment, Growth and Basic Human Needs: A One-World Problem*. New York: Praeger Publishers, 1977.

International Monetary Fund. *Recent Economic Developments*. Washington, D.C.: IMF, November 30, 1970.

————. *World Economic Outlook*. Occasional Paper, no. 27. Washington, D.C.: IMF, April 1984.

————. *World Economic Outlook Revised*. Occasional paper, no. 32. Washington, D.C.: IMF, September 1984.

Ishiyama, Y. "The Theory of Optimum Currency Areas: A Survey." *IMF Staff Papers* 22, no. 2 (1975): 344–383.

Islam, S. "Currency Misalignments: The Case of the Dollar and the Yen." *Federal Reserve Bank of New York Quartarly Review* 8, no. 4 (Winter 1983–1984): 49–60.

Johnson, G. G., and T. M. Reichman. *Stand-by Arrangements in the Upper Credit Tranches, 1973–75*. Washington, D.C.: International Monetary Fund, 1978.

Keohane, R. *After Hegemony—Co-operation and Discord in the World Economy*. Princeton, N.J.: Princeton University Press, 1984.

————. "The Big Influence of Small Allies." *Foreign Policy*, no. 2 (Spring 1971): 161–182.

Khan, S., and M. Knight. "Determinants of Current Account Balances of Non-Oil Developing Countries in the 1970s—An Empirical Analysis." *IMF Staff Papers* 30, no. 4 (1983): 819–842.

————. "Some Theoretical and Empirical Issues Relating to Economic Stabilization in Developing Countries." *World Development* 10, no. 9 (1982): 709–730.

Killick, T. *Development Economics in Action: A Study of Economic Policies in Ghana*. New York: St. Martins, 1978.

————, and M. Chapman. "Much Ado about Nothing: Testing the Impact of IMF Stabilization Programmes in Developing Countries." London: Overseas Development Institute, 1982.

Kochanek, S. *Business and Politics in India*. Berkeley, Calif.: University of California Press, 1974.

Krasner, S. *Defending the National Interest*. Princeton, N.J.: Princeton University Press, 1978.

Kraus, J. "Arms and Politics in Ghana." In *Soldier and State in Africa.* Edited by C. Welch. Evanston, Ill.: Northwestern University Press, 1970.

Krueger, A. *Liberalization Attempts and Consequences.* Cambridge, Mass.: Ballinger Press, 1978.

————. "The Political Economy of the Rent-Seeking Society." *American Economic Review* 64, no. 3 (June 1974): 291–303.

Krugman, P., and L. Taylor. "Contractionary Effects of Devaluation." *Journal of International Economics* 8, no. 3 (1978): 445–456.

Leith, J. C. *Ghana: Foreign Trade Regimes and Economic Development.* New York: National Bureau of Economic Research, 1974.

Lerner, A. P. *The Economics of Control.* New York: Macmillan, 1944.

Lewis, J. P. *The Quiet Crisis in India.* Washington, D.C.: Brookings Institution, 1962.

Libby, R. T. "External Co-optation of an LDC's Policy Making: The Case of Ghana, 1969–1972." *World Politics* 29, no. 1 (October 1976): 67–89.

Liddle, R. W. *Political Participation in Modern Indonesia.* New Haven, Conn.: Yale University Press, 1973.

Lim, R. "The Philippines and the Dependency Debate." *Journal of Contemporary Asia* 8, no. 2 (1978): 196–207.

Lindblom, C. E. "The Rediscovery of the Market." *Public Interest,* no. 4 (Summer 1966): 89–101.

McClelland, D., and D. Winter. *Motivating Economic Achievement.* New York: Free Press, 1969.

Marshall, A. *Money, Credit and Commerce.* London: Macmillan, 1924.

Maxwell, N. *India's China War.* Bombay: Jaico, 1970.

Millikan, M., and W. W. Rostow. *A Proposal, Key to an Effective Foreign Policy.* New York: Harper & Row, 1957.

Moggridge, D. E. *British Monetary Policy, 1924–31.* Cambridge: Cambridge University Press, 1972.

Morris, M. D. *Measuring the Condition of the World's Poor: The Physical Quality of Life Index.* New York: Pergamon Press, 1979.

Mortimer, R., ed. *Showcase State: Illusion of Indonesia's Accelerated Modernization.* Sydney: Angus & Robertson, 1973.

Mundell, R. A. "The Dollar and the Policy Mix: 1971." *Essays in International Finance,* no. 85. Princeton, N.J.: Princeton University Press, May 1971.

————. "The Monetary Dynamics of International Adjustment under Fixed and Flexible Exchange Rates." *Quarterly Journal of Economics* 74, no. 2 (May 1960): 227–257.

Mubyarto, S., and Boediono, eds. *Ekonomi Pancasila.* Yogyakarta, Indonesia: Faculty of Economics, 1981.

Nayar, B. *The Modernization Imperative and Indian Planning.* New Delhi: Vikas, 1972.

————. "Treat India Seriously." *Foreign Policy,* no. 18 (Spring 1975): 133–154.

Nehru, J. *The Discovery of India.* New Delhi: Asia Publishing House, 1961.

Newmann, J. "Inflation in Indonesia." Ph.D. dissertation, Tufts University, 1974.

Okazaki, H. "Japanese Security Policy: A Time for Strategy." *International Security* 7, no. 2 (Fall 1982): 188–197.

Organization of American States. *Latin America and the Reform of the International Monetary Systems.* Washington, D.C.: OAS, 1972.

Otani, I. "Inflation in an Open Economy: A Case Study of the Philippines." *IMF Staff Papers* 22, no. 3 (1975): 721–774.

Palmer, I. *The Indonesian Economy since 1965.* London: Frank Cass, 1978.

Patel, I. G. *Foreign Aid.* New Delhi: Institute for Public Enterprise, 1968.

Payer, C. *The Debt Trap.* New York: Monthly Review Press, 1975.

"Peru—Debtor in Disarray." *Economist,* July 30, 1977, p. 60.

Prebisch, R. "The Economic Development of Latin America and Its Principal Problems." *Economic Bulletin for Latin America* 7 (February 1962): 1–22.

Report to the U.S. Congress on Export Credit Competitiveness and the Export-Import Bank of the U.S. Washington, D.C.: Eximbank, 1982.

Roemer, M. "Ghana 1950–1980: Missed Opportunities." Development Discussion Paper, no. 148. Cambridge, Mass.: Harvard Institute for International Development, April 1983.

Rosenstein-Rodan, P. "Problems of Industrialisation of Eastern and Southeastern Europe." *Economic Journal* 53, nos. 210–211 (June–September 1943): 202–211.

Schelling, T., *The Strategy of Conflict.* New York: Oxford University Press, 1960.

Scitovsky, T. "A New Approach to International Liquidity." *American Economic Review* 56, no. 5 (1966): 1212–1220.

Scott, D. "Growth and Crisis: Economic Policy in Ghana, 1945–65." Ph.D. dissertation, Harvard University, 1967.

Shah, M. *Export Strategy for India*. New Delhi: Indian Council for Applied Economic Research, 1969.

Shaplen, R. "Letter from Indonesia." *New Yorker*, April 1, 1974, pp. 57–90.

Sohmen, E. *Flexible Exchange Rates*. 2d ed. Chicago: University of Chicago Press, 1969.

Steele, W. "Import Substitution Policy in Ghana in the 1960s." Ph.D. dissertation, MIT, 1970.

Steinbruner, J. *The Cybernetic Theory of Decision*. Princeton, N.J.: Princeton University Press, 1974.

Sturc, E. "Stabilization Policy: Experience of Some European Countries in the 1950s." IMF Staff Paper 15, no. 2 (1968): 197–219.

Tagaza, E. "Huge Payments Deficit Brings New Devaluation in the Philippines." *Christian Science Monitor*, October 6, 1983, pp. 17–18.

Tomasson, G. "Indonesian Economic Stabilization 1966–69." *Finance and Development* 7, no. 4 (December 1970): 46–53.

Triffin, R. *Gold and the Dollar Crisis: The Future of Convertibility*. New Haven: Yale University Press, 1960.

Uphoff, N. "Ghana's Experience in Using External Aid for Development 1957–66." Ph.D. dissertation, University of California, 1969.

Weiner, M. *Political Change in South Asia*. Calcutta, 1963.

Weinstein, F. *Indonesian Foreign Policy and the Dilemma of Dependence*. Ithaca, N.Y.: Cornell University Press, 1976.

Whitman, M. "Assessing Greater Variability of Exchange Rates: A Private Sector Perspective." *Papers and Proceedings of the American Economic Review* 74, no. 2 (May 1984).

Williams, J. H. *Postwar Monetary Plans and Other Essays*. New York: Knopf, 1944.

Williamson, J. *The Lending Policies of the IMF*. Washington, D.C.: Institute for International Economics, 1982.

Zysman, J., and S. Cohen. "Double or Nothing: Open Trade and Competitive Industry." *Foreign Affairs* 61, no. 5 (1983): 1113–1139.

Index

Ward, Barbara, 38
Wardhana, Ali, 113, 122, 136
Washington, 23, 26, 41, 46, 54, 61–63,
    66–68, 92, 119, 121
Washington Post, 23, 60, 178
Western Europe, 114, 121
White firm, J.F., 118
Widjojo, Nitisastro, 91, 94–95, 99, 108,
    110, 113–114, 128, 135, 198, 201,
    225n61
Wilopo, 92
Woods, George, 32, 41, 44, 47, 59, 61–62,
    64, 67, 71, 75–76, 206, 225n60
Woods-Mehta agreement, 44, 46–47, 49,
    68, 75–76, 197, 200, 206
World Bank, 11–12, 15, 23, 31–32, 38–39,
    41, 44, 55, 59, 61–62, 67, 69, 71–72,
    74–76, 92, 103, 107–109, 125, 159,
    171, 173, 185, 200, 212, 217
World War II, 14, 21, 29, 35, 53

Zagorian, B., 56
Zaire, 18